Praise for *What Your Employees Need and Can't Tell You*

With vivid accounts and research-based advice, Palmer charts the clearest course I've ever seen for managers seeking to navigate change. It's a tour de force.

—Robert Cialdini, *NY Times* bestselling author of *Influence* and *Pre-Suasion*

In this science-based playbook that is a must read for every manager of people, Melina Palmer lucidly reminds us that people management is a lot like raising children: "tune in, take turns, and talk more" are the 3 Ts that every great manager must follow.

—John A. List, *Wall Street Journal* bestselling author of *The Voltage Effect* and *The Why Axis*

Change is not a one-off event. As Palmer so clearly showcases in *What Your Employees Need and Can't Tell You*, focusing on the micro-moments and making little tweaks can make all the difference in whether a change is easy, natural, and celebrated—or a massive failure with demotivated employees left in the wake. Unlike other books or frameworks that may take a lofty, impractical approach to managing change in business, Palmer's science-backed insights are immediately applicable by any manager in any industry.

—Nir Eyal, bestselling author of *Hooked* and *Indistractable*

Melina Palmer has re-entered the chat… with a thoroughly researched and deeply engaging book which delivers the goods in her uniquely inquisitive, practical and supportive style. Melina has gifted a generation of leaders with not just a roadmap for effective and meaningful change, but also a car, the keys to that car, a full tank of gas, a roadmap-following playlist and a box of healthy snacks to make sure we reach our destination in good spirits and with great success. In other words, she's given us everything we need to set out and become champions for change in our organizations and our lives.

—Jeff Kreisler, head of behavioral science at JP Morgan, coauthor of *Dollars and Sense*, founding editor of PeopleScience.com

Melina Palmer has done it again! *What Your Employees Need and Can't Tell You* is the leader's practical (and engaging!) guidebook to managing exceptional teams using evidence-based nudges from behavioral science. I found myself taking notes about techniques to put into immediate practice with my own team. If you want to take your leadership skills to the next level, let Melina Palmer be your guide.

—Amy Bucher, Ph.D., author of *Engaged: Designing for Behavior Change* and Chief Behavioral Officer at Lirio

In her book, Palmer makes a convincing case for why change is possible and how you should go about it. Using insights from behavioral science and many fun personal stories, she paints an engaging and optimistic picture of behavioral change. Such a fun and educational read!

—Ayelet Fishbach, professor of behavioral science and marketing at the University of Chicago Booth School of Business and author of *Get It Done*

One of the hardest working and most prolific content generators in our field, Melina has once again presented us with a treasure-trove of insightful real-life use cases and practical advice—a must-read on change management!

—Dr. Benny Cheung, director at Dectech

"Thoughtful planning up front will always save time in the long run." As I read Melina Palmer's words, it hit me—this book is an investment. Any good investment should give you something greater in return. Spending time with this book will pay big dividends. And, the more time you invest in it, the more you'll reap over the long run. I write that because, as someone who teaches influence for a living, I know following Melina's advice will help you when it comes to understanding and communicating with people. Let's face it, we cannot accomplish anything apart from people so the most successful individuals will spend an inordinate amount of time learning whatever they can about how people think and behave. Congratulations on your investment. Now maximize it.

—Brian Ahearn, author of *Influence PEOPLE*

Change is everything. Knowing that, one can decide either to become a master of change or inevitably turning into its victim. This book is definitely helping to accelerate towards the former. Enjoy!

—Dr. Agnis Stibe, 4x TEDx speaker, artificial intelligence program director, professor of transformation, and creator of the STIBE method for hyper-performance

Half our life is spent "at work", and despite the advances in behavioral economics in other areas, there was no comprehensive way to use it for ourselves and our teams. Not anymore! *What Your Employees Need and Can't Tell You* is the book meant for every manager to help make change easy for their employees. It provides an easy, accessible method to understanding and using the power of human motivation and behavior at work to build more engaged, motivated teams. Highly recommended read!

—Anant Sood, cofounder of worxogo

This book is an amazing compendium of behavioral science presented in a practical way to improve management and business decisions through small, but impactful changes. *What Your Employees Need and Can't Tell You* opens possibilities for the butterfly effect that behavioral science can generate in your business. If you are ready to embrace change, look no further.

—Dr. Marco Palma, director of the Human Behavior Laboratory at Texas A&M University

Change is easier than you think, once you know how the brain works. In this accessible, actionable book, Melina Palmer reviews the most relevant behavioral science findings for making change management less painful and more effective. You'll learn how to be more thoughtful about change, how to "calm the elephant," and why successful change management is "not about the cookie." An eye-opening and practical guide to navigating one of the most perplexing challenges faced by leaders today.

—Vanessa Bohns, author of *You Have More Influence Than You Think*

Melina makes behavioral economics approachable, practical, and fun. By the end of the book, you have learned how to put things into practice to make an impact into your business and your life.

—Matthew Confer, VP of strategy and business development at Abilitie

This book takes you on a fascinating journey to your employees' subconscious. It's packed with actionable, science-based insights that you can immediately apply to manage change. A must-read for managers.

—Matej Sucha, managing partner of MINDWORX and editor and chief at InsideBE

A wonderfully researched and moreish journey into the workings of our brain and how we can lead others more effectively by better understanding it. Packed with insight, if you manage people (and want to do it well) this is a must-read.

—Sam Tatam, global principal of behavioural science at Ogilvy and author of *Evolutionary Ideas*

"We're making some changes" is one of the scariest phrases in business, but Melina Palmer proves organizational change doesn't have to be a war. *What Your Employees Need and Can't Tell You* is a change management cheat code. It reveals the words to say and things to do that will open your team to new possibilities.

—James Forr, head of insights at Olson Zaltman

A well-researched and highly-accessible account of common challenges facing employees. Valuable insight into how behavioral science can help organizations to finally address them.

—Nuala Walsh, CEO of MINDEQUITY, and founding director of the Global Association of Applied Behavioural Scientists

Yet again, Melina has an ability to combine some of my most favorite topics in practical hands-on advice. What it takes to create employee buy-in and motivation through empathic conversation and the science behind human behavior are topics close to my heart and mandatory in a world fueled with constant change. Palmer's mantra to "be thoughtful" is easily applied and powerfully showcased in her second book, *What Your Employees Need and Can't Tell You.*

—Nadia Haagen Pedersen, executive vice president at iMotions

What Your Employees Need and Can't Tell You is a comprehensive guidebook on leadership. It's filled with the right questions to ask yourself and your employees. Palmer breaks down each concept in a way that's easy to digest and then implement. It will challenge the way you perceive yourself and your employees. You'll gain insights on how to truly lead yourself, your team and your organization to success.

—Nikki Rausch, CEO of Sales Maven, neurolinguistic programming expert, podcast host, and author of *Buying Signals* and *The Selling Staircase*

What Your Employees Need and Can't Tell You is a terrific resource for any leader seeking to inspire and manage organizational change. This book brings fresh perspective to important change management principles and practices through grounding in an engaging discussion of the latest science behind how we think, decide and behave along with helpful anecdotes to bring experienced challenges and successes to life. If you're looking for an engaging and actionable toolkit for managing organizational change, look no further.

—Sam Evans, growth marketing and behavioral design consultant

This is a practical guide on achieving organizational change through applying behavioral economics. Melina Palmer's *What Your Employees Need and Can't Tell You* introduces key concepts, making them relevant, applicable, and a joyful read. Whether you are a team leader or a team player, you will find scientifically based insights to put into practice today.

—Wiam Hasanain, social impact and behavioral science advisor

Melina Palmer turns conventional wisdom about change on its head by using smart, science-based tactics. Every business has to change, and change often, but many struggle to get employee acceptance and support. Melina shows how to use behavioral science to reduce resistance to change and achieve successful transformation. Anyone who manages people needs this book!

—Roger Dooley, author of *Friction* and *Brainfluence*

Change management has never been so scientifically grounded. This book is made for anyone tired of the conventional business advice and thirsty for evidence-based behavioral insights. It's for you if you're ready to start focusing on what's important, and apply the science to create and maintain a culture of engaged and productive workers.

—Aline Holzwarth, applied behavioral scientist

Small changes make a big difference. Palmer's mantra to "be thoughtful" is easily applied and powerfully showcased yet again in her second book, *What Your Employees Need and Can't Tell You.*

—Scott Jeffrey Miller, *Wall Street Journal* bestselling author and host of the world's largest leadership podcast

Your brain will grow two sizes reading this book. Behavioral scientist Melina Palmer will persuade you that the job of any manager is to help employees navigate change, and then teach you how to do it. Science-based but real-world practical. Her sense of humor makes it an enjoyable read, and OMG the Cobra Effect!

—Zoe Chance, author of *Influence Is Your Superpower*

A smart, thoughtful guide to creating successful change in organizations. Drawing on the best behavioral science, Melina Palmer provides engaging examples and applications to help any manager master the art of change. A must read!

—Wendy Wood, author of *Good Habits, Bad Habits*

We live in a volatile and uncertain business world where things are constantly changing. Unfortunately, facing change in the workplace can be hard for both managers and employees. But it doesn't have to be! Behavioral science is an untapped tool to help managers navigate this change while bringing staff along. In this new book, Melina has made behavioral science easy to apply for any manager trying to improve their ability to lead. It's a must read for business leaders who want the best for their employees.

—Will Leach, CEO of Mindstate Group and author of *Marketing to Mindstates*

In life, change is the only constant. Although this is true, this doesn't make it easy for us to handle. Melina is an expert in behavioral science and has a deep understanding of how the brain works. And she uses this incredible depth of knowledge to provide helpful tips on change management that are actionable, accessible, and relevant. I couldn't endorse this book enough. I learn something new every time I talk to her and I know you will get a lot out of this book!

—Kwame Christian, director of the American Negotiation Institute, bestselling author, attorney, speaker, and host of the number-one negotiation podcast, *Negotiate Anything*

WHAT YOUR EMPLOYEES NEED AND CAN'T TELL YOU

WHAT YOUR EMPLOYEES NEED AND CAN'T TELL YOU

Adapting to Change with the Science of Behavioral Economics

MELINA PALMER

Coral Gables

Published by Mango Publishing, a division of Mango Publishing Group, Inc.

Cover Design: Morgane Leoni
Art Direction: Roberto Nuñez
Layout & Design: Katia Mena

For permission requests, please contact the publisher at:
Mango Publishing Group
2850 S Douglas Road, 4th Floor
Coral Gables, FL 33134 USA
info@mango.bz

For special orders, quantity sales, course adoptions and corporate sales, please email the publisher at sales@mango.bz. For trade and wholesale sales, please contact Ingram Publisher Services at customer.service@ingramcontent.com or +1.800.509.4887.

What Your Employees Need and Can't Tell You: Adapting to Change with the Science of Behavioral Economics

Library of Congress Cataloging-in-Publication number: 2022940963
ISBN: (print) 978-1-68481-015-4, (ebook) 978-1-68481-016-1
BISAC category code BUS103000, BUSINESS & ECONOMICS / Organizational Development

Printed in the United States of America

Contents

Foreword

When Melina graciously hosted me as her guest on the 111th episode of *The Brainy Business* podcast, I was struck by her passion and skill at helping her audience learn and apply behavioral economics in their work (and life). Certainly, we had fun nerding out on the research while discussing the complex and nuanced reasons why you should never simply go with your gut in making business decisions. Yet, she always focused on making the audience the center of the show, helping her listeners truly get the key lessons and takeaways that would help them make the best decisions possible. My experience was repeated and even intensified when she invited me back for the 175th episode to discuss my new book on leading hybrid and remote teams in the future of work. I was especially impressed as I knew Melina had just returned from maternity leave and was taking care of the "Brainy Baby."

I felt grateful to Melina as those two interviews improved my ability to communicate about behavioral economics and help people apply it to their business and personal life. So I gladly agreed to write the foreword for her new book when she kindly invited me to do so, confident I would learn more and become a better communicator from her expertise.

I'm also confident you will be grateful to her as you learn how to be an effective change agent in our increasingly disrupted future and empower your team to do so. Let's be real: Change is a constant in our business lives. That means we need to do away with the myth that there are times of change and times of stability. As Melina wisely points out, managers are always trying to implement some change or another. Such change might range from getting their teams to adopt a new quality management procedure to making the voice of the customer a more central component of product design and delivery or even deciding on a location-flexible working style that balances hybrid, office-centric, and remote work.

The competitive advantage of today—and even more so tomorrow—depends on your ability to thrive in the context of change. Yet as Melina highlights, doing so is a challenge if the story we tell ourselves and our teams about change is that "change is hard." Such **framing** around change leads our brains, and the brains of our team members, to fall for the **status quo bias** and create **sludge** that results in resistance to change (framing, status quo bias, and sludge are all behavioral economics concepts that Melina will explain in the book, and you can check them out in the handy glossary available for download in the resources section at the end).

So why read Melina's book, rather than the thousands of other books out there about overcoming change? Well, those books are full of myths that don't hold up in the face of behavioral economics, psychology, cognitive neuroscience, and other research findings. It may make leaders feel good to read a book that says you only have to convince your employees that someone moved their cheese and now they have to go and find it.

Guess what? Humans aren't mice.

Sure, it might make the author rich to give such a simplistic solution. I know that many business leaders at top companies started change initiatives by handing out copies of such books, which basically say: adapt to change, or else! Well, those are the change initiatives that tend to collapse due to the foot-dragging of resisting employees.

If you want to cultivate the ability to not simply survive but also thrive amid change, you better work *with* the human mind—not against it. And Melina shows you how. Her book is chock-full of critically important insights, lessons, and takeaways to transform you not only into a change agent but a change super-agent!

It's Melina's unparalleled ability to step into the shoes of her readers that empowers her to accomplish and inspire this. One of the most useful aspects of this book is how thoughtful she is about bringing about change effectively in a way that aligns with our brains.

For example, consider that most change initiatives have many complex components, launched at the same time as the organization is undertaking its day-to-day tasks. Melina instead recommends that change efforts start with decreasing the pressure on a team to deliver various projects and increasing the bandwidth available for change. Moreover, Melina endorses pursuing changes one at a time, rather than having a variety of changes launched at once, so the team can focus on getting the change right rather than doing it fast.

Likewise, Melina's approach is to change lives in a world of humans rather than mice looking for cheese. She describes research-based techniques to get buy-in from teams into change initiatives and develop trust in the team leader as protecting and promoting the team's interests. A key component of change that she highlights is how to ameliorate team conflicts and improve relationships between team members, which is critical for the journey of implementing change. A point I found useful, and I think you will too, is how to make change into something fun rather than a drag. And if you're in a hurry to implement a change effort tomorrow, you can skip to the "It's Not About the Cookie" chapter and then read the rest of the book.

In short, Melina is truly thoughtful about change—and everything else. You'll learn a lot from this book about how to make change happen in a way that works with who we are and how our brains function, rather than idealized—but false—stories about how we *should* work and think. If you want to help your team thrive in our increasingly disrupted world, dive right in!

Dr. Gleb Tsipursky, behavioral scientist, CEO of Disaster Avoidance Experts, and author of bestseller, *Never Go with Your Gut: How Pioneering Leaders Make the Best Decisions and Avoid Business Disasters* (Career Press, 2019)

PART 1

BIG PLANS AND MICRO-MOMENTS

CHAPTER 1

Culture, Change, and the Brain

Change is necessary. As Will Rogers points out, "Even if you're on the right track, you'll get run over if you just sit there."

But change is also hard.

Do you agree? Most people do. After all, we've been taught this for essentially our entire lives. "You can't teach an old dog new tricks," right?

As it turns out, old dogs *can* learn new tricks (and, according to some, they do so faster and easier than younger dogs because they aren't as easily distracted).[1] I'm here to tell you that while we have been taught it for years, change doesn't have to be hard.

If you approach change properly, it can be quite easy. People naturally and happily embrace change all the time, but we tend to ignore its signs.

I'm guessing you can barely remember a time before having your smartphone with you everywhere you go. You've conveniently forgotten what it was like to have to know exactly what you were going to do all day so you could print out directions from MapQuest before leaving or feeling bored in line and not being able to check your email, Instagram, TikTok,

Twitter, or play a quick game of Candy Crush to pass the time. The iPhone changed everything, but it wasn't the first smartphone. That was created by IBM in 1992—a full fifteen years before Steve Jobs made his infamous announcement at Macworld. There was some traction for smartphones in those fifteen years. Perhaps you had a Palm Pilot or Blackberry now collecting dust in the attic, but the speed of change was nothing like the iPhone (and before it came around, many people stubbornly rebelled against a seemingly difficult or unnecessary change).

I'm writing this a few weeks after the fifteenth anniversary of that iPhone announcement. As of March 2022, nearly 84 percent of people worldwide own a smartphone. (Not to mention tablets, smart refrigerators, in-car displays, and more.) How did you adapt to all those devices? Can you pinpoint where you decided to change and have a smartphone become an essential piece of your life? Was it the same day that you transitioned from simple black coffee to a five-dollar venti iced caramel macchiato? For most of us, these changes were seamless. We have completely integrated these products into our lives and change a little bit each day to incorporate new things we are excited about or that are properly introduced to us.

You may want to tell me that this change is different. That's not like a change at work because . . . why?

The iPhone didn't change the world by chance. It was the product of immense and meticulous planning. Steve Jobs was hyper-focused on design and making things "intuitively obvious."[2] How much time did you spend thinking about the right way to introduce your change at work? Did you consider how it could be easy, simple, and intuitively obvious? Or was announcing the change just one item on an ever-growing to-do list? Something you assumed people would figure out and eventually get on board with?

Change initiatives at work can be like smartphones, fancy coffee, and so many other easy adaptations we make daily. When you understand how to look at change and properly align it with the rules of the brain, change becomes easy and natural. I've done and seen it repeatedly across my career:

- magically working well with "difficult" people no one else can get through to
- getting other departments to convert from impatiently asking for things they *need yesterday* to planning 90–120 days in advance so my team wasn't constantly putting out fires
- having team members happy to move desks, excited to report to a new manager, or integrate a new process
- getting executive support to rebrand and shift the entire marketing budget into a new, unproven direction and then getting the entire company to rally behind it so we nearly tripled brand awareness in less than two years

Don't worry. I'll talk more about these examples and others as you learn about the brain, biases, concepts of behavioral economics, and my "It's Not About the Cookie" framework for change.

***

Speaking of the brain, what do you know about it?

Take a moment to consider what your brain does and how it works. What do you truly "know" for sure? How much of what you believe about your brain is built on assumption and wishful thinking? And, to take it a step further, how much do you know about the brain of your best friend, employee, or boss?

The truth is, even though we all have brains, we don't intuitively understand how they work.

Since 2002, we have uncovered more about the human brain than was learned throughout the preceding 200,000 years.[3] Technology and the combined power of a connected world have contributed to this learning, and there is still so much more to discover in the years to come.

One of the best things (in my opinion, at least) to come out of this time is the field of behavioral economics—which is built on the rules of the brain that help us predict what people will actually do instead of what we think they *should*.

I like to say that if traditional economics and psychology had a baby, you would have behavioral economics. Or, put another way:

Traditional Economics + Psychology = Behavioral Economics

In addition to being a proponent of making things that are intuitively obvious, Jobs also called simplicity "the ultimate sophistication." He went on to say, "It takes a lot of hard work to make something simple, to truly understand the underlying challenges and come up with elegant solutions." Remember that while you read this book.

Yes, many of the concepts and biases I will teach you throughout this book will seem simple. That is by design! My goal as an applied behavioral economist is always to make it so these complex topics are easy to understand and apply, so that anyone can begin to use them and see results right away.

Behavioral economics is a field rooted in science, the result of decades of research from multiple disciplines around the world: psychology, economics, neuroscience, and philosophy, to name a few. However, it is also an art. There are hundreds of rules, concepts, and stimuli working together in the brain to shape everyone's reality and decision-making. The concepts introduced in this book are proven, and we all experience them somehow, but choosing which to apply, when, and how to apply them? That's where the art comes in.

You can be a great manager and lead your employees through change in a way that feels natural: where they are happier, the business is more successful, and everyone wins. I promise it's not in a utopian land of unicorns and rainbows. This truly is achievable for all managers, regardless of background, personality type, or experience. If you are ready to learn, I will teach you the art of change (which is solidly based in and backed by science).

So, what is the trick to being naturally better at change (and helping those around you be more accepting of it)? It takes an understanding of the brain's rules and then working with those rules instead of against them. That's essentially it.

Now, please don't misunderstand me—there are no "silver bullets" when it comes to change. It still takes effort. Behavioral economics will give you the ability to shift your focus from being a victim of the reactions of others to updating the way you present the information to them so you get the reaction you are looking for more often.

Snowballs of Change

When you think about change in your organization, what comes to mind? You probably think of those big, gigantic projects that need a lot of people rallying behind them. Projects that involve converting to a new software system, shifting your entire company to be remote during a global pandemic, a massive cultural realignment, a new CEO, a merger. Right?

Of course, those are some of the changes I'm talking about in this book, but change is much more than that. The change referred to here looks at *micro-*

moments. The everyday changes that seem small are critical moments of opportunity. They are the snowflakes that come together to form a snowball of change.

The average person makes 35,000 decisions every day.[4] You, your employees, your boss—each making 35,000 daily decisions, the bulk of which occur below your conscious awareness (more on that in a minute).

Think about the typical approach to change management. How much time is spent behind closed doors refining a plan announced in an email, press release, or single meeting? Or, if the team is lucky, three or four meetings (because if you still have questions after that, you've crossed over into "problem" territory and get labeled as someone who needs to get on board or find a new boat).

What is the alternative?

Let's start by taking a step back. If the average person makes 35,000 decisions per day and we assume eight hours of sleep, you have sixteen hours of decision-making time. If we assume an eight-hour workday, half of the decisions (17,500) are at or about work. Taking that out, for a five-day workweek, there are 87,500 weekly decisions. Further out, we have 4,375,000 decisions by every employee every year (I've factored in two weeks of vacation if you're doing the math along with me). Of course, not every decision has the same weight and impact on the outcomes of our lives, but even the smallest moments begin to accumulate and are either working for you—or against you.

Your one hurriedly typed email didn't convince people to change their minds? That single conversation didn't move the needle? No wonder! There's a full-on tundra of past status quo moments working against your single snowflakes.

Creatures of Habit

All mammals have habits (whales, dogs, rats[5]), and research indicates that anywhere from 40 to 95 percent of our decisions are habitual.[6]

It makes sense when you think about it (breaking the daily decisions down the other way, you end up with 2,187 decisions every hour, thirty-six per minute, or a little more than one every two seconds). Clearly, you aren't making logical, deliberate choices about each of those micro-decisions. So, what does that mean for your work? Let's see:

- You sit down at your computer. What's the first thing you do? Why is that first? What if you did something else?
- Before that, where do you set down your bag, coat, or keys as you get situated in the room?
- Your phone buzzes or dings with a notification. What do you do? Did you consciously think to look at it, or was it more of a reflex?
- It's two o'clock and your energy dips. What do you do? You might grab a snack, play a game on your phone, or stop working on that important project to check email, Slack, or social media.

These are all examples of the many habits in your life—personal and professional—every day. In each of them, an association in the brain triggered an action (or a desire to act). According to habit expert Wendy Wood, that is essentially all a habit is—a mental shortcut we learn as we repeat our behaviors in a way that reliably produces some sort of reward.[7]

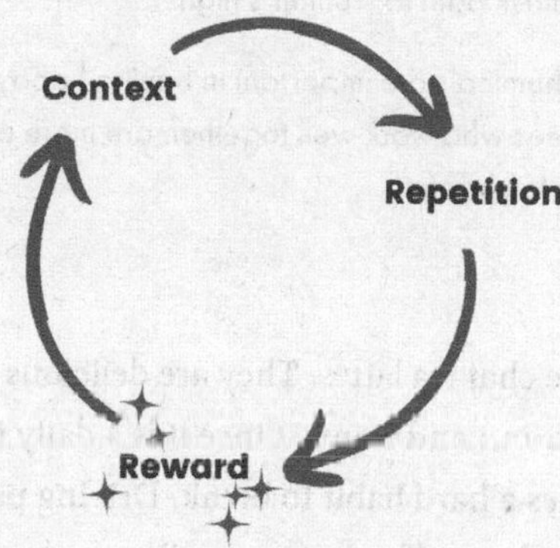

Habits are a mental shortcut formed from context, repetition, and rewards.

Whether it's dopamine, oxytocin, serotonin, or endorphins, our brains are constantly seeking feel-good chemicals.[8] Habits form because your brain is trying to find predictable ways to get **rewards**. This is why **repetition** matters, so the reward can be predictable. Over time, the brain starts to connect what we did to the **context** around it (where we were, who we were with, what time it was, what we saw, heard, or smelled). Eventually, that context makes it so the behavior automatically comes to mind, and the cycle continues, reinforcing itself again and again.

Once you see it laid out like this, it is probably painfully obvious, right? A total face-palm moment—and that should be a hint that we are getting on the right path. (The brain knows what it does. When you say, "You do this" and it says, "Yeah, I do that," it's usually a good sign.)

A DOSE of Chemicals

The brain loves four main feel-good chemicals:

Dopamine: anticipation, motivation, and goals

Oxytocin: empathy and social bonding

Serotonin: mood and pride

Endorphins: mask pain (a "runner's high")

The DOSE brain chemicals are important in having happy, engaged, motivated employees who work well together, are more productive, and respond positively to change.

As an example, I love chai tea lattes. They are delicious and full of sugar, which my brain seeks out and wants. Once it is a daily indulgence, it is expected and becomes a hard habit to break. Driving past Starbucks on my way to work, I may tell myself to be strong. "You're better than this, Melina. Do *not* touch the turn signal!" I give myself logical pep talks and try to rely on willpower. My eyes glance at the clock. I've got time and I really need a latte today (but this is the *last* time, I swear!). Tomorrow I'll start my new life when I have less on my plate, but right now I've already turned into the drive-thru.

Attempting to change the *response* is what our logical brain likes to think is needed, but it's wrong. Trying to will myself not to stop when my brain is already excited and knows it could get some reliable rewards is extremely difficult. If you want to change a habit or start a new one, you need to understand the context and reward to modify the right things. That's what is driving the behavior.

Something as simple as taking a different route to work so I don't drive past the Starbucks (changing the context) eliminates the cue and can change the habit.

Identifying Habits

So, how do you know if the thing you're doing is a habit?

Wendy's easy tip: Consider if you need to be focused on the task or if your mind can wander.[9] For example:

- Pouring your coffee in the morning while mentally responding to an email
- Scrolling through text messages during the video conference
- Listening to a podcast while driving
- Mentally preparing your shopping list while in a meeting with your boss

If you can accomplish the task without actively thinking about it, it's a habit.

And, when it comes to any business-related tasks—let's use scrolling through text messages during a video conference—which one is the habit? The reading of the texts or how you are showing up in the meeting? Or, more likely, both?

Thinking About Change

If you only consider change as the big, massive projects where you send out impersonal communication and expect people to jump on board quickly, you ignore millions of habitual micro-decisions. Are they building into a snowball that will support change when it comes? Or piling up into an iceberg of habit-driven indifference that will stand between you and the change you seek?

In my opinion, every conversation and interaction at work is a change initiative. Because we are in an environment with lots of change, we are always in the wake of a change that has already happened, some that are actively occurring, and others we need to prepare for.

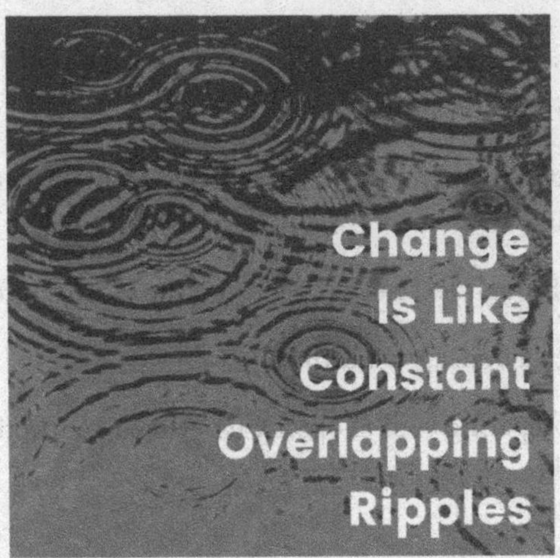

Even small changes cause ripples. Everyone is in a constant state of overlapping changes.

This is why I say a manager's main job is to lead employees through change. In businesses these days, we are constantly asking employees to adapt:

- Trying out a new process or procedure
- Working with a new teammate
- Reporting to a new manager
- Switching physical locations
- Rallying behind a new goal
- Researching a new possible project to pitch
- Absorbing the role of another coworker who has left
- Trying out the newest productivity tool or philosophy

This list could go on forever, but I believe you get the point. Employees are dealing with change all day, every day. Some are small changes, some are big, but they all matter. Whether you take the time to think about it in advance, all those micro-decisions are either working for you or against you. Wouldn't it be better to be thoughtful about them?

The way our brains respond to change can be trained like a muscle.[10] The more people get used to and accept little changes, the easier it is to handle the big ones when they come along. If your company has a culture of change, employees can be ready for anything that comes their way.

Now, when I say "culture of change," I do not mean some sort of unpredictable environment where nothing is ever the same. Quite the opposite. Too much change—change for change's sake—is a recipe for disaster. Because the brain is built on habits, it needs predictability to run efficiently.[11] Our brains get overwhelmed easily and overwhelm can have a huge, negative impact on decision-making.[12]

The War for Time

As Ben Horowitz shares in his book *The Hard Thing About Hard Things*, you need different management strategies during times of "war" and times of "peace."[13] During times of peace, you can look at proactive, incremental changes that allow you to get a little better each day. During times of war, it is more about triage and having enough bandwidth for the big things that matter.

When it comes to your team's performance, "war" is not just when you are battling large change initiatives. As you learn more about the brain, you will see that any time you create undue stress and pressure on the brain, it is essentially a time of war. **The biggest problem and barrier to your team naturally being accepting of change is time pressure: deadlines, projects, busy work.** When the brain is bogged down with this sort of stress, it is more likely to rely on biases that favor the status quo and to oppose anything that isn't predictable or known (like your proposed change, no matter how big or small).

In business, we are constantly working under deadlines. You need to complete this project by five o'clock, finalize that report before tomorrow's meeting, or get on board with a new initiative *right now* so you can pile it onto your already-overloaded plate. Because time is a scarce resource, it gets spread thin quickly, which can cause employees at every level to feel time pressure.

With unlimited time, most people tend to be risk-averse. Imagine you are assigned a big project to work on and need to report on it in six months. Most people will get hung up on little details when there is ample time. The risks of moving forward weigh heavily, and it feels like there will be plenty of time once you get that other thing out of the way.

Then one day, you wake up and realize, "Oh no, that project is due Friday and I've barely started!" It's a stressed-out frenzy of late nights and pushing other deliverables not to miss this deadline (creating a vicious cycle avalanche that can be hard to get out from under).

It likely won't surprise you to know that time pressure is a form of stress. It also floods your brain with chemicals that cause it to be overwhelmed.[14] You've felt it—you know the anxiety that comes from watching the seconds tick, tick, tick away before that meeting where your boss needs the report you are frantically trying to complete.

You feel anxious, worried, and stressed. Your hands might be shaking as you try to read the data and copy it from one document to another, impulsively checking the numbers four or five times before you hit "print" and then mutter, "Come on, come on" under your breath while the pages begin to come out of the machine.

That same stress occurs while you are working under any looming deadline. And while we may like to believe that we are better with this pressure, it simply isn't true. You may make quick decisions (because you must), but they aren't necessarily the best or most strategic. They are likely decisions to help your brain feel safe in the status quo it loves so much. This could be as simple as defaulting to the same ineffective report you've always used instead of taking the time to consider why you are bringing a report at all, what you want people to do with the information, or the best way to present it to help the company reach its goals.

Studies have shown that even though people can *feel* more creative on high-pressure days, they are *45 percent less likely to think creatively when time is scarce.*[15]

The lesson here is that spreading your team thin so they constantly feel the scarcity of time pressure will lead to less creative work and increase the likelihood that they will make mistakes because their brains are overwhelmed.

Prioritizing your resources and narrowing your focus so the team is less stressed will alleviate the effects of all the biases you'll learn about in Part II and make any change initiative easier.

Focusing on fewer things (the right things) will help your team be more innovative, effective, and productive (while also feeling better about it). Oh, and of course, more willing to change and adapt naturally.

So, what is a culture of change? To paraphrase Hemmingway, it recognizes sudden success is a product of gradual micro-changes. Our businesses need to adapt to survive in the economy of today and the future. After all, there is a reason this chapter and book opened with the quote, "Even if you're on the right track, you'll get run over if you just sit there." For our businesses to successfully change, our teams need to change with us—and it can be done in a way where they are thriving, engaged, and loyal to the organization instead of burnt out, spread too thin, and dreading the next meeting.

It is the job of management to help ensure that the right changes happen for the right reasons at the right times and that they are communicated to employees in the right ways.

What Makes a Great Manager?

I mentioned that having happy, engaged employees is important to a culture of change. That isn't just my opinion. Engaged employees are linked to an increase in innovation, productivity, and performance while also reducing costs across industries and company size.[16] The *Harvard Business Review* found that 71 percent of senior-level executives from organizations with five hundred or more employees (about half had over 10,000 employees) ranked employee engagement as very important to achieving overall business success. Unfortunately, only 24 percent believed employees at their companies were highly engaged.

According to JP Morgan in a 2022 article, the new Human Capital Factor (HCF), which takes into account employee pride, purpose, and psychological safety "has demonstrated that it may be more relevant to a company's stock performance than other investment factors."[17] The cofounder of Irrational Labs, who came up with the HCF, is behavioral economist Dan Ariely, who said "[Investors] often focus on 'what is easy to count' instead of 'what is important to count.'" It is time to pay attention to what is important instead of easy. Companies need to prioritize engagement and invest in their human capital.

So, what is the best way to predict whether employees will be engaged or not? It isn't company policy or good intentions—it's their manager.

According to Gallup, "Managers account for at least 70 percent of variance in employee engagement scores across business units." A 70 percent variance! This has resulted in staggeringly low engagement scores among workers: They say 30 percent of employees in the US are engaged at work and worldwide is even worse—a mere 13 percent.[18]

The article these stats are included in is titled "Why Great Managers Are So Rare." They say the biggest problem is that companies hire managers without the talent to do the job well 82 percent of the time. To put that another way, **four out of five current managers do not have the talent required to excel in the job** in a way that will help the company and its employees to thrive.

How reliable is the data? Gallup has studied performance at hundreds of organizations—measuring the engagement of more than 2.5 million work units and 27 million individual employees over two decades. Given that, it must be safe to conclude there is some truth in their statement.

According to Gallup, the problem is that most managers are hired because of their success in another role or their tenure with the company, as if putting in the time means they deserve to go on to the next step. However, the problem is, an individual's success with sales, programming, customer support, or graphic design doesn't translate to possessing the talent needed to motivate and engage employees. Gallup found that one in ten people has the natural skills to be a great manager, another two out of ten have the potential to be trained, and if the other seven out of the ten become the manager, things can go wrong quickly.

After their decades of research, Gallup says great managers:

- **motivate** employees to act;
- **engage** others with a compelling mission and vision;
- can **overcome** adversity and resistance;
- create a clear culture of **accountability**;
- build **relationships** that foster trust, open dialogue, and full transparency; and
- **make decisions** based on productivity, not politics.

How actionable is their advice? Their article explains that since one in ten people is likely to have the talent and most people don't lead more than ten employees, chances are one person on every team has the talent to be the leader! That's fine and dandy, but what are you supposed to do with the 82 percent of existing managers who don't have this natural talent?

Demoting them back to a previous job (so someone on their team who used to report to them is now their manager) will probably not go over well. Waiting anxiously for those managers to leave or retire will take way too long. And how can you be sure that the ones who leave are those without the natural talent for the job?

Do you have to accept a world where your employees are disengaged and hope for the best?

While Gallup concluded that only three out of ten people have the potential to be a great manager, that finding was based on data from an old way of doing things. It didn't include a framework for helping people proactively understand how the brain works to excel in management.

In *The Voltage Effect*, John List shares the science of what great ideas need to scale. One of the five vital signs is that you can't rely on only the best of the best—perfect fits—to make it work.[19] He gives the example of a pre-K program he co-created, which had great results in its petri dish. Unfortunately, it relied on great teachers to execute the program. Not all teachers are great. For the idea to scale, it needs to work even with average and bad teachers. It needs to be implementable by everyone, regardless of a natural talent for the job. I've kept John's five vital signs of scalability in mind while writing this book because every employee deserves a great manager who helps them be engaged.

This book is here to help every manager—whether they have the natural talent for the role or not—to be excellent at leading their teams through change. If you want to put in the work to be a great manager and are willing to learn and adapt based on the science I present to you in this book, I truly believe you can achieve that goal.

And for all the companies out there, imagine if you could make employee engagement levels higher and more predictable. Less turnover, higher productivity and profits. Wins all around. And unlike the statement Gallup made that you need to get rid of 70–80 percent of your managers because they will never be up to the task, this book and its philosophies are intended to help more of your existing managers become great at leading employees through change, one micro-moment at a time.

The best news is my framework is designed to make all managers more effective by enhancing their ability to manage employees through change. It is about understanding and working with natural human behavior—the micro-moments that make up all the interactions in the office. Small tweaks and shifts can prime and nudge your teams to be on board with whatever change you present and model you approach it with instead of constantly fighting against it without understanding why.

Whatever models you use for managing change and motivating employees. Whatever your software for tracking employee performance. Whatever your goals and how you track KPIs. Whatever your industry. Whatever your current engagement levels. If your company is made up of people managing people and you do not plan to remain stagnant, this book is for you. Are you ready? Let's do this.

CHAPTER 2

Unlocking the Secrets of the Brain

The last chapter gave a little hint at how the brain works, but before we get into the biases and concepts, it is important to explain the rules of the brain. This foundation is critical for understanding and applying my "It's Not About the Cookie" framework for change.

The Receptionist and the Executive

Let's say you want to have a meeting with Oprah. You can't just call her up and get an appointment on the calendar—you need to make it through a receptionist (or ten) first. The "gatekeeper," who keeps every little thing from making it to the remarkably busy Oprah, is a lot like the relationship between your conscious and subconscious brain.

Nobel Prize-winning behavioral economist Daniel Kahneman talks about the brain in two systems.[20] **System 1** (which I call the "subconscious" throughout this book and *The Brainy Business* podcast) is the automatic system. It is quick to react and can handle an incredible amount of information at any given time—to put it into computer terms, as much as eleven million bits of information per second.[21]

By contrast, **System 2** is what I refer to as your "conscious" brain. It is much slower and cannot handle nearly as much information. Compared to the subconscious' eleven million bits per second, the conscious brain can only do about forty bits per second (yikes).

Subconscious (System 1) = Receptionist

Uses proven rules to make tons of quick, automatic decisions

Conscious (System 2) = Busy Executive

Only really important stuff makes it to this level; slower, more evaluative decisions

While we like to think we're in control of our brains and decisions (and believe we are doing everything as a complex, logical evaluation), it isn't the case. The conscious brain cannot handle enough information to get through the plethora of decisions needed to survive.

Unfortunately, these two brain systems don't speak the same language. That is why employees say they are on board with an initiative but take actions that derail its progress. They aren't purposely lying to you (for the most part). It turns out people don't know what they will do. Even worse, they can't tell you after the fact why they *did* something because, again, the two parts of the brain aren't speaking the same language.

Should Is a Four-Letter Word

Here at The Brainy Business, "should" is a four-letter word. If you have ever found yourself saying, "People *should* get it" or "Anyone *should* be able to figure out this is the right choice," it's time to stop and reflect.

People do not always do what they "should" or what is in their best interest. Even if they *know* what is best, it doesn't mean they will do that thing. We all want to be healthier, and we know what it takes to reach that achievable dream: proper nutrition and exercise.

But do we do what we know we *should*? Often the answer is no.

This is the conundrum of the brain: The conscious "knows" what to do but can't get the subconscious to follow orders. NYU psychologist Jonathan Haidt[22] explains this with a fantastic example of someone riding an elephant.

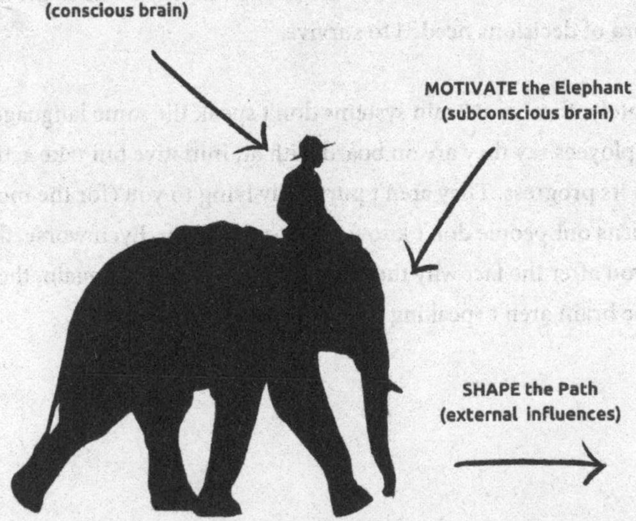

Elephant and rider image inspired by the work of Jonathan Haidt.

The rider (conscious brain, System 2) can have the best plan and all the logic in the world, but if the elephant (subconscious brain, System 1) is distracted or uninterested, it will win without consulting the rider. Pushing or pulling the elephant, yelling at it, or pouting won't get it to move. But the right **nudge** of encouragement—perhaps a pool of cool water on a hot day?—and look out, subconscious is on a mission!

Working with the brain—helping the rider and the elephant be on the same path—is always easier than pulling the elephant along. That is where The Brainy Business' approach to change management steps in.

This approach will help you unlock the brain and its concepts; you will understand how they can be combined and applied in all sorts of ways to those micro-decisions to help your team become naturally better at change.

When it comes to change management, the first problem is that the conscious "rider" of the person presenting a change is trying to talk to the employees' "riders" in their language when they need to focus on the elephant first.

Elephants don't understand human logic, and the subconscious brain is the same way. Start with the elephant, and the rider will help explain why it was a fantastic idea.

Learning the Rules

Think back to when you first learned to drive a car. It was likely a slow, tedious process where you were constantly second-guessing yourself. (Where do my hands go? Which pedal is that? Don't forget to check the mirror!)

It was slow because your conscious brain had to learn and set up rules for the process. Now that those rules have been established, it's much easier—you likely didn't even need to think about any of that the last time you drove, right? That's because driving skills have moved into your subconscious brain. While you drive, your brain is still making the same decisions and evaluations, but they are done quickly using established rules of thumb—things that have worked in the past.

Everything's smooth and easy—until you're driving over a mountain pass in the pouring rain between a semi-truck and a guard rail—then you can feel reality shift and slow . . . way . . . down. You're aware of every tiny shift in the wheel against your hands, every eye movement feels intense, your shoulders are raised, and you're hyper-aware.

That is the process of your subconscious handing the wheel over to your conscious brain (pun intended). Driving at this moment is too important and needs diligent focus to keep you safe. It's worthy of those forty bits per second (and something else needs to be relegated down to the subconscious level while driving takes precedence).

This is also why you turn the radio down while searching for a new address; the conscious brain can't handle that much input at one time.

Overwhelmed Brains Remain Stuck in the Past

How easily do our brains get overwhelmed? It takes a lot less than you think.

A study in the *Journal of Consumer Research*[23] found that remembering a few extra digits can impact decision-making. One group was given a two-digit number and the other a seven-digit number to remember while going through a series of tasks. One of the tasks was choosing their snack after the study was over. Those remembering the simpler number were more likely to choose the healthy fruit salad. Those remembering only *five more digits* were more likely to choose chocolate cake.

In another study, people were asked to imagine their car needed repairs; in one case, it would be $150 to fix it, in another $1,500.[24] Those who were well off had no impact when they completed unrelated spatial and reasoning tasks after the thought experiment. Lower-income individuals did fine when the imagined repair was small, but when they were told it was $1,500, their cognitive functioning was impacted, and they performed poorly on the tests. **Just imagining the consequences and next steps of a fictional repair bogged down their conscious brains so much that they had a hard time doing an unrelated reasoning test later.**

How often are you heaping mountains of decisions, facts, figures, and deadlines on your coworkers or employees, trying to help them make a better, more informed choice?

Imagine this: You have a meeting with one of your direct reports and don't expect you can get time on the calendar with them again for another week. You need to have an in-depth conversation about a big change coming up. The meeting is an hour long, and you also have a bunch of other stuff to hand off to them. So, you decide to spend the first twenty minutes unloading all that other stuff you want to give them a heads-up on. You ask for a bunch of facts and figures; dates, names, and project steps are flying around at high speed, so you'll have enough time for the real stuff. They are nodding along and furiously taking notes. For some reason, when you present the change information and tell them what's upcoming, they react poorly. Perhaps they get defensive, complain, or have an outburst. The conversation drags on and you now need to have three more meetings and multiple emails to get them back on board.

Perhaps you didn't have to "imagine" that, rather you are reliving half a dozen examples where this has happened to you.

The thing I want you to consider now is—how differently might that meeting have gone if you would have separated the most important thing and only focused on it going well? The information you unloaded at the beginning of the meeting was out of your convenience; it was faster and easier for you to word-vomit everything instead of organizing your thoughts and sending the less important stuff in an email or other correspondence.

Instead of taking forty-five minutes to write a thoughtful email and plan for the change meeting, you gambled that it would go well and you could save a few minutes by bundling it all together (no shame, we've all done it). To try and save those minutes, you ended up with several hours of meetings, emails, and stressful plans to fix the created problem.

As you will see throughout this book, **thoughtful planning up front will always save time in the long run.** The cognitive capacity of the conscious brain is a big reason why. When its forty bits of processing power get overloaded, the subconscious must step up and handle everything else. There are lots of biases, heuristics (rules of thumb), and concepts it uses to operate and most of them are wired to maintain the status quo (i.e., oppose change) because the subconscious operates on predictability and habit.[25] Not taking this into account makes every change conversation harder.

Nature, Nurture, or Both?

While the earlier driving example shows how your brain has created rules and biases based on your individual experiences, the subconscious' rules are also greatly influenced by our biology and have been developing for thousands of years.[26]

Consider the "fight, flight, or freeze" response we all have when confronted by danger. There's a reason our automatic process takes over in those intense situations—it needs to protect us based on what has kept us (and our ancestors) alive for generations. Any of our relatives who saw two reflective dots in the bushes during the night and thought, "Nah, I know you all think that's a tiger, but I bet you're wrong!" probably didn't make it through the evolutionary chain before being eaten by said tiger.

One example of this is our need to **herd**. Animals, including humans, herd for protection.[27] Anyone on the periphery is more likely to be killed by a predator than those on the inside, so it is beneficial to be as close to the center of the herd as you can. If you watch videos of sheep being herded by dogs, the outside animals run fast to get to the middle, while those in the center are less inclined to move—until they find they've drifted too far out.

They also follow each other almost blindly, the assumption being, *If everyone is running in this direction, they must know something I don't. Instead of waiting around to see what they are running from, I will run first and ask questions later.*

Humans do this too. It is in our nature. Nearly every teenager in the world has said something like, "But *Mom*! All my friends are doing it." To which Mom replied, "If all your friends were going to jump off a bridge, would you do that too?" That feeling of discomfort from not doing what everyone else is doing—whether it is going to a concert or holding a certain attitude toward a new project at work—is fueled by herding instinct.

We also learn by herding and observation. Babies watch adults and other children do things and emulate them almost immediately. This is how we learn to speak, walk, be safe, and find food. It is critical to our survival.

What Are *They* Doing?

Because we are a herding species, we are more likely to look for **social proof** to guide our decisions (especially in times of uncertainty). We instinctively look to the majority of others like us to determine how we feel about new situations.

This is why five-star reviews make us feel comfortable buying from a company we have never done business with, and labeling items as "most popular" will increase how many people choose them. They are forms of social proof, which help us make and feel good about a decision.

Even in seemingly illogical ways, social proof will encourage our behavior to take action. Imagine you see two job postings (assume the details of the roles are essentially the same). The only difference is that one says fifty people have already applied for the job and the other says five have applied.

Logically, your rider knows you should apply for the job with only five applicants—you have a much better chance of getting that job than the one with more competition. What do people do? They prefer and are more likely to apply for the job with more applicants. Matej Sucha and the MINDWORX team found that including social proof on job postings increased the likelihood that someone would submit their resume or CV by 138 percent.[28]

As another example, I want you to imagine you are brought into a meeting of people like you with a large corporation that wants to invest in some smart people, and they are using this group interview to find the best of the best. You sit down and are shown a slide with a simple equation on it, say, "What does two plus two equal?" You are the eighth person in the group, and as each person ahead of you answers four, four, four, you follow suit. Easy.

There are a couple more rounds of this and then another seemingly simple question, "What color do you get if you mix red and yellow?" You had an immediate answer in your head and were confident until the first person said "purple" with absolute confidence. "Purple?" you think. "How ridiculous." Then the next person says purple. And the next. And the next. You are getting anxious now. You thought it was orange, but these people must know something you don't. It's almost your turn—what will you say? Purple or orange?

Studies show that up to 75 percent of participants will give an answer they *know is wrong* to go with the group.[29] Three out of four!

You might say you wouldn't do it, but in the heat of the moment, your subconscious herding brain could take over and force you to say something you don't believe to keep from being ridiculed. There are multiple biases at play here that we will get into later, but it is important to know that our herding instinct is at the root of many actions, decisions, and behaviors of your team members.

I also want to note that herding mentality is more likely to come out when people feel vulnerable or unsure of themselves. Shaking up the status quo (again, presenting people with change) is when people are likely to feel uncertain and look to others for clues on how to behave even more than usual. If you do not consider herding and the brain's natural tendencies when presenting change initiatives, get ready for a stampede of elephants.

While I don't recommend calling people "elephants" or any other names, I will use this and other terms throughout the book to help reinforce the parts of the brain I am referring to and the general actions people take. These terms are used with the best of intentions for your learning.

The Past Shapes the Future

Both types of learning—those created through the generations and via our individual experiences—influence the rules the subconscious lives by and constantly applies throughout the day.

Almost everything you do in life is based on a prediction of what is coming next, based on the subconscious' understanding of the past; it churns through choices and usually does well. However, more often than we realize, the subconscious uses rules that don't perfectly fit the situation (as you will repeatedly see through the examples in the remainder of this book). With eleven million bits to process every second, it's no wonder that every decision isn't 100 percent on point.

For example, most of us aren't in danger of meeting tigers these days, but the brain still applies our fight, flight, or freeze response when we are "attacked" by a meeting with the boss or overwhelmed by the idea of changing our routines.

The most important thing for you to know as you evaluate your approach to change is that behavioral economics helps us understand these rules of the brain. The biases and concepts I will introduce throughout this book have been proven across culture, age, gender, income, education, and more.[30] They may appear in different degrees and are not the same for every person in every situation, but we all do each of these things to varying degrees in our lives every day.

Imagine seeing a chessboard for the first time and sitting down to play against a master, but you weren't allowed to know the rules and had to learn as you went. You might come up with theories and guesses for what each piece could do, or why and when to move one, but it would be incredibly difficult to make progress and you would rarely win.

How much could you learn at each point if you knew the rules going in? How different would that experience be?

To me, understanding behavioral economics and how the brain makes decisions can set you up to be the chess master instead of a fumbling novice. When you know the rules of the game and most of the world doesn't, what sort of leg up can you and your counterparts have in navigating and leading your teams through change?

Manipulation and Ethics

At this point, I'm guessing you may have a question about ethics and manipulation. The "chess master versus fumbling novice" analogy intentionally brings this to mind (it's called **priming**, which you'll learn in Part 2).

Whether you think about it or not, your behavior influences others. You can't stop or get away from that. As Vanessa Bohns shares in her book *You Have More Influence Than You Think*, this can be a huge benefit.[31] It's a funny little quirk, but research has shown we tend to believe that we pay attention to others more than they pay attention to us. She says, "We are constantly influencing people in ways we don't always notice. That means there is more opportunity and responsibility out there to use that influence for good and in ways that affect change." Not being thoughtful about it is more likely to make things worse than it is to benefit the recipient.

For our purposes, the information throughout this book is presented to help you think about your approach to change and helping people to be naturally better at it. And, while I often don't recommend pointing out to someone that they are being biased (it rarely goes over well), the insights from this book should also not be a secret. Everyone will be better off if they understand their brains and those of the people around them better. This isn't something only for the managers to know, something to be kept behind a corporate veil until someone is promoted. Everyone will benefit from the insights in this book, and the information should be widely spread throughout the organization.

I wrote this book to help you consider how you package and present information to help people be happier about, and more likely to support, change initiatives at work. It will help those around you be more likely to become engaged team players (though that doesn't mean never dissenting or presenting opposing opinions—we aren't in the market for a bunch of yes-people). The goal is for your organization and its people to have smoother navigation through the inevitable and constant seas of change.

Yes, any knowledge can be used for "evil" in the hands of the wrong person. I hope and intend that everyone will use the powers given to them here for good. Err on the side of helping people improve their lives, and please nudge responsibly. Do you solemnly swear to use these powers for good?

If so, please read on.

CHAPTER 3

Change Is All About You

When you think about change and helping those around you to be better at it, it always starts with you.

The subconscious brains of the people around you react to what is put in front of them. Changing how you present information will change the response. You can think of yourself as an elephant whisperer—but you can only achieve that if you engage your rider and train it to support the elephants.

This presents a challenge because your elephant will have natural reactions as well. It might get angry, annoyed, or feel stressed and overwhelmed. Those reactions need space to breathe, ideally before you present change to others because the way you present a change has a huge impact on whether it is accepted or rejected.

What is the real problem?

The way people respond to change.

OR

The way change is presented to people.

Much like the brain itself, change is unbelievably complex. There are a lot of moving parts and nuances. No two change scenarios are identical. One employee will behave differently in two different scenarios. Two employees could receive the same message and have different reactions.

Yes, this seems obvious and logical when you read it here—of course, people behave differently in different scenarios! So, why would you expect a one-size-fits-all approach to change to work for every person in every scenario?

Your brain is wired to look for the easiest path to success: the "Yes, I agree to accept change" box every employee can check and adhere to without faltering. While it is compelling to search for that perfect formula that can be applied every time, the algorithm of change management does not exist. Your team is not made up of ones and zeros. Context is key and each scenario deserves thoughtfulness (if any task doesn't justify thoughtfulness, I encourage you to ask if it is worth doing). Before having a meeting with someone (or sending an email or shooting a quick Slack message), you should know:

- why you are reaching out to them in this way at this time;
- where they are now;
- where you are helping them to go;
- some possible paths to help get them there; and
- points where errors are likely to come up and how you can help keep them on the path.

Asking the right questions and knowing the top brain barriers to be on the lookout for (and how to work with them instead of against them) is your path to change. While it isn't a formula, it can be applied consistently in every interaction—big and small. At first it will require a little conscious effort, but it will become a habit faster than you think (and those positive habits are great at snowballing).

It may be tempting to skip these steps as your brain looks to revert to the status quo, but I promise you it is worth investing in these areas if you want to master change. Every little moment matters, and they all add up. As Susan Scott said in *Fierce Conversations*, "The conversation is the relationship."

The Value of Common Language

In *Evolutionary Ideas*, Sam Tatam shows the importance of having a common language on a team.[32] With it, we can communicate more efficiently and effectively. If we had to ask for the "long, bent, yellow, slippery, morning staple" every time, it would take a lot longer to get breakfast, and it is more confusing than saying, "banana."

Sharing the biases and concepts throughout this book is a step toward a common language that can help your team be more efficient and effective at change.

Relationships Are Memories

Organizations rely on people working together toward a common goal. If you don't make and maintain good relationships with your peers, the members of your team, those in other departments, and your superiors, you will have a hard time influencing them (and leading change is all about influence).[33] We casually throw the term "working relationship" around often, but have you ever stopped to think about what it means? According to *Psychology Today,* "Like a character made of LEGOs, we're built of blocks of memory that all fit together to form our consciousness."[34]

This is true of our entire existence, not just our relationships with others, and it is directly tied to what I've already told you about the way the brain processes information. When you first learn something, it requires your slower conscious brain to figure it out. Once it becomes a memory, a habit, a rule, a bias, a heuristic, a common language association, it has moved into the subconscious processing space. Everything you have ever learned has gone through this process—how to walk, talk, eat, manage interpersonal relationships, drive a car, not throw a fit when other people pick up a toy you were *just about to play with*—each is its own LEGO block, building upon the other pieces to create our conscious existence.

Memories Lie

When you think about your brain and its memories, you may relate it to a filing cabinet, or think about it like a photo stored in the cloud. We like to think that each memory is an exact copy of what happened, in all its intricate detail, stored in a secure place to look at whenever we want and then put back in the same condition it was in when we took it out.

Unfortunately, that's completely wrong.

Our memories are basically inaccurate renditions our brains tell us, and every time we access them, we change them a little. So, the more you think about something, the less and less it's like the original version. Frustrating, right?

Every person's brain is constantly changing their memories to better suit their needs: making themselves look better, exaggerating certain parts and playing down the importance of others, all without our conscious knowledge. It can even create false memories: where someone believes something happened to them, even though it was only in a story or "fake news."[35]

At eighteen, I started working in an airline call center and quickly made my way into the customer care department. You know all those times you were annoyed at the airline and called to yell at someone? That was me.

It was fascinating to hear the stories people told about their experiences. The horror of the most terrible flight delay: "It was *excruciating*!" they would say, "I was stranded at the airport with no food and uncomfortable seating and the bathroom was a mess..."

A few clicks on the computer and, come to find, their flight was delayed for ninety minutes.

In case you didn't know, every person who calls to complain to an airline will ask for a free ticket—a slight exaggeration, but not that far off. I once had a woman ask for a free ticket because the flight attendants took too long to give her a can of soda on the flight (she was in row eight).

Perception is reality in these memories, and the experiences people have while stuck in the airport for a lightning storm will impact their view of the airline even though the weather is beyond its control. Logically, people know the airline is making choices to keep everyone safe. But the subconscious brain isn't keeping that in mind when it files the experience away as a memory.

Think about the old fishing tale example, where someone caught a minnow and twenty years later it was "a whopper—the biggest thing you've ever seen!" They are not intentionally lying (usually). In their brain, the fish gets bigger each time they tell the story, as they unknowingly level out some facts to exaggerate others. This is a natural tendency of the brain, and we do this in all sorts of experiences, not just to look good to other fishermen.[36]

Another funny quirk is that the brain doesn't always know the difference between what actually happened to us and something we *think* happened.

Do you remember that time you got lost at the mall when you were five years old? You were walking with your mom and a fluffy orange teddy bear caught your eye. It was fascinating because orange isn't a common color for a bear, and it looked so cuddly through the glass. In what felt like a second, you looked back, and your mom's black-and-white-striped dress was nowhere to be found.

Fear surged within you as you started to panic and looked frantically around at the legs of adults quickly walking by. They say it was only twelve minutes before you and Mom were reunited, but it felt like a lifetime.

Believe it or not, your brain has stored this little tidbit in your memory bank. Even though it is a fake memory, your brain doesn't always file it that way. In one famous study,[37] a third of people who were reminded of "that time they were lost at the mall" (which never happened) believed it to be true. One-quarter continued to claim the untrue story as a real memory after two follow-up interviews.

And because of **familiarity bias**, the more something is said, the more we believe it.[38]

If I went to the members of your team and said, "Don't tell anyone, but I heard from the CEO that the company is planning on a merger and your department will likely be eliminated . . . better start applying for other opportunities now before the word gets out!"

I might immediately follow that up with a "just kidding." But we can't un-ring the bell. People can't un-hear the thing they heard. And our brains like consistency, so once we have heard something, we believe it to be true and look for things that confirm that expectation.[39]

- When have you shared something with a trusted confidant before all the facts were in and found out later you were wrong?
- What have you said off-the-cuff in a moment of overwhelm that is sticking in the brains of your team?
- What are your most vocal team members saying to the rest of the group around the physical or virtual water cooler?

Hindsight may seem to be 20/20, but memories are not always what they appear and are likely to be exaggerated when people are stressed or worried about how they will be impacted. While curiosity can be great, it is also an un-scratchable itch.[40] And as Jon Levy said to me, "When the stakes are high, and there is a gap in what people know, they will fill the gap with whatever they can get their hands on and gossip, regardless of how inaccurate or wrong, is a tool that can reduce anxiety and reinforces social ties."[41]

This book is full of micro-moment missteps that result in big problems, taking time and other resources to resolve. Thoughtful sharing of information (facial expressions, virtual backgrounds, email signatures, and more) can make all the difference. (And, yes, I'll address each of these.)

Are Your Existing Relationships an Asset or a Liability?

If you have been in your role or organization for a long time, you have built a substantial collection of memories with the people around you. Each time you interacted with those people (walking down the hall, in a curt email, in a meeting where you were distracted, when you supported them in front of the team), millions of pieces of information have been sorted and filed by the subconscious brain, and their perception of you is constantly evolving with each new experience.[42]

So, as you consider how you will transition yourself and your approach to managing your team, it is important to know where you are coming from.

- How do people see you today? (Your boss, your coworkers, your direct reports, people in other departments)
- How do you want to be seen?
- How big is the stack of memories that exists? Are they working in your favor or constituting an obstacle to overcome?

Don't go with wishful thinking here. If you are going to change, you want to understand what needs to change around you and where to start. If there is a substantial pile of counterproductive memories working against you (say, being known for years as someone who resists change or as a *don't-bother-me-unless-it's-urgent* manager), you will not change those perceptions overnight.

That constant stream of micro-decisions took a long time to build, so you need to be dedicated to building new memories to replace the old ones. As I said in Chapter 1, if you are willing to put in the work, you can change this—and thankfully, it doesn't need to equal the amount of time that went into creating the memories that exist.

If you have ten years on the job, it won't take another ten or even five or three years to create a new memory set, but it will take consistent, thoughtful actions—from grand gestures to micro moments. Don't get discouraged here. It takes focus, but it is achievable and there are so many benefits.

Much like creating an exercise habit, you wouldn't expect that to change overnight. Saying "I'm a runner now!" doesn't make it true. Planning for your workouts doesn't make you more fit. Once you decide you will run a marathon this year, you need to put all your eggs in that basket to make it happen. You need to rechoose that repeatedly, multiple times a day. Meal prep. Accountability buddy. An app that tracks your progress. Running coach to help your form. Laying out (or sleeping in) your running clothes so you eliminate excuses. Changing your route to work so you don't drive past the tantalizing smell of your favorite doughnut shop.

Creating the running habit is built on the same micro-decisions I mentioned earlier. You want to stack as many of them as you can to become (and reinforce) that memory of who you are (a marathon runner) again and again in every tiny choice.

It's the same with your management style. To lead others through change, you need to be thoughtful about the memories, relationships, and micro-moments. You need to walk the walk, talk the talk, think the think, and be the be. To bring it back to the snowball, you need to put in the time to collect enough snowflakes before they can come together to form the new normal.

Change doesn't have to be hard, but it does take thoughtfulness, consistency, and focus.

Reflection Point

You chose this book for a reason, presumably to enhance your skills as a manager and to make the world better for your employees and the teams you are on. (Arguably, influencing teams of people who don't report to you is even more difficult and important for your career success—all these lessons work for those teams too). I want to take a moment here for you to set your intention. What is your goal upon reading and completing this book?

Being a great manager has a lot to do with supporting your team, but it starts with you. Do you enjoy your days? Are the bulk of your micro-moments positive, or are they mostly made up of stress, deadlines, feeling "busy" and going through the motions until you get to the next step on the ladder (where you can *really* make a difference)? You'll learn more about the biases at play that contribute to this thinking in Part 2, but I want you to take a moment to consider this now before moving on.

They say the best time to plant a tree was twenty-five years ago, and the second-best time is today. As I've already shown you, change isn't in the single, big moments; change comes one tiny moment at a time. If you dream of a day where you can be truly influential, where you can love your work every day and inspire those around you to be better—don't wait. Do something small today and do it again tomorrow. There are many examples of micro-shifts throughout this book that you can apply systematically to get a little better each day. Your brain loves to be better than the "you" of yesterday, so this will be right in your subconscious' wheelhouse.

The great opportunity doesn't have to depend on someone else or your next role—make the most of what you have right now. And, believe me, my roles haven't been all Instagram-worthy dreams. In college I had an internship as an inventory management specialist for an electrical wholesale distributor. The company had thousands of items in the warehouse, and it was my job to pick up a giant printed document each day, which had line after line of things like, "Bin 324: ½-inch copper screws (Total: 42,437)." It was then my job to go to that bin and start counting "1…2…3…" All day. Every day. Seriously.

But I enjoyed each day, had fun with it, and was quickly given the opportunity to create a marketing department for this family-owned business. Good things can happen when you find joy in the micro-moments.

To paraphrase the great Roy Kent (because *Ted Lasso* is amazing and should be quoted whenever possible): Most jobs are fine. Most people approach their work each day with a mindset of "fine." And there's nothing wrong with that. Most people are fine, but it's not about them. It's about *you*. You deserve a life that makes you feel like you've been struck by lightning. That energizes you and lights you up. Don't you dare settle for "fine" when it is wholly within your power to be more.

A Tree a Day

If you are skeptical about the difference one person can make with repeated small actions over time, I want to tell you about Jadav Payeng, also known as The Forest Man of India.[43] He was deeply saddened as a teenager in 1978 when he saw more than a hundred snakes that died after a flood because there was no shade to protect them. He got twenty seeds and twenty-five bamboo shoots and began to plant in the desert. But he didn't stop there. He vowed to plant a tree every day—something he has now done for more than four decades. In and of itself, planting more than 15,000 trees and plants for over forty years is miraculous. However, because the trees could then pollinate, reproduce, and create an ecosystem, the efforts of this single man have resulted in a 1,360-acre forest oasis in the middle of a desert that is home to five tigers, a herd of 115 elephants, over 100 deer, wild boar, many species of birds, rhinoceros and, of course, snakes.

One person dedicated to being the change and making a little effort each day has created a chain reaction that has allowed countless species to thrive in an otherwise desolate area. When you understand the biases and concepts introduced in this book and start with one small change a day, you will be amazed at how quickly it spreads throughout your team (and throughout your entire life).

Change takes dedication, authenticity, focus—and it starts with you. If you don't change your approach, how can you expect others to react differently? Let's plant some trees, shall we?

CHAPTER 4

And. . .It Has Nothing to Do with You

"There is nothing wrong with change . . . if it is in the right direction."

–WINSTON CHURCHILL

Yes, I dedicated an entire chapter to why you are the most important factor in helping others around you to change, and that is still true. However, it is *also* true that you can't help others to change by only thinking about yourself.

As you will learn in much greater detail in Part 2, our brains are biased to believe that we are better, faster, and smarter than everyone else. Our brains start, and often focus on, our standing within the group (or herd) and have an eye for self-preservation.

When presented with new information, the natural reaction is to think, "What does this mean to me? How does this affect my status quo? Where is the threat to my safety and survival?" Your subconscious brain is doing this constantly to keep you alive. Of course, everyone else's brain is doing the same thing.

While we are all impacted by the biases and concepts of behavioral economics, they don't always show up in the same way. Someone worried about their reputation or outcome will present information in a way that benefits *them*, instead of in a way that makes it easier on the recipient.

While I don't want to put the cart in front of the horse by providing a bunch of "what to do" examples before you learn the foundations, I do want to give a taste of how the "It's Not About the Cookie" framework can be applied after you've completed this book. This story shows how a micro-moment can have a huge negative ripple effect when not considered thoughtfully:

"Everyone, gather around," the boss said while rubbing his eyes and forehead to make his exasperation and exhaustion apparent. "I know many of you aren't going to like what I have to tell you now, but please don't shoot the messenger here. We've got some big changes coming and I need everyone to get on board even if you don't like it."

Have you ever given or received a speech like this?

Chances are you have. The problem is that language like this makes it so herding and social proof work against you instead of for you. It has used herding incorrectly in a couple of ways. Let's break it down.

Mistake #1: Nudging the herd in the wrong direction. The statement started with, "I know many of you aren't going to like what I have to tell you now" and "I need everyone to get on board even if you don't like it"—you have made it clear that most people (i.e., the herd) will not like this. The natural inclination of any subconscious brain hearing that is to assume this is bad and something to dislike. You have primed the audience to fight you on, or seriously question, anything you tell them next. In the case of a big change initiative, they may say things like their "gut" tells them something is wrong. Even if they can't articulate the problem to you, in our case, that is the subconscious' natural herding instinct, and it could be from something as small as this one sentence spoken offhandedly when the change was presented.

I like to call this unintentional normalizing.[44]

To show how this works, I want you to imagine it is your first day of college. The dean welcomes everyone and at orientation and says, "Cheating will not be tolerated. Eighty-five percent of people try to cheat at some time in their academic careers, but the school is on high alert, so don't even try it."

You may never have considered cheating as an option, until that day your professor presents a pop quiz you are completely unprepared for. As you look around the room, feeling the stress swell up inside you, you remember what the dean said and how you have never seen or heard of anyone else being kicked out of school for cheating. "If 85 percent of people try it," you think, "a lot of people must get away with it!" Cheating now feels like it is the safest thing to do because you are part of the herd.

You may not believe that this would sway you or anyone on your team. You are a good person who doesn't cheat, and you can't honestly believe you would do that. Like the purple and orange conundrum in Chapter 2, when presented with an uncomfortable situation, people are likely to follow the herd. It is important to note that even if you, and others in your organization, say and truly believe you would not be impacted by herding, social proof, or anything else in this book, that doesn't make it true. Everyone does this. It is human nature.

How to fix it: Know what you want people to do and emphasize the right herd. Before you present a change initiative, it is important to think about the ideal behavior you would like from everyone so you can find points to nudge them to stay on track.

Don't think about the problems or who might be difficult (**confirmation bias**). Instead, consider the best-case scenario in small and reasonable steps. This is one meeting or introduction to a concept. It is unreasonable to expect people will go from zero knowledge on the topic to on board and excited immediately.

And, honestly, if they do, that is another problem. Having a team that is overly agreeable without ever questioning an initiative is a sign of complacency, not necessarily of great communication. As Jay Van Bavel and Dominic Packer say in their book *The Power of Us*, dissenting is difficult for people; for that reason, they often only do so in groups where they care a lot.[45]

It is unreasonable to expect people will jump on board every time with no questions, regardless of what you say to them. For now, think only about this first meeting. Given the path you want them walking down, what is the first tiny step they should take?

It might be something like:

- being open to the idea;
- being interested in learning more; or
- know the initiative is coming and gathering questions to ask in an upcoming meeting.

Once you know what you want or need from your team in this first step, look for the herds that work in your favor. People will instinctively follow the herd, so where is the one that is in line with what you want them to do?

Pro Tip:

Don't use the crutch of herding to provide a short-term win for a long-term loss. Let's say someone on your team misses a deadline. They apologize profusely and appear to be beating themselves up about it. To console them, you say, "Don't worry about it. You know, people miss deadlines all the time around here and no one ever gets mad."

This can fix the short-term problem, sure, but you don't want to lean on herding today for a behavior you want to *change* tomorrow. If you tell someone that everyone else (or a majority) of people do something, they will feel comfortable continuing to do whatever it is and it will be much harder to get them to change later.

Thoughtfulness matters and shows how every interaction is about change. How is something you said offhandedly weeks, months, or years from now rearing its ugly head in a way that is making today's change difficult?

Mistake #2: Telling people *not* to do, think, or feel something. In addition to generally not loving being told what to do (a principle known as psychological reactance),[46] humans are bad at not thinking about things.[47] For example:

Do not think about white bears.

How'd you do? My guess is your brain is flooded with white bears right now. This is because of the way our brains retrieve information. To think of anything, we also think of what it is not—the items closely related to it.[48] (These are the LEGO blocks of memories and associations we talked about in the last chapter.) So, when you tell people "not" to be upset, or "not" to shoot the messenger, or "not" to rebel against your suggestion, it is *not* going to work well. (See what I did there?)

How to fix it: Like the first item, **don't add those negative thoughts into their brain space.** As a reminder, the original statement included, "I need everyone to get on board even if you don't like it." Even removing the last qualifier so it says, "I need everyone to get on board," would be better. It isn't great, mind you, but it is better.

Instead, look beyond what *you* need (see the next mistake for more on this) and consider what *they* need. And not their conscious, logical brain either. What does the elephant need? What can you say to calm the elephant to help achieve the goal you outlined in the first step?

Mistake #3: Hedging for your herd reputation instead of the project at hand. Look back at the full initial statement again and tell me who the speaker is most concerned about: "Everyone, gather around. I know many of you will not like what I have to tell you now, but please don't shoot the messenger here. We've got some big changes coming and I need everyone to get on board even if you don't like it."

This clearly isn't about the team, right? The speaker has chosen words that make it seem like they only care about themselves. They want to ensure this is easy for *them*. Subconscious elephants are then looking around at their peers in the herd to see who is looking out for their best interests—the boss certainly isn't. And, especially when the boss is seen as part of a different team (which they are making clear here), they are not going to get the benefit of the doubt.

How to fix it: Don't think about yourself. What do the recipients of this information need to get to the next step in the process (and the goal)? My friend Nikki Rausch has a great tip for fixing this off-putting language, which is to look for the "I statements."[49] In those three sentences, the speaker used the word "I" or phrased the language about themselves and what "we" (presumably the higher-ups) need *five times*.

There is no concern for the people receiving the information and what they need to hear to understand and support the change. When you stop and look at it, of course people react badly to a statement like this!

They feel undervalued, unappreciated, and like no one is looking out for them (so they better be on high alert for all the stuff in this change that could be negative for them). One seemingly small miscommunication like this early in a change initiative can derail the entire project. Ten thoughtless seconds can pack thousands of snowflakes into the iceberg.

Trying to rewrite that existing text by removing the "I's" is difficult. Instead, you need to start from scratch with the recipient in mind. What do they need to hear right now to help them feel comfortable?

Let's pull in everything we have learned from these three mistakes to write a new potential introductory statement:

"Many of you have said at one time or another that you don't like the current software system: I have heard you say it is too slow, unreliable, or has unnecessary steps. If you have ever been annoyed with the system, here's some great news. Keeping all your insights in mind, a project is now underway to implement a new, faster, more reliable, and efficient system to help make your job easier. For everyone who wants to provide feedback on what would make the new system ideal, we're setting up interviews next week. Right now, what questions can I answer for you?"

Of course, the introduction needs to be catered to the situation, but notice the shift in the focus, tone, and approach. The new statement emphasizes what the listener cares about (making their job easier), letting them know their concerns have been heard even when they weren't formally asked for ("I have heard you say..." and "keeping all your insights in mind"), and it focuses on something the herd has agreed upon in the past that helps support your initiative (the old system is bad). This also includes some ability for them to be involved in the solution (which increases engagement and intrinsic motivation) and gives them room to be heard with a thoughtful question.

Let's Ask People What They Want

You've likely heard of the gold and platinum rules. In the past, people said to use the golden rule and treat others how *you* would like to be treated. The platinum rule is to treat others how *they* would like to be treated. Asking them what they want seems like the best step in pursuing the platinum rule. The problem, of course, is that people are bad at knowing what they want.

For example, students who took a photography class were presented with two of their photos at the end and asked to choose one to keep. One group was told they could change their mind whenever they wanted—come back and swap for the other photo until the end of time. The other group was told their decision was final—once you leave, this is being sent to another country immediately.[50]

Which group do you wish you were in?

Most people *think* they would like to have the option to change their minds, but those people were more miserable in their decision. They agonized over whether they did the right thing, impacting their overall happiness. As the study's authors said, "When you've made an irrevocable decision, you rationalize it. Once something's gone and gone forever, the mind gets to work figuring out why what it got is really better than what it lost."

We think we know what will make us happy or why we might dislike an initiative, but we are often wrong.

The good news is while people can't always tell you what they want and how they want to be treated, behavioral economics gives you insights into what the brain is seeking so you can live the platinum rule. Yes, sometimes you should still ask because incorporating people into the process helps them be more intrinsically motivated and productive. However, understanding the brain's biases will help you realize where people are saying one thing and don't realize they mean something else.

What's Next

Part 1 of this book was dedicated to:

- The two systems of the brain and how decisions and habits work
- How relationships are memories
- What makes a great manager and how anyone can get incrementally better to achieve that goal

- Why thinking about change should not be reserved for giant, company-wide initiatives but is fostered as part of the culture one micro-moment and decision at a time (snowflakes, snowballs, and icebergs)
- Why you need to plant a tree a day—do something now instead of waiting for the perfect forest opportunity to come tomorrow

So what's next?

Part 2 is all about **awareness** of the biases in your way and concepts of behavioral economics to work with (or navigate around) them. This part is not about action. However, you will find little, easily implementable changes (which I call "**Micro-Shift Moments**") sprinkled throughout. To keep it from being overwhelming there isn't one for every bias and concept you'll be introduced to. Instead, they've been carefully curated to start getting little wins as you go so you can begin to build a culture of change for yourself and your team.

Part 2 is divided into three sections of three chapters each. These are in an intentional order, based on how I want you to think about implementing change. You need to **calm the elephant** and reduce the cognitive load before thinking about the **status quos and shortcuts** you want to work with or navigate around. That should be considered before you add in the dynamic of an **us versus them** mentality and how it impacts your teams.

The chapters themselves are themed by a problem, statement, or behavior you might see in the workplace.

In one chapter, there might be four biases and two concepts outlined within its content and there could be just one bias or concept in the next. Some items may pop up in more than one chapter. I want to note that this book does not cover every bias, heuristic, or concept that exists, nor will it outline everything that could ever come up in your working life. This is a curated collection of the topics I think are most important for someone who wants to apply behavioral economics to be a manager who excels at leading employees and teams through change. It is robust enough to do the topic justice without including so much to cause overwhelm.

Where to Focus Your Attention

If you don't remember and relate to things, you can't apply them to your life and work. At its core, this book (and all my work) is about application. While there are many academic citations and formal names used throughout this book, in my opinion it is less important that you know the specific name of the bias, heuristic, or concept (this book and its glossary can be your handy resource guide whenever you need it). This is why I use the terms "subconscious" and "elephant" or "conscious" and "rider" instead of "System 1" and "System 2." Those latter terms are a System 2 process and if each time you see them used you must stop and think, "Now, is that the fast one or the slow one?" it will use up too much of your conscious bandwidth for you to get the point—the concept being shared and why it matters to you as a manager.

Looking at a scenario and asking a good question (*I wonder why that happened?*) and being able to think about what *might* happen in advance is so much more important than winning a game of "Name That Bias!" (Though that does sound like fun; note to self, next project: create the *Name That Bias!* game—ha!)

Instead of getting super bogged down on exact terms, I want you to know that these things exist and understand how they work together. As you go through the content, I recommend you focus on the intent and theme of the chapter itself. Consider:

- What does it mean?
- How does it impact behavior?
- How has each member of your team exhibited this behavior?

- When have *you* exhibited this behavior?

That last one can be harder for many, as it is often easier to see biases in others than it is to see them in ourselves (one of our many biases at play). That being said, it is important to take time to reflect on yourself and others for each of the biases, heuristics, and concepts in this book. Know that I will often use the terms "you," "your brain," "the brains of your team," "our brains," "the human brain," and the like. I mix up the language to keep it interesting but know that everything you read applies to you, your team, your boss, your friends, family—you get it. And, when I say "your employees," the lessons apply to any team of any size—they don't have to report to you. Influencing others who don't report to you can be even more difficult but just as important.

Take time to reflect as you go (there are "Reflection Points" to help remind you), as thoughtfulness is a key theme throughout this book.

Part 3 introduces my "It's Not About the Cookie" framework and how anyone can apply the behavioral economics lessons from this book. It is a step-by-step process that can be applied for any level of change—from a single aspect of one person's job changing (implementing a new process or moving their desk) all the way to a huge change initiative that impacts the entire organization (rebrand, restructure, merger). It builds upon the biases and concepts introduced in Part 2 and adds complexity by starting to combine them to achieve various outcomes.

Behavioral Baking

In my first book, *What Your Customer Wants and Can't Tell You*, I introduced an idea called "Behavioral Baking" to think about applying behavioral economics to business. Flour, sugar, butter, and eggs can be combined in all sorts of ways to create lots of things. If you want to be a baker, you need to know what each ingredient does and what you plan to make. You can't throw everything in a bowl and hope it becomes brownies (well, I guess you *can*, but it's not a great strategy), so you need a recipe to follow.

You may have some flops along the way, but you would never say, "I tried baking once; it's not real." That would be ridiculous. You would look at what happened (my cake is dense; I will try less flour next time or aerate the eggs longer) to adjust your behavior the next time. It takes thoughtful application and dedication with little tweaks as you get better and better. When you start baking, you will probably start simple—say with a boxed cake mix. As you get better, you can mix in some spices or add in some chopped nuts or chocolate chips. Eventually, you might get comfortable enough to start baking things from scratch. You will learn at every step of the way and maybe have a misstep here or there, but it is all progress on your baking journey.

It's the same as you start to apply behavioral economics to your change management approach. The biases and concepts introduced to you are the ingredients. What you want them to combine to make (cake, cookies, pie crust, bread) are your goals, and the framework is your recipe to get there.

Now that you know what to expect, let's talk about the biases blocking your way and some concepts you'll need to overcome them.

PART 2

BIASES AND CONCEPTS

2.1
CALMING THE ELEPHANT

As noted in Part 1, the most important thing you can do to help pave the path of change is reduce the cognitive load. This will help your team have the mental bandwidth necessary for changes (and helps give you more time to focus on important stuff instead of wasting time on clarifications and busywork). So, what can you do? This section builds upon the analogy of the brain being like a person riding an elephant (hence my phrasing of "calming the elephant"). When the elephant is distracted, it is more likely to rely on the biases and heuristics (be less open to change) and cling to the status quo.

You have likely had someone say that no matter what they try or how much they focus on something, they can't change. (Perhaps you have felt this yourself from time to time.) Common advice might be to suck it up and figure it out.

The problem is your rider is trying to shout logical arguments at their elephant, forcing it into submission to change its behavior and shift its focus. Metaphorically or literally yelling at someone while their brain is overwhelmed will not get you the result you want. Progress cannot be made until you have calmed the elephant.

Not to confuse things with a new animal, but this example from Stephen Wendel in his book *Designing for Behavior Change* is too good not to share.[51] Imagine you are walking along the beach and see a fish flopping on the sand. You have a few options to help the fish; you could:

- explain to the fish how its gills work and why it should be in the water;
- yell at it, "Get in the water! Hurry up; you're dying!";
- dig it a trench so it can swim back to the water; or
- pick it up and put it in the water.

In business, the first two approaches happen more often than we realize. And while option three is great when the time allows because it will make it easier for people to do what they want to do anyway (their jobs), it is not helpful when the fish is already out of the water. It's a little preoccupied with, you know, *dying* to be able to listen to your logic. It is also aware that it needs to get to the water, so shouting at it with the obvious result and no support to make it happen isn't useful. Digging a trench would have been nice when you had the time to plan (i.e., in times of peace). In times of war, like when the fish is dying, taking the time to dig a trench is too little too late.

Picking up the fish and putting it in the water every time isn't the solution; as I have said, the goal isn't to become a micromanager of your teams. However, if you've got a bunch of fish flopping on the beach, you need to get them back into the water before you can start to talk about the future.

Human Example

I once had a struggling employee. She missed deadlines, showed up late for meetings, and had general performance issues. This was her first professional role, and I could have chalked it up to a lack of experience. Instead, I looked for other explanations of what might be going on. I've always made time to meet with my employees regularly. These one-on-ones always started with: "What's the most important thing we should be talking about right now?" per advice from Susan Scott in *Fierce Conversations*.[52] In this particular meeting, when asked that question, my employee responded, "I wish we could talk about my wedding!"

I replied, "Sounds good; what would you like to talk about?"

She was understandably surprised, but I was serious, knowing that this might be her distracted elephant problem. We spent the next thirty minutes of this one-hour meeting discussing the color of the bridesmaid dresses, which invitation styles she was debating between, and other decisions causing her stress. Once she had been able to make a few of these decisions, she noticeably relaxed. She followed up on a few of her outstanding tasks, we planned the rest of the week, and I was pleased to see that she could focus again now that her subconscious elephant was calm.

Many might say that this conversation wasn't my problem. Her inability to focus and get through those decisions aren't part of our business, and therefore, we shouldn't care. I disagree.

Our brains don't separate problems and thoughts in this way. They can only take so much at any given time (**cognitive load**), and once that glass is full it spills out and creates problems in all other areas of life. While it is not a manager's job to focus on every aspect of someone's life and hold responsibility for them meeting their deadlines, showing up on time, or having focus...when a little caring and thoughtfulness over thirty minutes (that we would be spending anyway) can have such an impact, I say, why not? There is more harm in ignoring the elephant than in taking the time to ask a thoughtful question, thoughtfully listen, and then move on.

Reducing the cognitive load by being thoughtful is your key tactic for calming the elephant (or getting the fish back in the water). The three chapters that make up this section are dedicated to showcasing what that means, some ways to spot the problem (using the titles of the chapters and details throughout), and related concepts you will need when you start to implement in Part 3.

CHAPTER 5

I'm Not Biased

Let's get this out of the way—everyone is biased. We will never eliminate bias from our organizations, HR departments, team members, or ourselves. This is an unrealistic, unattainable goal that is set up to fail. Here's why.

As you learned in Part 1, the brain relies on the subconscious the vast majority of the time. The subconscious uses rules of thumb to make quick, efficient decisions. Without this process being used for most of our choices, our brains would use up too much energy and we would cease to exist.[53] The subconscious needs predictability to work. When things aren't predictable, the brain needs to defer to the conscious to make a slower, more deliberate decision (which is still informed by lots of other biases that have worked in the past).

The term "bias" has gotten a bad rap. I suppose we have a bias about biases, so let's correct that now. Biases themselves are not bad; we need them to survive.

However, there are times when biases do not serve us or our organizations well. Being aware of them is an important step in not letting them run the show and wreak havoc on our businesses and interpersonal relationships. As a manager, when you can spot biases and know how to navigate them, you can help your team thrive through change.

Naïve Realism

Naïve realism is the belief that, unlike other people, we see reality exactly as it is.[54] We are objective and unbiased. The facts of the world are clear and should be obvious to everyone else. Anyone who agrees with us is rational and everyone else is either uninformed, lazy, irrational, or biased.

There's a reason this is the first bias—it is foundational to every bias and lesson in this book. Knowing this exists will help you learn and challenge all the biases at the right time to be a better leader.

As an example, if you find yourself having conflicts with a lot of people and thinking no one understands what you are saying, or if you are often wondering, "How can they not see it? It's so *obvious*!"—it's time to look inward.

Try to have a little perspective and look from that other person's point of view. We are all biased and irrational (yes, even you) and much more often than we realize (i.e., all day, every day). Remembering this can improve communication and effectiveness.

When you feel like you are the only objective one in a sea of biased individuals, stop. Do a thought exercise and say, "How would I prove myself wrong?" One way to do this is to imagine you are an attorney and you have been given the case against you. It is your job (and you will presumably be paid a large sum of money) to find the flaws in your argument. What would you attack first? Where are the weak spots? What would a jury of your peers find convincing?

If you can't find anything—keep looking. There is always another reasonable perspective, I promise.

Egocentric Bias and Naïve Cynicism

Have you ever been on a project and felt like you put in way more work than everyone else? That you are being a team player and everyone else is being selfish and in it for themselves? So has everyone else, and it goes beyond work.

When couples were asked how much they contributed to household chores, including making breakfast and managing the finances, the averages exceeded 100 percent. In other words, people believe they do more than they do and downplay what someone else is doing (I didn't see it, so it didn't happen).[55] This is called **egocentric bias.**

As another example, two people who did not know each other were tasked with playing a cooperative video game together for five rounds, which was about thirty minutes of playing time.[56] They were told that the point of the experiment was to see how much people could assess, monitor, and remember their performance and that of others. So, once they were done playing, they completed a survey and were asked to indicate how much they felt they and their partner contributed across eight categories and what they thought their partners would say. Four of the categories were positive, like "points scored" and "power-ups earned," and four were negative, like "falls" and "missed shots."

When rating themselves, both sides were fair and indicated that they both contributed to the good and the bad of the game.

However, when asked what they thought the other player would say, things got biased. People predicted (incorrectly) that the other person would exaggerate the good things they did and downplay the bad stuff. Because of **naïve cynicism,**[57] we expect other people to be more biased than we are. We believe that our perception is reality and that others will not recognize the effort we put in (and not acknowledge their faults). It is easier to remember when we did things—the shots we made and the power-ups we got—than it is to estimate how often the other people did those same things. We also tend to focus on ourselves much more than anyone else, but that's a bias for another chapter.

Our brains can have an internal Instagram filter we put over our stuff and see everyone else in the harshest, worst lighting possible. We also assume others will do this much more often than they do, so we expect that they will be motivated by their self-interests and treat us unfairly if it is to their advantage when that often isn't the case.

False Uniqueness Bias

The human brain is wired to make us believe we are more unique than we are—that we are special, our problems are special, and we need unique solutions. [58] There are two important sides to this bias:

- When the trait is **positive**, we will **underestimate** how many others do the same.
- When the trait is **negative**, we will **overestimate** how many others do the same.

As an example, if you always get your annual reviews submitted on time, regularly read books to enhance your knowledge, or take the time to meet with your direct reports regularly—you will *underestimate* how often other managers do these same things.

On the flip side, if you are consistently turning in your annual reviews late, take on too many projects so you are working a lot of late nights and weekends, or are consistently canceling meetings with your team at the last minute because something more urgent and important came up—you will *overestimate* how often other managers do these same things.

Why do we change our tune based on the desirability of the action?

One side enhances our view of ourselves: We like to see ourselves as better, faster, stronger, and smarter than everyone else and *underestimating* how many other people do the good things we do makes us feel special. On the other hand, because we are a herding species, we don't like to stray too far from the group in a way that will make us stand out. This is especially true for negative stuff, so overestimating how many other people do the same less-than-optimal things makes us feel safer and more protected, like we are part of the herd.

Consider this: If all the other managers treat their employees like they are less important than priorities coming from above or laterally (i.e., by consistently canceling meetings with them because something more urgent/important came up), why should that have any impact on your approach to meetings with *your* team? Don't justify easy behavior by saying that "everyone else does it" or "that's just the culture around here." You can set a higher standard for yourself. As a manager, how much of your job should be making your employees a priority? Or making your team thrive? Forget about what the other managers do and set your non-negotiables.

Micro-Shift Moment: Research shows that shifting your self-talk from first person ("I got this!") to second person ("You got this!") increases the likelihood of success.[59] Shifting your language from "can't" or "shouldn't" to "don't" will also make you more likely to follow through. *Can't* is a state of deprivation, while *don't* is more empowering. Instead of saying, "I shouldn't cancel that meeting," try, "Your team relies on you. Don't cancel meetings with them."[60]

What Should Our Goal Be?

So, if we can't eliminate all the biases, you may be wondering what you should be striving for. First is to know that everyone is wired to believe:

- You put in more effort than everyone else (and they are unlikely to see or recognize that).
- While others are biased, you are not. You see reality as it really is. Those who disagree with you lack common sense.
- You are motivated with good intentions; others are more selfish and out to take advantage of you, the system, and any advantages they can get.

And remember, everyone else thinks this in reverse (i.e., you are the biased one).

Behavioral Concept: Priming

We can't change these biases from being a subconscious default. Trying to stop that is like if you tried to tell your brain the color "red" will never be associated with the word "apple" again. You can't tell your brain to unlearn that any more than you can try and say, "Don't herd anymore, brain" and have it say, "Oops! My bad. I'll stop doing that."

Over the years, I've found that experiencing a concept is the best way to understand (and eventually use) it. In that spirit, consider the poem below:

> Behavioral economics concepts get shared the most,
>
> on *The Brainy Business* podcast (where I am host).
>
> Listen in the car as you drive to the coast.
>
> Learn lots of new concepts; across social media you'll post.
>
> Say, what do you put in a toaster?

I am guessing you have seen a trick like this before—maybe you even thought, "You won't fool me, Melina! I know you want me to say *toast*, but the true answer is *bread*" (or bagels or whatever).

Here's the thing: you know on a *conscious* level the right answer is bread, but you still need to remind yourself, "don't say toast" because you've been primed to give the rhyming answer. Your conscious brain *knows* it's wrong, and you may have stopped yourself from saying "toast" aloud, but you could not stop "toast" from being that first, automatic response.

Priming is a constant influence. Beyond rhyming, all the senses perpetually take in information (a huge amount of those eleven million bits processed by the subconscious every second). Since sight takes up 70 percent of the body's sense receptors, I'll focus on that.[61]

We don't realize it, but our eyes are constantly moving (three times per second on average) and checking the environment for threats.[62] If nothing of note is going on, no alert is sent to your conscious brain because it doesn't need to know, but that doesn't mean it isn't impacting your behavior.

For example: do you have a special time you always seem to notice the clock? Maybe it's 11:11, 12:34, or 5:55. It may feel like a sign of some higher meaning that you always look up at that exact moment. In reality, your eyes saw the clock hundreds or thousands of other times on those constant scans. You don't remember because no other random time mattered enough to flag the conscious brain.

Now you may be wondering, if our eyes are constantly scanning the world around us, why don't we see big blurry blobs all the time? It's because while sight is taking place in the eyes, *vision* occurs in the brain.[63]

We have evolved so we can focus on something *and* constantly scan our environment for threats or potential stimuli through saccades. Saccades are why things like flipbooks work—our brain weaves together a stream of basically still images and predicts what is missing to make it look and feel constant. Cool, right?

The main lesson here is how much the brain is guessing—even at things right in front of you. At any given time, your eyes can only make out about a keyhole-sized circle in fine detail. Everything else is of, as neuroscientists Stephen Macknik and Susana Martinez-Conde say, "shockingly poor quality."[64]

This is also why we prefer the **status quo**: The brain's job is to keep you safe and evaluate as much as possible with existing rules to fill in the blanks. Predictability and efficiency go hand in hand. And even when you (or your colleagues) don't consciously notice an object or image, it still influences behavior.

For example, while I love sarcastic humor, I make it a point not to have anything snarky in my office. TGIF messages or "Hang in There" cat posters are a constant negative prime that could be impacting your performance (and anyone on your team for whom it is in view).

You can't say, "People shouldn't read that much into it." The instinct is fixed, so take the time to be thoughtful and intentional about what you surround yourself with. As Rachel Lawes, an expert in semiotics, says, "Where there is choice, there is meaning."[65]

You choose the items in your office, and each is a sign or symbol communicating something to the brains of the people who see it, whether you consider the message in advance or not. It can be priming their demeanor in the meeting or how they feel about you (forming memories that work for or against your goal).

Micro-Shift Moment, Personal: Look around your space. What is in your line of sight? On the walls, on your desk, in the distance, on your computer desktop, in your notifications (that red bubble saying you have 2,486 unread emails is priming you to feel busy, overwhelmed, and stretched too thin—it is also a default setting that can be changed so you don't have to see it). What isn't serving you well? Get it out of there! I'm not making you throw anything away (though there is a lot of stress created by clutter, so I am all for it if you choose to). For the purposes of this micro-shift, think of it as "out of sight, out of prime." Try being in a prime-friendly space for thirty days; what changed?

Micro-Shift Moment, Others: Have a trusted colleague take a screenshot of you during a video conference at a random time (you don't want to be posing and trying to put a filter on it, you want the reality). Step back and look objectively at the entire space. Is it cluttered or disorganized? How is the lighting? Is there anything on the walls? Should there be? Do not rely on a virtual background or blur setting and assume that will solve your problems. It sends the signal that you don't trust them enough to see your space (don't worry, we revisit this example again later).

Creative Primes

At a 2018 event for 150 executives, McKinsey put priming to a practical test.[66] The task was to work in pairs to come up with ideas for the coming years' leadership program, something we all have done before.

The teams were split into two groups; all had the same task, but each side had a few differences in execution.

- **Group 1 (Warm)**
  - Received friendly instructions ("Hello!" "We need your help," and "Thank you")
  - Were provided hot tea or coffee to drink and were encouraged to offer drinks to others
  - Were to write their ideas down on sticky notes using colored pencils

- **Group 2 (Cold)**
  - » Received firm instructions ("Please adhere to these instructions during the session on ideation" and "You should ensure you are properly hydrated during the session")
  - » Were provided ice water to drink
  - » Were instructed to write "clearly listed and numbered" responses on white lined paper

So, what happened?

The "cold" group came up with thirty-two ideas, which were mostly logistical and structural (i.e., don't schedule too many speakers too quickly; make sure breakfast and lunch are on the agenda). The "warm" group generated seventy ideas, which were much more innovative (i.e., host a post-apocalyptic simulation; team building via white water rafting).

A few primes are included in that test. Let me break down four things to try:

1. **Leverage visual associations.** Our brains are literal.[67] If you want your group to come up with more innovative ideas, take some time to consider what comes to mind when you think about the concept of innovation (or creativity) itself. What brands or companies come to mind? Concepts or words that flash in your brain immediately?

   Write them all down. Once you have your list of literal associations (i.e., colorful, abstract, out of the box, open, Apple), find ways to incorporate those visually into your meetings and planning sessions to encourage the behavior you are priming for. Using Apple as an example, you could put their logo up on the wall, sure. But, because our brains are so literal, you could also put a bowl of apples on the table, and it might still spark innovation by subconsciously reminding participants of the company.

2. **Make it colorful.** Ditch the lined paper. How could you replace legal pads or Word or Excel documents with opportunities to take more free-form notes? Including colorful pens and Post-it notes for in-

person meetings (or emojis and interesting software for virtual ones) can encourage people to be more creative without realizing it.

3. **Get rid of rigid.** Bureaucratic, cold instructions force the brain into a regimented box and stifle creativity. If you want to prime people to be more open, make sure your instructions reflect that. Incorporating friendly, open language can encourage your team to find more creative paths to new solutions.

4. **Encourage generosity.** While warm beverages have been shown in some studies to be linked to feeling warmer toward others, this isn't always the right drink choice. However, you can always encourage people to be generous and offer a drink to others. This action can promote a spirit of collaboration that is foundational for teamwork and innovation.

Bad Priming

"Be in my office at two. We need to talk."

This email came from my boss at around ten o'clock in the morning. As you can imagine, I began to freak out. This email would be terrifying at any time, but I'd only been working for her for a couple of months, so it was extra scary. What had I done wrong? My brain began to scan through all my current and past projects. Had I forgotten something? Was there a ball I'd dropped somewhere?

Understandably, I assumed the worst and spent the entirety of the next four hours distracted and preparing to defend any possible mistake. By 1:55 p.m., I knew what was going on with every project, interpersonal relationship, and tiny detail that may have prompted this meeting. If a battle was coming, I was ready for it.

Counting down the seconds until 2:00 p.m., I did everything to calm my nerves. I knocked on the door and she gestured for me to take a seat. My heart was pounding with anticipation when she said, "I wanted to let you know that I will be out of the office tomorrow, and I'm listing you as my contact while I'm gone."

Dumbfounded, I realized that was it. That was the reason for this impromptu "we need to talk" meeting. Other things were said to me in that meeting, but I don't recall what they were. My brain was too busy coming down from the flood of chemicals that had fueled my day.

Thankfully, this didn't turn into an incident, and I realized that my boss often sent emails like this. In the years I worked for her, it was never about anything big. This was how she communicated, so I adjusted to it.

But can you imagine if I *had* done something wrong? Is there any way this meeting could have possibly gone well? I was on edge. My brain was buzzing, and the elephant came in fully ready to charge. Even now, more than a decade later, reliving that incident to write it out here, I felt my heart rate speed up. In this case, she primed me to expect the worst.

Like the rhyming words making you more likely to want to say "toast," priming shows us that what happens before a decision point is important and can significantly impact how someone reacts.

The Popcorn Principle of Priming

I like to call these negative primes "burnt popcorn moments." Much like that bag of popcorn someone burnt in the corporate lunchroom, that email derailed my entire day and I have remembered it for years because it was so jarring. When you create your communication around change, it is important to ask yourself, "Will this come off like burnt popcorn?"

That statement you make, email you send, facial expression, or offhanded comment in the hallway can all be priming the experience that others have next. If you are sending out burnt popcorn, you are priming them to be annoyed or concerned with whatever you will share. (And on the flip side, much like the delicious scent of freshly popped popcorn at the movies priming you to get a bucket and soda, if you are thoughtful about your interactions, they can be a positive prime, helping keep people on the path to change.)

That email from my old boss shows how badly things can go awry from one off-the-cuff email. She was a busy person and could justify that there was value in her saving time by sending short emails. But remember that the communication you put into the world when approaching change is *not about you.*

Sure, she saved a minute or two by not writing a more thoughtful email or saving it until she had the bandwidth to focus on what she was doing, but if she had thought about me and what I needed to hear at that moment, it could have prevented a lot of wasted time on my end.

When kept in a vacuum (i.e., not thinking about the recipient), it is hard to make the case for all the emails and communication points you would need to be thoughtful about every day. If you spent an extra minute or five on every email you send, how much more of your valuable time would be lost? It would add up quickly.

However, when you consider the minimum of four hours of productive time *I* lost that day because of that minute she saved? It is a clear case for taking the extra few minutes to save 240 or more.

Take a moment to think about the communications you have sent and received from your colleagues. How many were sent in haste and caused future problems and clarifications? According to Nick Morgan, author of *Can You Hear Me? How to Connect with People in a Virtual World*, our biased brains have led us to believe that other people understand our messages 90 percent of the time. Sadly, the real number is only 50 percent.[68]

That means half of your emails are misunderstood by the recipient. Half!

That leads to an average of seventeen hours per week each person spends clarifying previous information (this was a stat from 2016; imagine how much this must have grown since so many more people began working remotely in the COVID-19 pandemic). What's more, 62 percent of emails employees receive are not considered important.[69]

When you look at it that way, all those quick emails are costing real time and money for your teams (creating the **time pressure** problem introduced in Part 1). And those are your regular, run-of-the-mill emails; when significant changes are being presented, burnt popcorn emails will cause a bigger disruption in the flow of productivity.

Think about the ripples of the email you are about to send (or Slack communication or offhanded comment). I always encourage people to read their communication with the worst possible intent before sending it (remember those biases that opened the chapter). If this was sent to your work nemesis (whether you have someone in mind or this is a fictional exercise), how might they read it? Or imagine that same person sent you that email; how would *you* read it?

Being more thoughtful about your communication can reduce miscommunications and follow-ups. A little thoughtfulness now can save hours on the back end. And, because you will be sending less communication overall, it makes it so people are more likely to pay attention to your important emails when they do come through. Win-win.

Let's Stop This Negative Prime

We have all gotten the email with a PS that says something like, "Please excuse any typos; I'm sending this from my phone." I believe this was even a default option from the phone manufacturer at some point.

Stop for a moment and think about the subtext (prime) of this message: "You are not important enough for me to take the time to review and proof my email before I hit send. Please do the work yourself, and of course, forgive me because I'm busy and important."

Ick.

This seemingly innocent line, intended to be light, humorous, and even thoughtful—is missing the subconscious mark. If the email is important enough to send, take time to give it a read-through and ensure you didn't make mistakes. If it is not urgent or so important you need to be sure it is accurate, then save it for later (even in a draft form) and consider if it is part of the 62 percent of unimportant emails. Does it need to be sent at all?

When you are more thoughtful about the emails you send, it will reduce the number of clarifying communications required (reducing workload, time pressure, and stress). Oh, and (**Micro-Shift Moment**) if you have that "please excuse my typos" line on your settings, please take the time to change it now. I'll wait.

Word Choice Still Matters

Even after I told you that half of your communication is misinterpreted by the people receiving it, do you still feel like *you* are a better communicator than most people so that doesn't apply to you? Be honest.

Well, so does everyone else, so I want to bring it back to your attention again: You are not as good at communicating as you think. Even if you are good at this, how might you change your word choice if you assume that half of people will misinterpret what you say? (And, even if you are better than others, there is still plenty of room for improvement.)

It may feel like individual words here or there shouldn't have a big impact on how someone interprets your overall message, but because they prime the experience that comes after, they can have a massive impact. And the order we hear things matters so much because the first items influence how we feel about everything that comes next. As an example, let me introduce you to two people, Alan and Ben (and some of their key traits):

Alan: intelligent—industrious—impulsive—critical—stubborn—envious

Ben: envious—stubborn—critical—impulsive—industrious—intelligent

I'm guessing you like Alan more than Ben.[70] Even though the same six words were used to describe each person, we like Alan more because of the order we heard these traits. The meaning of the words that came later in the list (and how we interpreted them) changed because of the words that came first. (More on this when we discuss **confirmation bias.**)

Another study tested two competing stereotypes that live within the same person. All participants were Asian-American female undergraduates with similar SAT scores who took a test with twelve difficult math problems.[71] Their pre-questionnaire included the priming words. One group was primed about gender (Is your dorm co-ed or single-sex?), and another was primed by ethnicity (Do your parents or grandparents speak languages other than English?). Both were compared to a control group. This shouldn't have any impact on their math test, right? Well, here's how they did:

- Asian Identity: 54 percent
- Control: 49 percent
- Female Identity: 43 percent

I would guess that most (if not all) of these women would say they don't agree with the stereotypes in the test. They might consciously fight against them, but the subconscious brain's automatic association still impacts behavior. They were all equally capable but being primed with a simple, seemingly harmless question meant an 11 percent reduction in scores.

How often are you inadvertently biasing surveys you send to employees by asking priming questions too early? Are your company's new hire procedures setting some off on a worse path than others? Could one wrong statement at the beginning of a staff meeting be causing your team to perform 11 percent worse than they could if you had chosen your words more thoughtfully? Daniel Coyle, author of *The Culture Code*, has an example where asking people three simple questions at orientation (What happens on your best day? What happens on your worst day? What are your special skills?) instead of talking about yourself and the business increased employee retention by 207 percent.[72]

Assume everything matters. This applies to the words and images in your communication and whatever was said or done right *before* your conversation.

While you can't control everything, it is worth looking at what you can control.

What happened right before you planned to have your big change conversation? Is it something that primed them to be ready to process this right now, or is their elephant on high alert because of something unrelated? If now is not the time, can you delay the conversation to ensure they are ready to hear whatever you have to say? If not, what could you do to prime the conversation early with better words, images, or sounds that could make it easier on them later in the meeting when you present the information?

Reflection Point

Once you know the most important outcome, you can start looking for primes that incorporate all the senses to make it a reality. (We will do this together in Part 3.)

One of the most important things to remember about priming is that people almost always say they were not influenced by the primes or didn't see them. This is why understanding the concepts of behavioral economics introduced throughout this book is so critical: People cannot tell you what they will do and what influenced their reactions.

If you want to help people be naturally better at change, consider what is going on with their elephant and communicate with it. The coming chapters will give you more tips to find and consider opportunities to nudge the elephant along the path. But for now, consider if the primes around you are setting people up to be calm and relaxed or stressed and overwhelmed. What needs to change?

CHAPTER 6

Three Weeks? We'll Do It in Two!

How many of these common items are you guilty of?

- Your "to do" list is unreasonably long, ten or twenty (or fifty!) items deep, even though you know you can only complete two or three in a day. If you keep a written list, there are items you have recopied onto a fresh page at least three times because you are sure that *this time*, you will be able to finally have the satisfaction of crossing it off the list.
- Someone asks how long a project will take you to complete. You look at the items required, and even though the last ten times you did a project like this it took five hours, you decide to round down and say you will be done in four.
- You ask a team member how long they need for a project, and they say, "Four hours." You reply, "Ooh, any chance you could have it in three? I've got a big meeting this afternoon."
- You look at the clock and see there are two minutes before your next Zoom meeting starts, and you say to yourself, "Two minutes? Let me knock out a few of these emails really quick" and find yourself showing up to the meeting five minutes late because you lost track of time.

My guess is that, if you are a human person, you have done some version of every item on this list at least once in your life—perhaps all in the past week? And, even if you can't relate to the exact scenarios here, you have done something in this vein before. Four main factors work together to create this problem: optimism bias, planning fallacy, time discounting, and bikeshedding.

Optimism Bias

Optimism bias is likely a term you've heard before, so let's start there. Classic example: Are you a better-than-average driver?

If you said yes, you are in good company. Eighty-eight percent of people do, but clearly that can't be true because no more than half can be above the average.[73] And even as I say this, you likely think, "Ha! All those other silly people thinking they are above average like me."

It is surprisingly hard to internalize and accept that you could very well be part of that *other* group. Stop and reflect on it for a minute. Do you believe it? Even now? (Or now?)

You do not need to be an optimist to be impacted by optimism bias and, yes, there is a negativity bias, which will come up in a later chapter. You (and your colleagues) employ optimism bias to think you are better than others at all sorts of things:

- Emotional intelligence
- Completing tasks quickly
- Completing tasks correctly
- Thinking strategically
- Listening to others
- Understanding the "real" problem

- Planning for projects

I could go on and on, but you get the point. Optimism bias impacts nearly every decision you and your colleagues make in business.

Planning Fallacy

Planning fallacy is all about our tendency to underestimate how long it will take to complete a task, how difficult it will be, the costs, and the items that will distract us along the way.[74]

As Kahneman (the first behavioral economist to win a Nobel Prize) says, we do this over and over because "successful execution of a plan is specific and easy to imagine," and while we focus on the few paths to things going right, we forget to account for the seemingly endless list of ways things can go awry.[75] When we don't allocate for how the plan can go off the rails, we are likely to be victim to planning fallacy.

One study asked college students how long they thought it would take them to complete their thesis papers.[76] The average prediction was thirty-four days. They were then asked to give estimates for how that might change if everything went amazingly smooth (in which case they predicted it would take only twenty-seven days) and what if things went crazy and there were lots of delays (in which case they estimated forty-eight days).

What really happened?

It ended up taking an average of fifty-five days! A full week longer than the worst-case scenario prediction and three weeks beyond the original thirty-four-day estimate. Whether it is term papers, work projects, high-profile construction projects, home renovation budgets, or a slew of other examples, we do this constantly.

It is important to know that planning fallacy is more than mere procrastination. It isn't about setting better deadlines. Our brains are programmed to continue to do this even when we set up plans, are familiar with the task, have motivations or incentives to finish on time, or have planned with a team. And sadly, while you might be tempted to think that your team can hold each other accountable to not fall victim to this, the problem has been shown to compound on teams instead of making them better at overcoming it. To look good in front of the herd, you might feel pressure to undersell how long it will take you to complete something and expect you will do better than usual.[77]

So, Do We Just Have to Accept It?

Thankfully, no. There are options to overcome planning fallacy. Let's use the time estimate as our example here. When it always takes five hours, why do you say you only need four?

There are a few reasons. First, you expect to be more efficient than you have been so far because of that optimism bias we talked about a minute ago.

So, when predicting how much time you will need, you are looking at what you expect, which is intrinsic (inside) and likely to be downplayed. Your brain likes to think it is constantly getting better, and it feels good to predict you will be faster than before (while creating superior output, of course).

This combines with the issue of the extrinsic (outside) delays. We tend to ignore all those little things that will inevitably come up: calls, other meetings running long, a colleague stopping by to ask a question, the "ding" on your phone that prompts you to check Instagram, a child needing a snack while you are working from home . . . your brain basically assumes none of those things matter enough during the planning phase and that they won't be a factor.

Each little thing by itself isn't that big of a deal—five minutes here, three minutes there, ten minutes over there—but those add up fast.

When you don't plan for those external pieces and factor them into your time budget, you fall victim to planning fallacy.

One thing that has proven helpful in this case is to have people determine their timing as if a coworker were taking on the project.

If you were to think about the coworker completing the project, you would have less of the intrinsic stuff and can clearly see the external pieces. Especially if you choose a coworker whom you think is slower than you.

Micro-Shift Moment: If your instinct is to say, "I bet I can do that in *only* twenty-five hours," it is probably best to plan for thirty. Instead of suggesting you will deliver the project at end of day Friday, suggest noon on Monday. In most cases, it will not make a big difference on the recipient's end, and it gives you a significant buffer to complete over the weekend if needed (and if you get it done on Friday, you look like a hero for sending it early—win!).

Time Discounting

Ever decided on Saturday night that you would buckle down and start a diet and exercise plan "on Monday"? Maybe you spent all Sunday planning and were psyched when you set your alarm that night but felt like a different (and unmotivated) person when the alarm went off?

That's time discounting at work (or as I like to call it, the "I'll start Monday" effect).

Studies have shown that the brain sees our future self (whom you are committing to get up at five o'clock to run) as a completely different person.[78] It's easy to commit *Future You*, but when *Real You* faces the harsh reality of the alarm, it is easier to hit snooze (making it Future You's problem again).

If you want to overcome time discounting to start applying behavioral economics in your business, the best tip is to find something you can do right now. That is why there are Micro-Shift Moments sprinkled throughout this book, and why focusing on micro-moments is so important anyway. If you continually look to the future and say you will do something when things are better, easier, when you have more influence, when you have a different boss, when there is more time, or fewer projects, this is **optimism bias** and **time discounting** working together to keep you firmly in the **status quo** (where your subconscious is most comfortable). When you feel like you want to put something off until tomorrow, ask why.

Then follow that up with, "What can I do right now to prove to my brain this is important?" (And do it.)

Of course, know this is a natural tendency for team members. What can you do to help them overcome this natural tendency? When can you help the team do something today instead of assuming *Future Them* will be excited to do it tomorrow?

Bikeshedding

Bikeshedding is where trivial items feel like they are unbelievably important, and we tell ourselves that we can't dedicate time to some bigger, scarier thing until we solve them.

This tendency got the name bikeshedding because it was first observed in a team that was tasked with designing a nuclear plant, but they spent an inordinate amount of time focused on the design of the bike shed.[79] Spending so much time on the bike shed is clearly ridiculous to an outsider. However, now that you understand the subconscious loves predictability, it shouldn't be that surprising.

Designing a nuclear plant is scary; there are serious consequences if you mess that up. And, until you start that project, it is easy to let your optimism bias tell you that you will get it done faster and easier than it will really take.

Imagine that much like the thesis-writing students previously mentioned, you are assigned a big project to work on and need to report on it in three months. Most people will get hung up on little details (i.e., bikeshed) when there is ample time. The risks of moving forward weigh heavily, and it feels like there will be plenty of time once you get that other thing out of the way.

Then one day you wake up and realize, "Oh no, that project is due Tuesday and I've barely started!" Cut to a stressful slew of late nights and pushing other deliverables not to miss this deadline (creating a vicious cycle, a snowball effect that can be hard to get out from under). Which, as you already know, it may feel like you are at your most creative and productive, but you aren't.

Spotting and reducing bikeshedding is important, and knowing it exists is a big part of the battle, but because our brains like to get themselves distracted, it is also important to **plan** for that time. Just like knowing these biases exist and knowing they will never be completely eliminated, you need to know that your brain will want to bikeshed and need breaks. If you and the team plan for them, they won't derail your day and get everything off track.

This may mean working in breaks to give your brain a little bikeshedding treat to keep working.

Behavioral Concept: NUDGES

The concept of a nudge in behavioral economics is what you might expect: a gentle touch or tap—a way to get attention or help things get back on track. This is built on the work of Richard Thaler, who won the Nobel Prize in economics in 2017 and co-authored *Nudge: Improving Decisions about Health, Wealth, and Happiness* with Harvard professor Cass Sunstein.[80]

One of my favorite examples of nudging comes from the book's early pages:

Assume you gave every kid in the school the funds and ability to order whatever they wanted from the cafeteria—no adults will ever know. What do you expect they will do? Make a beeline for the cookies and ice cream?

In real life, we find that choice is influenced by context. Whatever was at the front of the line was 25 percent more likely to be chosen—and consequently 25 percent *less* likely to be chosen when moved to the end.

Want kids (and adults) to pick carrot sticks instead of French fries? Put one at eye level and the other out of sight (and, as you now know about **priming**, out of *smell* as well).

Consider how you might approach cafeteria design given this knowledge.

You could set it up to make the students "best off"—but who defines that? One could argue that the students would be "better off" if the school sold cafeteria space to the highest bidder so there was more money to invest in other educational programs that otherwise don't have the funding. If you don't like the idea of choosing, you could make the cafeteria design random, but you might be condemning some kids to obesity if they are in the unlucky "dessert first" model. You may say you want to mimic what people would choose on their own, but we now know that doesn't exist because, as the example demonstrates, choice changes based on how the options are presented.

What choices you present and how you present them is the burden of the **choice architect**. While it may be tempting to become an ostrich, not considering the architecture of the choices you are presenting in advance doesn't mean you aren't influencing behavior. You are. It is being done without intention and could be making things worse (or better) without you realizing it.

- The way you create and name files and folders (physical and virtual) is choice architecture.
- The order results appear from a search on your intranet are nudging people toward a choice.
- Putting options for your next project in alphabetical order will have a different outcome from listing them in reverse alphabetical order or by who suggested them.

It all matters. Small details that seem like they *shouldn't* matter (there's that word again) can hugely impact behavior and choice.

According to Thaler and Sunstein, "A nudge is any aspect of the choice architecture that alters people's behavior in a predictable way without forbidding options or significantly changing their economic incentives. To count as a mere nudge, the intervention must be easy and cheap to avoid. Nudges are not mandates. Putting the fruit at eye level counts as a nudge. Banning junk food does not."

To summarize:

1. Everything matters.
2. There are no neutral options.
3. You cannot avoid being a choice architect—any format will influence the choices, so it is best to be informed and deliberate.
4. Nudges can help simplify complex choices and help illogical humans make good decisions.
5. Nudges are not mandates—they need freedom of choice to count as a nudge.

NUDGES is an acronym created by Thaler and Sunstein to feature the different types and aspects of nudging.[81] They include:

- iNcentives
- Understand Mappings
- Defaults
- Give Feedback
- Expect Error
- Structure Complex Choices

While they all matter, for our purposes, I have chosen to focus on two aspects that incorporate three of the nudges. First, defaults, to show their power. Second is a combination of expecting error and how you give feedback to help keep people on track. (Curious about the others? There is a seven-part series of the podcast with details on each.)[82]

Defaults

Most people will stick with the default, regardless of what it is.

When the state of Washington started including a five-dollar donation in all vehicle tab renewals, which can easily be removed at the time of payment, they changed the default. In its first year, the switch raised an additional $1.4 million for the state parks. Pretty impressive for such a small change, don't you think?[83] That's the power of a well-structured default.

Whenever you are presenting options, asking people to change, looking at a process, or anything else—always consider the default. Is it serving your ultimate goal? If not, can you remove or change it?

Expect Error and Give Feedback

Brains are busy and they make mistakes. We forget our keys, leave the card in the ATM, drive away without putting the gas cap back on, or forget to put on our seat belts. (This extends beyond driving, of course, but look at how many flubs we might make in a single trip!)

Speaking of cars, you know how it dings when you forget to buckle up? That is a **feedback nudge** put in place because the manufacturers expected you to make an **error** at some point.

Too often we expect our employees, vendors, and others on our teams to be perfect. We have little tolerance for them forgetting things and may sit and watch, waiting for them to make a mistake we see on the horizon. While I am not recommending you become a micromanager and worry about every little step others make (that would drive anyone crazy), I do want you to make it easier for people not to mess up by expecting errors and helping to keep them on track.

I like to think of this like bumpers in bowling. If you know where someone could fall into the gutter, and you can easily create something to help nudge them back onto the lane, why would you not?

When our brains get overwhelmed—say we have a lot of projects and changes to our routines and are living in the middle of a pandemic—they are more likely to make mistakes. If you add the stress of perfection or tell them how important it is that they do not mess up because all eyes are on this project, it can quickly backfire by freaking out the elephant and increase their likelihood of making a mistake.

If you have an important project that the team needs to be on their A-Game for, line up a bunch of nudges to help keep them on track in a way that feels supportive, not like you don't trust them.

Yes, it can be that simple. However, it is important to choose your feedback wisely. If your car dinged and beeped and had lights flashing at you for every little thing, it would become too much; you'd start to ignore the alerts so none of them would have any impact. Once you know the project warrants the nudges, start to set up your bumpers.

Here are some ideas to get you started:

- If there is an important deadline you need others to hit, expect they are busy and might forget. Send them a reminder email twenty-four hours in advance (or longer if the project requires more time).
- Create a checklist of important, repetitive tasks and have the team hold each other accountable for using it.
- If you think someone doesn't understand their assignment, reach out with a clarifying question or ask them to explain the project to someone else on the team.
- If you know people will underestimate how much time the project will take, build in buffers for when you need it and when you ask for them to give you a draft.

Helping people know they are on the right path by providing a little feedback nudge goes a long way in overall experience and ensures things stay on track.

Why Explain It to Someone Else?

People who aren't meeting expectations tend to know what they *should* do. Telling them to do those things can be demoralizing. One study of nearly two thousand high school students found that when they advised younger peers on how they could be successful in their classes, those giving the advice got better grades that term![84] One eight-minute online activity where they wrote out advice for someone else was like a pep talk to themselves (think back to what I said about self-talk earlier) and got them out of their ruts.

Behavioral Concept: Anchoring & Adjustment

When your subconscious brain doesn't know the answer to something, it takes a guess. Some might call this an "educated" guess, but often it is working off rules of thumb—which is where all these concepts in behavioral economics come from. As it is processing at eleven million bits per second, it is using these judgment calls a lot to guide you through your day and life.

When introducing this concept, I always go with a little question-and-answer game. While I can't hear your responses, I trust you not to Google the answer. Just go with your gut. Ready?

> Are there more or less than ten thousand penguins in Antarctica?
>
> How many do you think there are?

Do you have that number in your head?

There are twelve million penguins in Antarctica! Was your number a lot *less* than that?

Let's try another one.

> Are there more or less than one thousand countries in the world?
>
> How many do you think there are?

There are 195 countries in the world. Was your number *higher* than that?

What Happened?

Your subconscious took the number I threw out to you and assumed I must know something about penguins or the number of countries in the world.

What if I had simply asked, "How many penguins are there in Antarctica?" without the preface of "Is it more or less than ten thousand?" Would your number have been different? Or what if the anchor I gave was one million? Or ten million? One hundred million? One billion?

When I asked the question about countries, your lazy brain's conversation with itself might have been something like, "Hmmm, let's see how many countries I can name. No, that will take too long, and it's a lot of work." If I hadn't given an anchor, it might have used some other rule of thumb—like estimating. You might have thought, "Well, I know North America has three, then there is Australia and New Zealand out there too . . . think of a map . . . maybe there is an average of twenty countries on each other continent? Or how about I pad that a little because I am probably forgetting a bunch? So let's say thirty per continent. That means 120 plus the handful I named, so I'll guess 125." Not too far off.

But because I gave you the high anchor of one thousand, your brain skipped that whole estimating thing and went with the easiest possible path:[85] "She must know something about countries, which is why she gave me that number to start with. That seems high, but I don't know a lot of countries. I'll go with six hundred." (Or wherever you ended up.)

Anchoring at Work

Recently, I saw a post on LinkedIn that someone reshared from Arianna Huffington, which says, "In a world where you can be anything, be the person who ends meetings early."

On the surface, this is a silly thing that most of us can appreciate and get a laugh over. However, there is a deeper lesson on anchoring from this statement. When you tell people a meeting will take thirty minutes, you have set an anchor. And while there are some things we wish would go longer than their allotted time, typically work meetings aren't in that category. Most people don't want more time in meetings than they have already mentally budgeted.

So, if you say it will be thirty minutes and take fifty-six, people are obviously annoyed because you went way over the time you anchored. They might be longingly looking at the clock for every minute that goes past that half-hour mark, wondering when you will be done. Anything important you have to say in those "extra" twenty-six minutes has been tainted by this irritancy. If you're hoping to present any difficult stuff in those twenty-six minutes? Be prepared for the negative repercussions.

And if you get a reputation for going long on meetings, this can impact the entire aura around the event—every meeting you schedule comes with a precursor of dread as they wonder how much time they should *really* block out for this thing.

I've heard people say you should ask for something you know people will agree to and go from there. This can be a valuable technique in specific situations. However, when it comes to anchors, it can be much more damaging than valuable. I get pitches on LinkedIn or over email from people asking for "just five or ten minutes for a quick coffee chat."

We all know that isn't a five-minute conversation. They are hoping that if they get me on the phone, they can keep going and I will feel obligated to stay in this conversation for however long it takes. This is a strategy for annoyance and bad relationships.

Instead, especially with your team at work, put in a little thoughtfulness so you can be the person who ends meetings early *and* gets lots accomplished. Think ahead, outline the goals for the meeting and a rough agenda.

Determine how much time you need and give a 10 percent buffer (remember, this chapter is about **overcoming planning fallacy, optimism bias, time discounting, and bikeshedding**). Schedule the meeting for that longer time and plan to wrap up five minutes early.

If you need those five minutes, no worries, you have them. If you need more than that, identify that you are not going to finish on time when there is about 20 percent of the meeting left and transition to talk about next steps and what everyone should work on before you meet again. Don't hold people hostage in meetings that don't end on time. Even if you only think you will need five extra minutes, it is a courtesy to have the conversation when there is still an opportunity to end on time. Those who need to leave can do so, and if people choose to stay to wrap up the agenda, it wasn't something done without their consent.

Think back to the thirty-minute meeting that went for fifty-six minutes—ugh. Now, let's imagine the flip of this. What if you scheduled sixty minutes and it only took fifty-six? People will be delighted! When I end a meeting early, I often say that I am giving someone the "gift" of those minutes back into their day. And it really does feel like that.

Changing to a more realistic anchor that will allow you to be the hero makes all the difference.

Bringing It Back to Time

Time is probably the most valuable resource your team has. Left to our devices, we will overschedule and overcommit ourselves to a stressful, overwhelmed, error-prone existence. It doesn't have to be this way—even if you are in a culture that has made this abundant (remember the last chapter—just because all the other managers overcommit and underdeliver doesn't mean you should too).

As a manager, when you are trying to determine who to assign a project to on your team, resist the urge to pile it on without considering the consequences. As we saw in the research around doctoral students predicting how long it would take them to finish their dissertations, even when told to think about the worst-case scenario, humans are bad at predicting how long something will take.

Your team members feel extra pressure to not let you down, so they will likely tell you they have the time. They will tell you they've got it under control—and they probably believe that is the truth. However, you know they will be prone to underestimating how long something will take and the obstacles that will get in their way. Expect that error and give feedback to 1) Help them more accurately predict the time a project will take and 2) Level-set your expectations. When someone says they need three days for something, don't ask them to do it in two (and instead plan for it to take four).

Pro Tip: Don't just assume and not explain it to them. This is an opportunity to help them understand their biased brain (though, don't say, "Your brain is biased, so you're telling me wrong." That probably won't go over well). Instead, when they tell you they need three days, ask some thoughtful questions:

- What else do you have on your plate this week?
- Do you need any support shifting priorities?
- And (in a way that doesn't sound like you are bad-mouthing another team member) ask them to estimate how long it would take someone else to get it done.

When Will You Have That for Me?

You're handed a new project or task and the person asks, "When will you have that for me?" Your brain will speedily start doing some calculations and make assumptions about how quickly they want it. As the person being asked to do something, your anchor is set on an expectation that they want this immediately—every day or hour you think to request feels like a big ask, so you try to cut some corners. In other words, optimism bias and planning fallacy take over and make you feel inclined to give a stretch-goal response that superhuman *Future You* is more than capable of achieving.

"I think we can probably get that back to you by the end of the week."

"Wow!" they say, "I was sure that would take at least three weeks, but I would love to have it for Monday's budget meeting. I'll email Paul right now and let him know we can add this to the agenda."

Shoot. You've now committed your team to doing something that other teams are anchored on. It will be stressful, and you might end up missing some other deadlines—for something they didn't even expect! (I guess what they say about assuming really is true.)

There is a simple fix for this, making all the difference. When someone asks you, "When will you have that for me?" Reply with, "When would you ideally have it back in your hands?" (Yes, *ideally* is an important word choice here.)

They are now doing their mental calculation and trying not to sound unreasonable. "Hmm, I hope it isn't too much to ask, but do you think you can have it for me by the 23rd? That's about three weeks from now."

"Absolutely," you respond. "We should be able to make that happen."

Here is the list of benefits of this approach:

- They feel like they are asking you for a favor; if they ask for something unreasonable, you can say that it isn't possible and try to negotiate. In my experience, both on my own and for countless clients I have taught this to, the other person will almost always ask for something further out than you would have expected or thought they wanted.

- In that first example, if you said you would have the thing by the end of the week (anchoring) and it takes you ten days, they will fall somewhere between annoyed and furious. Even though they had an original anchor of three weeks, you took that off the table when you said you would have it by Friday. In the second scenario, when they ask if you can do it in three weeks, they will be delighted if you have it ready in ten days (and if not delighted it won't work against you). This puts a positive snowflake or two into your relationship snowball.
- We will talk about the IKEA effect later. For now, know that when people can contribute to the plan, they like it more.
- You also bought your team extra time to help budget for the optimism bias/planning fallacy/time discounting/bikeshedding situation that is bound to come up—with time to spare. Even while you are practicing being better at this, you can reduce stress and deadline pressure by using the "When would you ideally have it by?" question.

Mastering Meetings

For your first order of business, I challenge you to master meetings. That means:

- Show up on time, prepared and ready to go.
- If you called the meeting:
  - Think through what needs to be covered before you send the invite, think through how much time things should take (overestimate) and schedule enough time (remember, it is better to ask for sixty minutes and end early than to schedule thirty and take fifty-six).
  - Send an agenda in advance.
  - Plan to end five minutes early.

  - » End early and give people the gift of time back (I don't think anyone has ever complained that a meeting ended early—unless it was being tracked for CPE credits).
- If someone else called the meeting, do all the prep work in advance.

And as reducing unnecessary work is a big key here—if the meeting doesn't justify doing all this prep work in advance, ask if it is worth having.

Nudging People to Arrive on Time Without Saying a Word

Arriving late to meetings is common in many corporate cultures. Even when it is frowned upon, in the double-booked, stretched too thin world, this can quickly become an accepted standard swept under the rug.

If this was a problem in your organization, you might create a grand initiative and project team to come up with a plan to solve this problem. Working with the brain presents an easier way.

Dr. Agnis Stibe, an expert in transformation and hyper-performance, explained to me how one of his Executive MBA students used **social proof** and **herding** to **nudge** an entire team to naturally change their behavior on their own without saying a word.[86]

At the student's company, people were only showing up on time to 65 percent of their meetings. After learning about social proof in Dr. Stibe's class, this student devised an experiment. One day when the team showed up for their meeting, they were greeted by a chart on the screen with all their names along the bottom. Everyone who arrived on time got a block that corresponded to the color of the meeting. Everyone who showed up late got an "empty" space, which is noted by the horizontal line across the top. This made it clear how many meetings each person had attended and how many they were late for, as shown in this image. There was no way to make it up if you were late and it remained at the following meetings.

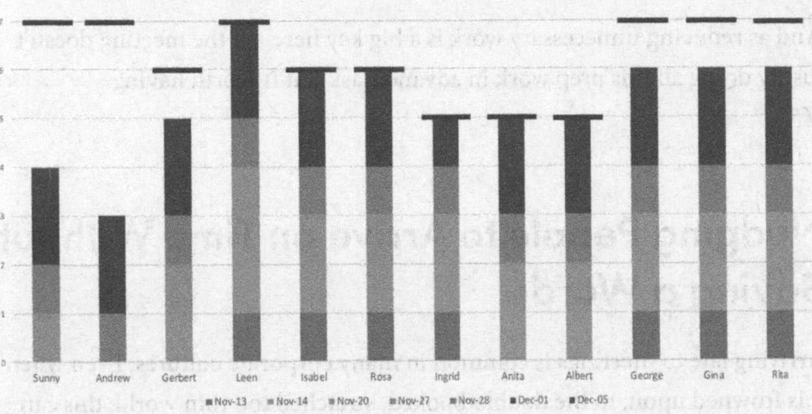

When a chart reminds everyone who has been late, the social proof nudges people to change their behavior.

In less than six meetings, the team went from 65 percent on-time arrivals to 100 percent.

I'm guessing you look at this and think, "Yikes! I hope they don't do that at my company." Even if you tend to be on time, it would make most people feel uncomfortable to have their attendance placed up on a chart for all to see in this way. But why?

The remarkable thing about this example is everyone already knows whether you're late or not—they see you show up. You know you are late; they know you are late, so why does a chart make a difference? It creates social pressure that makes you feel disconnected from the herd. As the laggards could see their peers showing up on time more often, it became more uncomfortable to be late than to be on-time. You can almost feel their anxiousness at the idea of getting another blank space.

No one had to say anything; there wasn't any other negative consequence added—it just made the error visible in an uncomfortable way, and change was achieved naturally.

Now, you don't always want a surprise like this or a big public display. But when used sparingly and intentionally, it can be effective.

Reflection Point

The lesson for you is to think outside the norm. You don't have to create a big incentive plan (positive or negative) or go through a complex policy change with lots of approvals from around the organization. Sometimes, making the negative behavior you want to change visible is enough to nudge the group. Easy, cheap, and effective. Where could your team benefit from a little nudge?

CHAPTER 7

Questions? Concerns? Good. Let's Get Started.

On January 22, 1986, at 3:43 p.m. EST, a high-profile launch of the space shuttle was scheduled.[87] Waiting on another mission's delayed return, the launch was pushed back by first one day and then another. Weather looked bad on the 24th, so it was delayed again. Additional bad weather forecasts led to another delay. They would now launch on the morning of January 27.

Millions of eyes were on this mission, including President Ronald Reagan, as this was the culmination of his Teacher in Space Project, announced a full two years earlier. Eleven thousand teachers applied from around the country and two were selected to train for this mission. Christa McAuliffe was the lucky one to be on board. Barbara Morgan was her alternate on the ground. Both women trained for months alongside the crew to prepare. McAuliffe would teach two programs to kids around the country from space as the kickoff for a touring lecture series to get children excited about careers in science and math.

The White House, press from every state in the nation, and millions of American families were all watching (and likely complaining about the delays causing inconveniences to schedules).

With this added pressure, it must have been infuriating and concerning for NASA management when there was *another* delay of twenty-four hours when a hatch wouldn't close properly. It was sawed off and reattached. The mission could finally depart the following day, on January 28.

Imagine the mindset of the management team when discussing the next morning's launch after a week of what probably felt like bumbling public delays and reschedules. Pressure to make it work and not delay again was likely expressed with a few raised voices and colorful language. Multiple engineers warned of possible failure due to the predicted low temperatures and other factors on a conference call the night before the scheduled launch. Eventually though, they deferred to the group, and the mission got the green light to launch the next morning.

That night, a severe cold snap hit Florida. NASA awoke to a launch pad covered in ice. Thousands of icicles can be seen in photos of the equipment at the John F. Kennedy Space Center at Cape Canaveral that morning in chilling black and white. While running tests for launch, a hardware interface module that monitored the fire detection system failed, causing another delay. Two hours later, at 11:38 a.m. EST on January 28, *Challenger* was finally ready for takeoff.

Seventy-three seconds later, it exploded.

Mission control, attendees on the ground, and 17 percent of the American population with eyes glued on their TVs (including President Reagan) watched in horror as the catastrophe unfolded. Debris rained down into the Atlantic Ocean for over an hour and all seven members of the crew, including the schoolteacher Christa McAuliffe, were killed.

The *Challenger* disaster is a common case study for engineers, ethics boards, managers, data analysts, and more. Its far-reaching tragedy of errors has a lesson for nearly anything you want to teach. A full book could be written on the subject, but here we will limit to two main biases: the false consensus effect and groupthink.

False Consensus Effect

People think that others think and believe the same way they do. Whatever we believe is thought to be common sense, and so anyone who disagrees has something wrong with them. In the study that coined the term in the 1970s,[88] students were given a few scenarios and two options for responding to it, for example:

You were speeding and pulled over as going thirty-eight miles per hour in a twenty-five zone and given a ninety-eight-dollar ticket (adjusted for inflation from the original study). You believe the finding to be accurate. When looking at the ticket, you notice the cop's description is inaccurate: weather, visibility, time, and location of the incident are all wrong. Do you pay the fine by mail or contest it?

Think about it yourself:

- What would you do?
- What do you think others would do?
- What kind of people would choose each option?

Regardless of the topic or the options, whatever they chose, participants believed most people would agree with them. Those who would pay the fine believed that almost three-quarters of people would do the same (those who would contest believed more than half would do the same). In addition, the descriptions participants gave for the people who would choose the alternative were negative and extreme. Across a series of these examples, when describing the "others" who would choose the opposite option, they used words like laziness, miserliness, and selfishness.

Those people aren't choosing something different than me; they *are* different than me. There must be something wrong with them (you can likely see similarities to **false uniqueness bias** here).

Businesses are victim to the false consensus effect constantly, of course. Whether it is a boss or other dominant voice in the room who assumes everyone agrees with them (Why wouldn't they? It's common sense!) or in the decisions made about what people care about in a change initiative or product features, or anything in between. Because people overestimate how much others will agree with their perspective, this bias can cause problems if left unaddressed.

Even if your company isn't dealing with life-or-death decisions like the *Challenger* example, there can still be catastrophic failures for businesses that ignore the voices of individuals to defer to a manager, team lead, or HiPPO (highest paid person's opinion).

Why Is Everyone Quitting?

I'm writing this book during what is being called The Great Resignation; people are quitting their jobs in droves. November 2021 was a record month with 4.5 million Americans quitting their jobs.[89] For context, this is about 3 percent of the working population, and the 2019 average was 3.5 million people quitting each month.[90]

The full cause and scope are still unknown at the time of writing, but some important notes are that not all industries are impacted, the pandemic has some influence (vaccine mandates are one contributing factor), and (perhaps most importantly) one thing that isn't as oft-reported is that *hiring is still exceeding the quitting numbers.*

That indicates that many employees are quitting because they have found better jobs. How do we define "better"?

This is an example where many companies fall victim to the false consensus effect. You may think wages are all that matter (because that is what you think would matter to you) or perhaps you are only looking at your 401k plan or other benefits package. For the employee, they might be willing to concede on wages for a work-from-home benefit. In his book *Returning to the Office and Leading Hybrid and Remote Teams*, Gleb Tsipursky (the kind forewordist to this book) noted that nearly a quarter of people were willing to take a pay cut of over 10 percent to be able to work from home at least some of the time.[91] Nearly half of respondents said they would leave their current employer if they didn't continue to offer remote work. If you assume the "obvious" problem is the only or most important one, you fall victim to the false consensus effect. The consequences could be dire, as many companies are experiencing today.

To combat the false consensus effect, you need to think about different perspectives and recognize that they are fully reasonable even if they are different than yours. Think back to the eleven million bits per second of processing power of your subconscious brain compared to the forty bits of the conscious brain. If we put that another way, it means for every one piece of information your subconscious felt was important enough to focus on, 275,000 other things were filtered out. Is it possible that one of the 275,000 is also valid even though your subconscious didn't focus on it? Of course. And it is more likely to be a number much higher than one—it could be in the hundreds or even thousands.

When you approach problems as a chance to think differently—and know that, even when you disagree, you might both be right—it makes it possible to find more interesting solutions and opportunities (both in quality and quantity). As Rory Sutherland says in *Alchemy*,[92] "the opposite of a good idea can still be a good idea." Within those 275,000, there are at least ten or twenty valid reasons you aren't considering.

- What is most important to the employees?
- What else might motivate them?
- What aren't you thinking about?
- What hidden interests are there that could be important?

Groupthink

Where there's a false consensus effect, groupthink is usually not too far behind. I like how an article in PeopleScience explains groupthink by saying you've likely seen this "when a bad idea seems to take hold of coworkers and they hold on for dear life."[93]

After the *Challenger* disaster, a group called the Rogers Commission was assembled to investigate the accident. Members included astronauts Neil Armstrong and Sally Ride and the Nobel-Prize-winning physicist Richard Feynman. Groupthink and "go fever" at NASA were explicitly blamed for the tragedy during the Congressional testimony.

Feynman's thoughts on the problem are worded in a way that steps out of the myopic view we tend to get when working on a project. He reframes the issue so eloquently it is hard not to cringe at the obviousness of the problem. This is the introduction to his comments:[94]

"It appears that there are enormous differences of opinion as to the probability of a failure with loss of vehicle and of human life. The estimates range from roughly 1 in 100 to 1 in 100,000. The higher figures come from the working engineers, and the low figures from management. What are the causes and consequences of this lack of agreement? Since 1 part in 100,000 would imply that one could put a shuttle up each day for 300 years expecting to lose only one, we could properly ask 'What is the cause of management's fantastic faith in the machinery?' We have also found that certification criteria used in Flight Readiness Reviews often develop a gradually decreasing strictness. The argument that the same risk was flown before without failure is often accepted as an argument for the safety of accepting it again. Because of this, obvious weaknesses are accepted again and again, sometimes without a sufficiently serious attempt to remedy them, or to delay a flight because of their continued presence."

If mic drops were a thing back in 1986, it feels like Feynman would have earned one for this statement. I mean, how do you argue with that? It is so shockingly obvious it would make anyone tuck their tail between their legs and retreat to the corner.

In the heat of the moment, we lose our perspective. We defer to the group. We **bikeshed** and get wrapped up in seemingly important things (not being embarrassed with further delays, the press and the president's office calling to ask when this thing is going to *just take off already*, the consequences to the next flight that might get delayed too if we don't hurry up). We ignore safety procedures and established policies and assume that things will continue to work now because they worked last time. We hope to kick the can down the field and deal with it next time when we will have more time (**optimism bias/time discounting**).

The *Challenger* disaster shows how flawed that logic is, doesn't it?

In their case, the explosion was determined to be caused by two rubber O-rings that were supposed to seal the rocket boosters, which lost their resiliency and failed due to the extreme cold. It sounds as though a slew of other things could have compromised the mission if those hadn't failed, but we will never know what might have happened if the temperature hadn't been a factor.

I want you to take away from this two important things:

- Time pressure, short deadlines, and high-profile change projects make it more likely for groupthink to be a factor—that is also when it is most important to not fall victim to it.

- The logic that something has worked before (or hasn't failed yet) so it will work now is flawed and (to put it a bit harshly) lazy.

Reflection Point

Take a moment to consider the meetings you had in the last week or month—how often have these scenarios played out to some degree in that time? If you consider every conversation a change conversation, how and where have you been promoting groupthink due to stress or pressure? What problems are you willfully ignoring or hoping you can limp through, playing Russian Roulette, hoping you'll make it through today and it will be someone else's problem tomorrow?

Don't Worry, We Have a Whistleblowing System

You may feel inclined to believe you have already set up a system for whistleblowers so people can bring attention to issues like this and overcome groupthink, the false consensus effect, harassment claims, unethical decisions, and other stuff.

First, I want to make it known that multiple people were pointing out and raising concerns about the problems at NASA for years in advance of the *Challenger* disaster—including the night before the launch (and I am guessing the morning of). At the end of the day, they deferred to the group (by choice or force) and the mission still took place.

The **bystander effect** also contributes to teams not acting when it is needed.[95] This finds that people are less likely to offer to help a victim they can see is in trouble when other people are around. The more people around, the less likely anyone is to help.

In business, this means that the more commonplace a problem is, the more it seems people know it is going on, or the more people there are on the impacted team, the less likely individuals are to say anything about it.

To my knowledge, no one quit their job in protest or pulled a contract not to be involved with something they knew was doomed to fail. It may have felt like they cleared their conscience by going on the record somewhere, saying they tried. How often have meetings with disagreements in your office ended with someone saying, "I want it on the record that I disagree with this, but sure, let's go ahead"?

Do you think, in hindsight, those engineers who (I'm assuming) said something like that in advance of the disaster felt like they had a clear conscience? Like they did everything they could? Like they did the right thing?

I'm guessing not. They likely felt riddled by guilt for long after; some of them might still feel that today, decades later.

Now, to your whistleblowing program. You might say that it was built with knowledge and learnings from *Challenger*, Enron, and others. You might feel confident in your "no tolerance" policy for problems like this. Right?

In a 2021 *Harvard Business Review* article, behavioral scientist and MindEquity founder Nuala Walsh shared her research on how companies can motivate employees to blow the whistle. This was focused on motivating bystanders to act when they see wrongdoing.[96] Despite popular movements, she indicates how so few employees blow the whistle and those that do often experience extreme consequences. For example:

- 82 percent suffered harassment
- 60 percent lost their jobs

- 17 percent lost their homes
- 10 percent attempted suicide

With stats like these, it shouldn't have been surprising that her research found most people classify whistleblowing as an act of courage rather than duty or responsibility.

Your brain is likely telling you that it isn't like that where you work. People are better where you are, and more people would stand up and say something if they saw something. Even without the threat of consequences, the bystander effect and status quo bias can keep people from acting.

Nuala's experimental research presented 923 employees with a hypothetical example of professional bullying. Participants expressed outrage and anger about the wrongdoing—in fact, 91 percent declared a willingness to report it. However, at the end of the experiment, everyone was tested to see who would take the first step, finding out *how* to report it. If the majority were outraged, why did only 9 percent take that tiny first step in the process—clicking a website for more information? Herding instincts, the bystander effect, moral blindness, and many other biases play into this lack of action. One proven tool presented in Nuala's REFRAME model that can help leaders is greater consideration of how you frame the problem and the conversations.

Behavioral Concept: Framing

Tonight is spaghetti night. Realizing there's no meat for the sauce, you quickly run to the store. They have two stacks of ground beef, side by side:

Which type of ground beef is more appealing?

Which one do you choose?

If you are like most people in the world, you would choose a package from the 90-percent-fat-free stack. But why? Any logical person (or quick reflection) would realize, "That is saying the same thing!"

Even if the 10-percent-fat option was less expensive, it might be hard to convince your brain to buy it because it sounds worse to the subconscious brain.

The main lesson from framing is that *how* you say something is more important than *what* you are saying.

In business, we are constantly presented with information that we disseminate to our teams. Often, we assume they will sort through all the information to find what is relevant to them; they should be able to find the truth in that data. How often do you pass along numbers or information as you found it?

There is a good chance you are trying to sell people on 10 percent fat ideas (an uphill battle). If you took some time to consider the frame and looked for the 90-percent-fat-free message, it could go over a lot easier. You may also be framing questions in the meeting to promote the false consensus effect and groupthink. Consider these questions that are all commonly used in meetings:

- No one has any questions, right?
- Before I move on, does anyone have anything to say?
- I see this as the obvious choice, but if anyone wants to throw anything into the ring…?
- Questions? Concerns? No? Good. Let's move on.

All of these are framed to promote the biases of this chapter. And, because we are a herding species and people want to stay safe, it can be hard to speak up even when they have a concern. What if instead you said:

- Let's poke some holes in this; what have we not yet considered?
- If this was wrong, what else might we try?
- If we were at a start-up without any constraints on legacy systems, how would we solve this problem?

Those reframed questions encourage thoughtful answers. The conversation and where you end up will be different. Plus, this type of inclusiveness can build trust with the team, which we will talk more about soon.

Micro-Shift Moment: When people ask you how you are doing, don't say, "Busy." The brain gets what it expects and, as you know, will filter out information that doesn't fit the paradigm you have established as important. If your default answer is "busy," your brain will find lots of ways to show you that is true, all day every day. Similarly, don't answer, "Fine." As noted by the earlier Roy Kent example, you deserve better than fine. The simplest response could be, "Very well, thanks. How about you?" I prefer to go with "Fantastic!" but that isn't everyone's style. My friend and colleague Marco Palma from the Texas A&M Human Behavior Lab says, "Living the dream!"

There are many possible responses to this question, so you should find one that fits your personality and goals.

Before we move off of framing, I want to revisit Richard Feynman's findings and how he reframed obscure numbers so they meant something. Our brains are lazy and when presented with lots of numbers and stats, we get a little distracted and they can get lost in the eleven-million-bits-per-second shuffle. We can't sit and evaluate every little thing, so sometimes even obvious errors in judgment can fall through the cracks. The way he explained a 1 in 100,000 chance of failure to show how ridiculous that is, was an important reframe: expecting to launch a shuttle every day for three hundred years and only losing one? Really?

That is an inaccurate assumption. When said that way, it is hard to ignore or explain away. Reframing the information made all the difference. How you say something matters more than what you are saying.

Words Matter

There are many common sayings in the business world. Things everyone around you is saying so you have adopted as your go-to phrasings. Some of these are fine. Others are terrible framing and send the wrong message. Here is one phrase I have made it my mission to eradicate from normalcy:

"Does that make sense?"

These four words are thrown around constantly, added to be polite and give someone an opportunity to ask a question or clarify something you've said. Unfortunately, it is not encouraging people to respond to you *or* ask questions.

This phrase has ruffled my feathers for years. When you stop and think about it, this is such an offensive phrase. I either must say/admit that I am not smart enough to understand what you have said so far or, more often, gloss over it and say, "Mmhmm," without asking any questions I might have that would make me look dumb in front of the rest of the group. The framing of this question contributes to the **false consensus effect**.

This question puts people on the spot and discourages a thoughtful response. Many people use it so often that it is their version of "umm" when giving a speech—a qualifier at the end of every point, making people feel bad (whether they consciously realize it or not) over and over again. (Lots of snowflakes for the iceberg.)

A simple reframe to this common sentence promotes conversation and doesn't make the listener feel bad: "Did I explain that well?"

This makes it about *you*. It is perfectly okay for the person listening not to understand *and* speak up about it . . . because it isn't about them.

Remember that just because a lot of people are saying something a certain way doesn't mean it is good and that you should do it too (**herding**). Often with my work in behavioral economics, I find that a small tweak can make a huge difference for people. You might be doing everything else right, but this one thing you are saying or doing—a bad frame, perhaps—is throwing things off. (Hence, micro-shift suggestions.)

Take a close look at the things you (and others) say often to find those small opportunities for impactful changes. Albus Dumbledore called words "our most inexhaustible source of magic. Capable of both inflicting injury and remedying it." Practicing framing goes both ways—you want to start with a good frame to understand what might make it bad, as well as start with bad ones to see what could make them better.

- Is there anything your boss, coworkers, or others often say that is always rubbing you the wrong way? Why do you think that is? How might you say it differently, and what phrases might you say that make others feel that way without realizing it?

- Find someone you admire at work, either in your business or whom you see in the media. What are some of their common phrasings? If you like them (or don't), how might it come across if it was said differently?

Reflection Point

As we close out this section and its three chapters dedicated to the importance of calming the elephant, how can you reframe the way you think about a stressed employee? Or one who has been making a lot of mistakes? Or those you know are going to be a problem?

How can you reframe your perspective (remember, change is all about you) and work with some of the biases and concepts you learned about in this section to have a different outcome in the future?

2.2
STATUS QUOS AND SHORTCUTS

This next three-chapter section is about the status quo and shortcuts the brain looks for to find the easy way through. As you already know from previous chapters, the brain is biased to prefer the status quo, and it is even more likely to look for this when it is overwhelmed (which is why we started with calming the elephant). This section will introduce other biases and important behavioral concepts to help you and your team navigate change.

The other tendency we haven't specifically called out yet is looking for shortcuts. As our brains run on predictability and we like to herd, it is common to look to others to see what has worked for them and want to apply those silver bullets to our situation now.

We like to say things take hard work and dedication, and we pride ourselves on our ability to put in the work (as you'll see in this section, we even have a bias where we think more time spent equals a higher value, which isn't always the case). However, when it comes time to grind it out, we want the quick fix: the simple formula, equation, or cheat sheet to get there fast.

- Get a million followers in three days doing this one thing that takes two minutes.
- How to go viral (with little to no effort or money).
- One sentence that will make everyone instantly and permanently better at their jobs.

Reflection Point

Before jumping in, take a moment to reflect on the biases and concepts you learned about to consider how they might contribute to the upcoming section. (What does **false uniqueness bias** say about our tendency to say we care about hard work but want the quick fix? How are we **priming** our teams to look for the **status quo**?)

And when you're ready, let's look at a new batch of biases and concepts for your team.

Want a refresher on any of those terms? Check out this handy virtual glossary and other resources at thebrainybusiness.com/employees-need

CHAPTER 8

We Tried That, It Doesn't Work

We already had a cautionary tale from NASA; let's have a more positive example this time. While NASA has had over two hundred missions, I'm guessing one of the top three you could name includes Apollo 13. We can perhaps thank Tom Hanks and the rest of the movie's cast for that. As you likely know, unlike the *Challenger* disaster, it was a mission facing almost certain peril where a team managed to rally together and overcome amazing challenges to bring the crew home alive.

Reading the logs of the event is an amazing experience. Talk about trust and autonomy; the number of decisions and new approaches needing to be undertaken in split-second intervals is nothing short of a miracle. If anyone on that team couldn't be trusted, if there was suspicion that anyone wasn't in it for the good of the team, it could not have been a success. Things had to happen too quickly and with no margin for error. It's a triumph of trust memories that were built long before in the buildup to Apollo 11 and the first steps on the moon. Flight director Gene Kranz, thirty-five years old at the time, said to his team, "Whatever happens, I will never second-guess any of your calls. Now let's go—let's go land on the moon."

That one simple statement was so well **framed** to **prime** a culture of trust—it's truly remarkable.

But this is a new chapter, and I want to focus on another aspect of Apollo 13. Shortly after an oxygen tank exploded, they realized they would have to abandon the main spacecraft and move to the Lunar Module (LEM) and turn it into a makeshift lifeboat. One big problem was that it was designed to sustain two men for forty-five hours, and they needed it to sustain three men for ninety: no small task. To make matters worse, there was a lack of communication between the teams designing the LEM and main spacecraft. They were siloed teams, and they never imagined anything from one area would need to work on another. Each worked happily on their projects, which didn't matter until it mattered. (Think back to Feynman's statement about using the "it worked last time" or "it hasn't gone wrong yet" flawed logic.)

In this case, the CM lithium hydroxide canisters used to scrub carbon dioxide out of the air were square on one system and round on the other.

They didn't fit together naturally and the team needed to figure out how to get a literal square peg to fit in a round hole under limited time with only the items available in the spacecraft, and they had to explain how to make it work to a team without experience with this specific sort of work who were about 200,000 miles away with communication systems a lot like a walkie-talkie. (And you thought trying to communicate with your team over Zoom was hard.)

When presented with the problem, the engineers and other team members on the ground all explained why it couldn't be done, what might go wrong, how they had never simulated that, and that they didn't want their departments to be responsible for making a guess, that the pieces weren't designed to do what needed to be done.

To this, Kranz replied, "I don't care what anything was *designed* to do; I want to know what it *can* do." A remarkable reframing that may have saved three lives.

Functional Fixedness

The bias that was plaguing the engineers is called **functional fixedness**. This is the "When all you have is a hammer, everything looks like a nail" problem.

Imagine you are presented with a candle, some thumbtacks, and a box of matches. Your task is to affix the candle to the wall and light it.[97] When presented with this problem in the original 1945 study and when replicated multiple times over the years, people try to use the thumbtacks to stick the candle to the wall (which doesn't work) and often get stuck.

They see the box that the matches (or tacks) came in as a *container* and don't even see the obvious solution of lighting the candle and melting a bit of wax to stick it to the box, then using the thumbtacks to stick the box to the wall. Easy.

Functional fixedness puts the box into a box, so to speak, and it is hard to see it as anything different than how it was presented. Interestingly, a subsequent study found that five-year-old children didn't have the same barriers; they solved the problem much faster than the adults and even six- and seven-year-olds. They don't yet have that container association in their brain, so it isn't a hindrance (the way it was delivered to you acts as a **prime**).

This highlights an important balancing act for you and your teams. As I've already discussed, there is a lot of value in common language. It is much easier to say, "Are we **bikeshedding** here?" than it is to try and explain what you think might be happening and get someone on board and essentially bikeshed about bikeshedding. In the case of functional fixedness, we see how something can become constrained by its associations—where that is all we see. The last section's biases help you to feel that what you believe is the problem (or solution) is all there is, and you get stuck—often coming up with the right answer to the wrong question.

Asking, "What is 5 + 5?" is not the same as, "How many ways can we make 10?"

What's the Problem?

Einstein said if he had an hour to save the world, he would spend fifty-five minutes thinking about the problem and five minutes solving it. Consider the ratio for the last problem/project you worked on. Did you even spend five minutes of your respective hour considering the problem before jumping into solve-mode?

Working on the wrong problem is expensive (time, money, mental bandwidth) and not understanding the problem is where most businesses go wrong. Invest in understanding the problem and everything else magically gets easier.[98]

The Curse of Knowledge

It's your first day at a new company and you are beyond excited to be there. Like a giddy child on the first day of school, you have your metaphorical pencils sharpened, notebooks organized, and brain ready to make the impact you've been dreaming about. This is the first day of the rest of your life.

In your first meeting, someone says a word you've never heard before. "What did he say?" you think to yourself. "Was that a company name or an acronym of a process or something?" You make a mental note to ask what that word means when there is a break in the conversation. Unfortunately, that moment never comes (and by now three or four other terms have been said that you have also never heard). That jargon is now swirling around in your head, weighing down your conscious brain and using precious resources so you don't forget. After a while it gets to be so long from the original mention that it would be weird to bring it up now, so you sit uncomfortably and decide to keep quiet and look like you are involved in the conversation while instead thinking about what you are making for dinner later that night.

This cognitive overload has made it so you can no longer contribute, and that excited child is feeling deflated and self-conscious. You want to look smart and valuable to your new team! If you weren't expected to know those terms and jargon going in, they wouldn't have assumed you did, right? If you ask a question, you risk them realizing you're a fraud and firing you for not being a fit. If no one allows you to ask or acknowledges the potential problem by giving you a "jargon cheat sheet," you may never fully bounce back.

The company isn't being intentionally coy or testing you (in general). Instead, they have forgotten what it is like to be new and all the things they have learned during their tenure here and possibly in previous roles. They suffer from a curse of knowledge, something responsible for so many miscommunications in business, both internally and with customers.

Reflection Point

Do you have any underperforming team members who had "such potential" that you have essentially written off? They could have been primed with a negative early experience like this, which set them off on the wrong path. Understanding the memory iceberg/snowball problem, you can see where some focused effort can help bring them back if you have anyone in this category. Thankfully, you don't need to pinpoint where the path diverted to get them onto a new one. Instead, know that it can be fixed if you put in the effort. While not everyone is a fit for every position and organization, few people are ever too far gone to be a great team member.

You Can't Unring the Bell

Once you have learned something, you quickly forget what you knew (and didn't know) on the way in. You can never unknow the things you know and even upon reflection can never fully be back into the shoes of a newbie. As Adam Hansen put it in our conversation on episode 176 of *The Brainy Business*, "Once you have the equivalent of a PhD in any particular topic, when you think about teaching that 100-level class, you are presenting information at a 200- or 300-level course at best."[99]

The things that blew your mind and were amazing to learn ten years ago will still be novel to those learning them for the first time today, but you have heard and seen them so much you don't even remember that you didn't know that once.

At this point you may be thinking, "Who cares? They will learn eventually; it's called on-the-job training." As with the other biases in this book, you need to look beyond your expertise and assumption that the only detriment is people taking time to ramp up to your level of knowledge. After all, it's called the "curse" of knowledge for a reason. It's not a good thing for business, so you should take advantage of the lack of expertise when it is handed to you.

For one simple example, problems you have learned to ignore after years of exposure may be noticeable to them—valuable information for any company that takes the time to absorb this fresh perspective before it becomes a victim of the curse of knowledge.

Beyond thinking about how you can get them up to speed as quickly as possible, consider what opportunities exist and ask, "How can we learn from the fresh eyes in our organization right now?" You have a small window to learn from them in these moments before their perspective becomes infected by the curse of knowledge too—and as you know, you can never get it back. Reframing the curse of knowledge to look at its benefit could be called the *blessing of the uninformed.*

Because I Said So

Remember when you were a kid and asked your mom or dad, "Why?" and their answer was, "Because I said so"? That likely didn't make you feel great. It is the same with your new employees who aren't given support to bring them up to speed and ask, "Why?" only to be told, "Because that's how we've always done it. Trust me; this is the right way."

If you want to learn from the fresh perspectives of new employees, you can provide mechanisms to gather this information in a way that helps them to feel valued and supported. Beyond that, it is important to make sure in those early interactions they don't get lost in a sea of jargon that makes them feel demotivated.

In my corporate life, whenever bringing on new employees, I would explain in advance that we didn't always realize how often we used jargon in meetings, so they could expect two things from me:

1. If there was something key I wanted to be sure they understood (it was foundational to the overall understanding of the meeting), I would stop the others in the room to explain what a term, acronym, vendor name, or process shorthand meant. By explaining this to the new employee in advance, I let them know that this was about *us* and not them. It was expected that they would not know everything right off the bat, and I had the comfort level and ability to slow down the meeting to ensure everyone was caught up. So then, if I ever stopped the meeting to ask my new employee, "Do you know what we mean when we say X?" they didn't feel put on the spot and were empowered to admit that they didn't know because this was made into a safe space for them.

2. If there were ever terms or names mentioned in a meeting that they didn't understand but I didn't stop the meeting, I told them to make a note for us to have a follow-up conversation. After the meeting in their one-on-one, I would take the time to ask about terms or jargon they were not yet familiar with and give them an opportunity to ask any questions they had collected over the week.

This simple approach doesn't cost money and has so many positive benefits. It can: overcome the curse of knowledge, help new employees feel supported, create psychological safety,[100] kick off a culture of curiosity that looks for opportunities to grow, and more. It also helps the organization learn and grow by taking advantage of the blessing of the uninformed.

Dunning-Kruger Effect

The Dunning-Kruger effect shows that those who are unskilled tend to *overestimate* their abilities and skilled experts *underestimate* theirs.[101] People who promise the moon and sound too good to be true are probably being run by **optimism bias** and **planning fallacy** . . . and they might not know what they are doing.

Think about a kid who graduates from high school and believes they know everything. They are at a point on the Dunning-Kruger scale, called the "Peak of Mount Stupid" (truthfully, this is the official term used, one reason I love this concept so much). When they get to college and find out they don't know nearly as much as they thought, they fall into the "Valley of Despair." As they build up expertise, they gradually gain confidence back in a way that is often less than the unrealistic confidence they felt when they didn't know what they didn't know. (And, in many ways, this starts a new Dunning-Kruger effect when they graduate college and think they know everything again and then start a new job and realize all that they don't yet know.)

Confidence and competence have a paradoxical relationship; this is known as the Dunning-Kruger Effect.

Getting back to **nudging**, you can easily **expect this error** for new team members—you can anticipate it. If you can see someone summiting Mount Stupid, about to plunge into the Valley of Despair, what can you do to help **give feedback** and guide them on that journey when they need you? Timing is everything when it comes to nudges. Someone on the top of the mountain is not nudgeable. Being in the Valley of Despair may mean someone is in a uniquely coachable position where they are ready to hear feedback, try new things (even though they are the same things you have been trying to tell them for ages as they were enjoying their time on the mountain), and improve.

It is also important to know that their time in the valley is one of cognitive overwhelm. To put it another way, their elephant is freaking out. Giving them too many things to change while they are feeling the stress will make the problem worse, so you need to be selective on what advice to give them (more on narrowing down your priorities and nudgeable moments in Part 3).

Reflection Point

1. As you build knowledge, you will gradually underestimate your abilities, skills, and all the effort and training that went into what you now know and can do. Just because it is easy for you doesn't mean it isn't of value to someone else. Especially when someone is new, overshare information to help with where you both are on the Dunning-Kruger scale.
2. As you are added to a team in an area where you aren't an expert, if you are confident that you know the answer and these people are missing something obvious, consider how the Dunning-Kruger effect (and other biases) might be influencing your confidence.
3. Know there is a reason why I brought this up alongside the curse of knowledge and functional fixedness in the section about status quo bias—you don't want to get too hung up in the knowledge you or

anybody else has. Just because it has worked before doesn't mean there isn't something better out there.

Functionally Fixated Teams

When you first show up to tackle a new skill or concept, you are so excited to learn you'll likely bring every mental tool you might need just in case. You're a sponge, ready for whatever life throws at you. This may seem naïve to someone with more experience who looks at your enthusiasm with a shake of the head, thinking, "I remember when I was a newbie like that; I didn't know anything! I'm so much better off now."

As you become an expert, you declutter that mental toolbox. Instead of having everything available to look at and use, over time you throw away the drills, wrenches, and duct tape while you perfect your hammer. Focused on your hammer, you might enhance its materials, make it stronger and more ergonomic—everything you do is about creating that ideal hammer.

The problem, of course, comes when you are asked to work with someone who only uses screws or has a firm rule about not creating any holes. A hammer is useless in both scenarios, and if all you can do is argue about the value of your hammer while the other department members are trying to talk over you to convince you to use drills or nonpermanent glue, this quickly becomes a standoff where no one is willing to budge; everyone believes their way is best and the others are illogical jerks who are unwilling to listen to reason.

I can appreciate that it may feel like I've taken the analogy of functional fixedness and "when all you have is a hammer, everything looks like a nail" a bit far. However, when you look at your business interactions, how often are you arguing a point you know to be true while others are fighting just as passionately for something they believe in? Or how often have you proposed a great idea only to be told:

- "We tried that once and it didn't work, so it can't work now."
- "We've always done it this way."
- "Our customers only buy from us in this way."
- "You're new to this space, so you couldn't know all these reasons why. . . ."

Remember back to the 275,000 things your brain filtered out for every one that gets through and that it is biased to feel safe in the predictable status quo. Do not default to the "that didn't/can't work" response and let that guide your decisions.

Remember that everyone else doesn't have to be wrong for you to be right. Often asking a new question can help the brain feel less stuck. For example, "How can we make the best hammer?" will get you somewhere different from "How many ways could we stick things to the wall?"

That picture could be hung with a nail, screw, Command Strips, or something else you haven't thought of yet. Each has its pros and cons and is worth evaluating. Even if you only have a hammer, you can still add a perspective of the other available tools. Sometimes, you benefit from knowing someone with a "drill" and someone else with "adhesive strips" to have a conversation with and other times you need to try and emulate their perspectives without them being there.

The Problem with Buggy Whips

One of my favorite articles is from the *Harvard Business Review*, titled "Marketing Myopia."[102] It has a small mention of a company making buggy whips in the early 1900s. If their mission was to "make the best buggy whips in the world," by the time automobiles come around, they are essentially dead. No one needs buggy whips in a world of cars.

If instead they took a step back and said, "What do people really want?" they could have had a different mission. People don't care about better buggy whips (*even if that is what they said they wanted*). They wanted to get somewhere and currently, a horse and buggy was the way they knew it could be done. If the company realized they were in the business of "making things go," they could adapt to the times and start making engines instead of buggy whips. Being too focused on the problem or solution you see, the functional fixedness of myopia, has caused many a business to die out unnecessarily.

To paraphrase my professor who introduced me to this paper: people don't buy drills; they buy a way to make holes—this is currently the best way to make them, but it won't be that way forever.

The Value of Story

You have probably noticed that I use a lot of stories while explaining concepts—that is not by accident. Our brains have learned to pay attention to stories. We teach children through fables and are captivated by the hero's journey, no matter how it is adapted.

Well-told stories connect with the brain's memory center, and people are more likely to remember what they learned in them. Every culture, all the way back to ancient times, has had some form of storytelling.[103] Stories are part of our nature; you should use them whenever possible as you communicate with teams.

What makes stories so special?

Dr. Paul Zak, founding director of the Center for Neuroeconomics Studies, has found that the neurochemical **oxytocin** is at the center of storytelling.[104] He and his team discovered that oxytocin signals the brain it is safe to approach someone—that they can be trusted. The release of oxytocin triggers empathy and motivates us to be more cooperative.

Zak's team discovered that oxytocin is released in character-driven stories—even on video.

But this only works when you grab the viewer's attention and hold it with tension. A good story is engaging and pulls you in, whether it's the new blockbuster or a business tip. This is why the first few moments of interaction are so critical. If your meeting starts by saying, "Hi there everyone, Melina here again. I'm excited to talk to you today because..." the audience is already gone. Whereas an intriguing question, powerful image, or unique facial expression could get someone to stop, lean in, and say, "Hmmm. I wonder what'll happen next."

We will talk more about small steps in Part 3, but for now, know that each moment in the story (whether it is a video, conversation, or written narrative) has the job of getting the viewer to the next moment—ideally, building up to the moment where they are ready to take the action you've designed in your process. Sometimes the story's only goal is to get them interested enough to be open to the change. Other times, you want them to take action—like start using the new system and try it once before the next meeting.

As Michelle Auerbach said when she was on the show, "Emotion is needed to make decisions, and stories evoke emotions."[105] If you want your team to make decisions and feel compelled to take actions they will follow through on, being thoughtful about the right story to use is critical.

The example of Gene Kranz and Apollo 13 opening the chapter isn't there by coincidence—none of the stories in this book are. They are carefully curated to make a point and help the reader get to the next step. The stories make you think and relate to your teams. They help you to ask questions and be thoughtful. They help you decide to keep reading, learning, and eventually implementing what you learn here.

I teach a class through the Human Behavior Laboratory at Texas A&M University called Creating BEtter Presentations (no, that isn't a typo; BE is capitalized to show how you use behavioral economics to accomplish the task).[106] In this three-week course, I show the students how every presentation is made better with a thoughtful story arc: where are they now, where do you want them to go, and how can you help them to get there. We look at the importance of chunking information along the path, find opportunities for good priming and framing, and know that less is almost always more.

When presenting a change, even when no money is exchanging hands, you are still selling someone an idea you need them to buy in on. This is why I use the same framework for pricing strategy and sales as I do with change management. Storytelling is essential to getting people to relate, understand, retain, and make decisions.

If you don't spend enough time thinking about the goals in advance, you share too much irrelevant information (even things that might be necessary to know *eventually* can be a huge hindrance if shared at the wrong time and all at once). As you know, the subconscious gets overwhelmed easily and giving too much information causes a problem called the **paradox of choice**. When we are presented with too many options and information, we become paralyzed—it is better to stick to the status quo and often do nothing at all than to choose something and be potentially disappointed. This is the focus of our next chapter, so let's jump in.

CHAPTER 9

I Want to Do My Own Research

Disclaimer: doing your own research (or having people on the team do their research) is not a bad thing. Often, not enough research is done, and people follow their herding instincts and other biases to the land of complacency.

However, when all the research has been done, the information has been shared, and it is the go/no-go moment, but people suddenly feel the need to go back to the drawing board, there might be something else going on. First, of course, you should do some evaluation to ensure you aren't asking someone to go from A to Z without all the steps in between (i.e., consider whether *your* biases are making you think they "should" be ready, when you're forgetting about the **curse of knowledge** or something else that could be blocking the way). Once you have confirmed that this is a decision-ready situation, it is time to see what might make their brains cling to the status quo.

Negativity Bias

The first bias I want to bring to your attention is negativity bias, our tendency to focus on bad stuff more than good stuff.[107] Consider employee reviews. I've had a lot of employee reviews over the years, with most of the comments being positive. However, I still remember my first review. My boss told me she "begged" people to give her some constructive criticism for me because everyone had only nice things to say (I promise this isn't intended to be a humble brag). She finally got someone to give an example of something for me to work on, and I remember who said it and what was said to this day (about a decade later).

What about all the nice things that were said? They blur together and are easier to forget because of negativity bias, which we have developed over time to keep us safe. This is why pointing out the pitfalls of an approach or idea (essentially, advocating to maintain the safer feeling status quo) can be celebrated as saving us from a potentially bad outcome before we made a mistake.

Focusing and dwelling on the bad, either that has already happened, or that could happen in the future, is rooted in our negativity bias and can keep us stuck in the status quo.

Ambiguity (Uncertainty) Aversion

People tend to favor the known over the unknown, including any known risks over unknown ones.[108] This is our "the devil you know is better than the devil you don't" bias.

Have you ever heard of graduation goggles? Most people hate high school and likely complain about it for most of the years they spend there, saying things like "I can't wait to get out of here" or "When will this nightmare be over?"

That happens until there is maybe a month left of school and you realize that change *is* coming. It's inevitable now—you may be moving states or to another country for college or find a job and new friends or a significant other. You might be moving out for the first time. Whatever your scenario, that is a lot of change and suddenly you become nostalgic for what you will leave behind.

Every walk down the hall has a "this is one of the last times I'll do this" vibe and you might start to say, "You know, this wasn't that bad," or even go so far as to start saying these were your golden years and "I'm gonna miss this place."

You know, that place you've hated for four years and couldn't wait to get out of . . . what happened?

Status quo bias and ambiguity/uncertainty aversion.

Now that the change is upon you, the stuff you know and everything you are used to looks pretty darn good.

This same phenomenon can make it hard to leave a job for a new one even if you get a great offer. You start to second-guess, and your brain will convince you of all the great stuff you've got going for you: a promotion that might be around the corner or a new level of vesting in your retirement or your friends that are there or whatever.

This feeling that "the devil you know is better than the devil you don't" is inherent in choices we make every day to maintain that status quo.

- Taking the same route to work
- Sticking with the same projects, processes, or roles
- Buying the same toothpaste (and even brushing with the same hand in the same way)
- Wearing the same staples when you've got a closet full of unworn options
- Resisting a new idea we know is good because it has unknown risks

This fear of the unknown keeps many businesses stuck in what they have always done. If you have people who have loved an idea and been a proponent up to the last moment and then they pull support and start to backpedal, this may be at the root of the problem.

What can you do? Because of **time discounting**, we can find it easier to commit to something we know is a good idea when we are in a cold state (i.e., not in the heat of the moment) so **precommitment** can help keep projects moving forward.

Even when people want to do something, they often get complacent and simply don't when the critical moment comes (because the status quo feels easier). As an example, one study found that 86 percent of people who said they planned to change their retirement allocations in the next few months had done nothing four months later.[109] How can you help people do what they say they want to do? In one example, the Save More Tomorrow program had participants commit today to saving in the future. They were asked if they would like to have a portion of future salary increases automatically go toward retirement—78 percent of those with the opportunity joined. After the fourth pay raise, 80 percent were still participating, which increased their retirement savings by an average of 10 percent over the forty-month period.[110]

How you present the choice makes a big difference in whether someone feels ready to move forward. You learned about nudges and a little about choice architecture already, but let's revisit the two terms now because while they are closely tied, they are not the same.

A *choice architect* is someone who indirectly influences the choices of other people. This means you set up the mechanism by which others will select their choice—and the *choice architecture* is the mechanism you select.

A *nudge* is something you would use to influence the decision, in the way the choice architecture is set up, to help the individual trying to decide to do the best job possible.

Here's an example:

Imagine you work in HR and have been tasked with boosting enrollment in the retirement plan and encouraging participants to contribute more to get the 10 percent match. Without copying the Save More Tomorrow approach, how can you help everyone do what they want and know is in their best interest?

By putting on your choice architecture hat and giving a little nudge.

Perhaps you put together a form that all employees need to complete. (Note: The form is mandatory; a retirement contribution is not.)

Presenting Choices

Which comes first? The first item in the list will have the most weight in the brain, so it is best to put the recommendation at the beginning. Is there a **default**?

What is the question you ask on the form?

Remember, everything matters, including the way you **frame** the question. Consider how you feel compelled to respond to each of the following:

- Regarding a retirement allocation, I would like to: ___________
- How much would you like to contribute toward your retirement?
- Experts recommend contributing 15 percent of your salary to a 401(k); how much would you like to allocate?

Do you hear the difference?

Choice architecture and nudges are complex—this example includes framing, priming, anchoring, social proof, and herding, to name a few, and this is just the *question*!

What are the options you include in your choice architecture? How do you word them? Do you simply have two checkboxes for "Yes" or "No" and then a line to write the amount they want to contribute?

What is the default if they do nothing? Do they stay at their status quo of no contribution? Or do they get the recommended "expert" opinion and start contributing 15 percent? That could be extreme and may be unconventional, but it is an option and worth considering (even if it scares your **herding** brain).

Maybe you list the choices as:

- Yes, I want to contribute the recommended 15 percent.
- Yes, I want to contribute, but let's start at 10 percent.
- Yes, I want to contribute at 5 percent.
- Yes, I want to contribute some other amount: ________.
- No, I do not wish to contribute yet.

As you can see, there are many options in wording to help nudge people to contribute higher amounts, but again, it is easy to opt-out and say "no thank you" by checking a different box on the same form.

People still have free choice. They still have all the information (perhaps even more useful if you include the recommended contribution of 15 percent—a detail they may not otherwise have).

And, while you may feel compelled to provide as many options as possible, resist that urge! As noted in the previous chapter, too many choices will result in a **paradox of choice**. When there are too many options, people will get overwhelmed and often do nothing (there is too much uncertainty and possible risk, so it is easier to make no choice). To keep with our HR benefits packages, people are given a lot of options and the common strategy is to divide equally among them. So, 50-50 if there are two options or 25-25-25-25 for four. And when there are too many choices for that to be a meaningful contribution, they are more likely to do nothing.[111]

There isn't a perfect number of choices that apply to every scenario, so being thoughtful about the end goal matters. You can then invest time in making it "intuitively obvious" for people, so they are more likely to make a choice instead of saying they need to do more research when you know they have all the information needed to move forward (this is a sign of the brain defaulting to the status quo).

Behavioral Concept: Reciprocity

It's three-thirty on a Friday in December. You're wrapping up emails and closing out projects to enjoy having the entire next week off for the holidays. A soft *knock, knock* breaks your focus. Glancing up from the screen, you see Nancy—a friend from human resources—holding a neatly wrapped box. "Sorry to disturb," she says, "but I know you'll be out next week and wanted to make sure you got my gift before you leave this afternoon!" Grinning from ear to ear, she reaches to hand you the bow-clad box.

You have no gift for Nancy and feel the guilt bubbling inside you.

Unable to control the urge, the words come tumbling out. "You won't believe it—I left your gift at home! I can see it there, right by the door. I'll have to bring it by after the holiday."

Why do you feel compelled to have a gift for Nancy now, when five minutes ago you could've left without a second thought? Why will this moment now haunt your entire holiday?

Reciprocity.

Receiving a gift—even a small one—compels us to give something in return. Not doing so just feels . . . wrong.

And the funny thing is, we aren't good at valuing the gifts we receive, so people tend to give back bigger than what they got.

Consider the little gift some restaurants give you at the end of your meal. And I do mean a *very* little gift: a mint or fortune cookie. Do you think this "gift" impacts your tip? Probably not, but the studies show giving a single mint increased tips by 3 percent, and giving two mints did more than double tips; they went *up almost five times* to a 14 percent increase.[112]

Given the cost of the mints, this is a great return on investment for the restaurant and shows that the consumer's brain feels obligated to pay back for the "gift." Though, this doesn't keep going up exponentially (meaning, you shouldn't casually drop a mountain of mints on the table and expect people will tip more than the cost of their bill). However, one thing is completely free and caused tips to skyrocket. Can you guess what it is?

Thoughtfulness.

When the waiter gave one mint with the check and started to walk away but then stopped, turned back, and said, "You know what, for you nice people, here's an extra mint," tips increased 23 percent!

While the mints matter, you don't need to give physical gifts to all your employees to get them on board with change (as you will see when we get to motivation, that can often backfire and make things worse).

When looking at change management, the "gifts" you give are thoughtfulness, transparency, kindness, and effort. Think back to what you learned about priming and the value of putting a little more effort up front to reduce unnecessary emails and conversations to clarify points. Taking that time and putting in the extra thought is a gift to your employees, one they will notice and feel compelled to reciprocate in the form of loyalty, effort, and support. This includes trusting you when they are scared to jump into the unknown. Considering how you can be generous with others can pay off huge for your current project and those yet to come.

The Economic Value of Trust

In episode 148, I was fortunate enough to interview Stephen M.R. Covey about his bestselling book, *The Speed of Trust*.[113]

One of my favorite things about this book is, probably not surprisingly, his equations, which tie in with the economics of trust. Trust might feel like it isn't a quantifiable value for a company. The organizations that even take the time to look at its value would probably categorize it as an intangible asset. You shouldn't.

As Covey says, this one thing changes everything. The rules are simple; as trust goes down, projects are slower and more expensive. Whenever trust goes up, we can get things done faster and for less money. Here they are in equation form:

Reduced Trust = Reduced Speed + Higher Cost

Increased Trust = Increased Speed + Lower Cost

Consider how quickly things can happen when you work with people you trust. Deals are made quickly, teams work efficiently, things click, and people feel great. His book describes a twenty-three-billion-dollar acquisition of McLane Distribution, a business deal between Warren Buffett and Walmart. This type of deal would typically take many months and cost millions to pay for accountants, auditors, and attorneys. They made the deal after a single two-hour meeting and a handshake.

He also shares a story of when Herb Kelleher, former CEO of Southwest Airlines, was presented with a three-page memo outlining a massive reorganization. Kelleher read it there in the hallway, asked a question (to which the team member gave a satisfactory answer that he shared the concern and was already working on it). In less than five minutes from being presented with the document, he gave the go-ahead, and the project could begin.

Without a high level of trust, interactions like these could not happen. You may be thinking, "We could never do that here." It isn't something that happens overnight, that's for sure. But continued investments in those micro-moments can build up trust over time. Remember back to the Gene Kranz example in the last chapter. Something he said in the buildup to Apollo 11 landing on the moon was creating a culture of trust critical to saving the astronauts of Apollo 13. To borrow a set of terms from Stephen's father, the late Dr. Stephen Covey who wrote *The 7 Habits of Highly Effective People*, every conversation is going into the mental bank account—it is either a deposit or a withdrawal.[114] You want to be making lots of deposits and building up that trust account so when you are ready to make a withdrawal, the account isn't negative.

Your investment in giving the gift of transparency and trust to your team can help them establish autonomy—one of the key factors of intrinsic motivation, which we will talk about more in Chapter 15.

When you think of the company 3M, what product(s) come to mind? If you are familiar with the brand at all, I am guessing Post-its is on your list. Did you know that Post-its, now the flagship of 3M, were created during "experimental doodling" time at the company, which lets every employee dedicate up to 15 percent of their time to projects that aren't directly related to their job?[115]

It's a common case study, so you might know that one. But what about Gmail, Google News, and Google Translate? They came out of a similar program at Google of "20 percent time." Atlassian claims zero turnover in engineering because of their similar policy. It's important to note that when they started to implement this flex time at Atlassian, many managers resisted and said they wanted to get reports from their team members to make sure they weren't messing around during this time—they were told no.[116] Autonomy requires trust. Trust helps teams overcome the fear of the unknown and try new things.

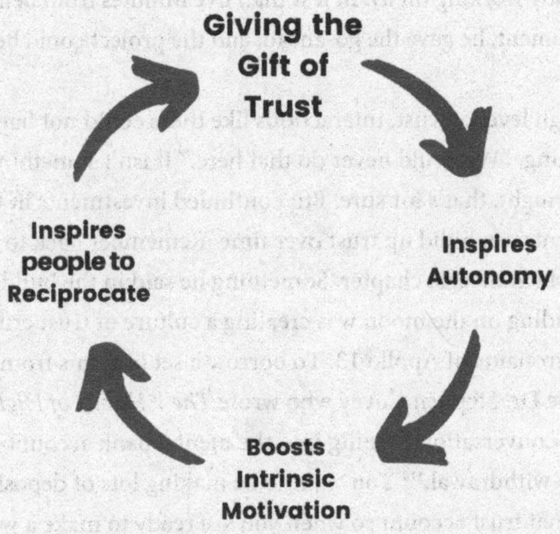

Reciprocity is a gift of trust that inspires autonomy and makes people intrinsically motivated, making them want to give back with reciprocity again.

Give the gift of trust freely; throw out that adage that trust needs to be earned before it is given. As Covey and I discussed when he was on the show, people are afraid of the few who could ruin it for everyone, so they put policies in place that hinder trust. Most people will do the right thing; your team wants to make you, themselves, and the company proud. Use the philosophy that people are trustworthy until proven otherwise and give them lots of chances to prove you right.

CHAPTER 10

He Always Meets *His* Goals, Just Do What He Does

It's World War II and the Allies are looking for ways to ensure more planes (and their pilots) survive their missions, knowing this could be the difference between winning and losing the war.

While it would be nice to reinforce an entire plane, there is a reason tanks can't fly. Too much of the super-strong metal would mean the planes couldn't get off the ground, so it was important to be strategic and pick the right spots to reinforce that balance. To figure out the best places to reinforce, the generals decided to have the planes analyzed.

The analysis was led by a mathematician named Abraham Wald, and as part of the research process he had the Air Force look at all the planes to see where they had damage—bullet holes and the like—and mark the spots on a card for each one.

Stacking those cards on top of each other quickly showed the damage clustered on the wings, tail, and some of the central body, and there were some notable blank spots with no damage.

In seeing these results, the generals did what all our brains tend to do when we see information like this, saying something like, "Capital analysis Wald, we now know where all the gunfire is hitting and can reinforce the spots with the most holes—thanks!"

To which he essentially (thankfully) said, "Uh . . . no."

Survivorship Bias

Do you see the problem with that conclusion? The problem with reinforcing the spots on the planes that have received the most bullets is that it doesn't account for a large—and important—part of the data set.

As the title of a great Ted Talk on **survivorship bias** explains, this conclusion is *missing what's missing.*[117]

In the case of the WWII planes, the analysis can only include the planes that *made it back*. Planes are hit everywhere; there is nothing special about those points on the planes that weren't hit in that gunfire couldn't reach them there . . . meaning they wouldn't need to be reinforced.

In fact, the reasonable assumption is that those are the parts that matter *most*—the engines, the cockpit—and when the planes were hit there, the damage was fatal, so they didn't return to be part of the study.

That means those blank spots are where you want to reinforce the planes, to make them stronger in those places so they can take fire there and not go down.

They, of course, took Wald's advice and reinforced the planes in the proper spot. For this and many other reasons, the Allies won the war.

When you hear and see it pointed out in this way, the flaw in the thinking is incredibly obvious. However, since most of us aren't in the business of planes taking heavy fire, this concept may seem inconsequential, an interesting anecdote at best. But of course, as you will see, this bias shows up constantly in companies.

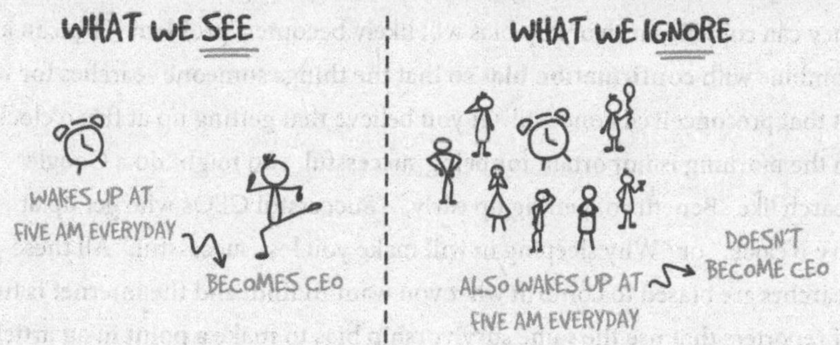
SURVIVORSHIP BIAS
WHAT WE SEE
WHAT WE IGNORE
WAKES UP AT
FIVE AM EVERYDAY
BECOMES CEO
ALSO WAKES UP AT
FIVE AM EVERYDAY
DOESN'T
BECOME CEO

Are you missing what's missing? Survivorship bias cartoon, courtesy of 100 Behaviors[118]

As this cartoon shows, we love looking for a shortcut to success and because we are a herding species, we look for how others have been successful in the past to try and emulate them and be more successful ourselves. We want to learn from others' mistakes and save ourselves time and turmoil.

The problem, of course, is that when you ask people what made them successful, they don't know all the aspects that came into play. The conscious rider is trying to explain what the elephant was thinking and will miss what is missing (among other things). A reporter might interview a bunch of successful people who say they get up at five o'clock in the morning and that is why they are successful, making that a tip for others to follow so they can be successful. This ignores all the successful people who don't wake up at five o'clock and those who wake up at five o'clock and are not particularly successful (and all the other things the successful people did that were not about the time they got out of bed). Survivorship bias ignores these important data points and makes incomplete conclusions that are then used to make other decisions. It is a bias that runs rampant in businesses.

Confirmation Bias

Whenever someone is looking for a shortcut or seeing what others did so they can copy it, survivorship bias will likely become a problem. This can also combine with **confirmation bias** so that the things someone searches for will fit that preconceived concept.[119] If you believe that getting up at five o'clock in the morning is important for being successful, you might do a Google search like "Benefits of getting up early," "Successful CEOs who get up at five o'clock," or "Why sleeping in will make you less successful." All these searches are biased to confirm what you want to find, and the internet is full of reporters that use the same survivorship bias to make a point in an article.

In your business life, you might see or hear:

- Do some research to find out how XYZ did that and we will do the same thing.
- Suzie always does this when she is in meetings, which must be why people like working with her.
- Our best two projects did this; that must be the key to success!

These are all natural reactions and you have likely done, seen, or said each of them at least once in your career (or if you think about it, you have likely done something like each of these at least once in the past week either in articles you searched for, thoughts you had, or conversations with team members). Any time you are looking for a path to success without considering the others that don't fit that mold—or when you or your team want a shortcut—assume survivorship bias will be at play.

While using a mental shortcut isn't always bad (as you know, we need our biases to survive), if you don't know and look out for survivorship bias, you will often reinforce the wrong areas of the plane. As long as no one fires at those critical points, you'll be fine, but one metaphorical bullet is all it takes to bring you down.

Reflection Point

The great thing about survivorship bias is that it doesn't have to be difficult to overcome. All you need is a little thoughtfulness and some well-intentioned questions. For example, let's use those same scenarios above:

- Do some research to find out how XYZ did that and then we will do the same thing.
    - » Has anyone else done the same thing and not been successful?
    - » How does their scenario vary from ours?
    - » What critical data might we not be able to see (or are we not thinking of) that impacted this outcome?
- Suzie always does this when she is in meetings, which must be why she gets so much done.
    - » Who else does that in meetings and isn't as productive?
    - » Does she "always" do that thing? What happens when she doesn't?
    - » Who else is productive and doesn't do that?
    - » Is the cost of training or doing whatever we think Suzie is doing going to scale across the rest of the team and would it be profitable for the outcome it creates? (In other words, is the juice worth the squeeze?)
- Our best two projects did this; that must be the key to success!
    - » What failed projects also did those things?

» Are there any similarities or differences between these two projects and others that should be considered before jumping to any conclusions?

These are not the only scenarios, nor the only questions to ask. Instead, I advise you to *be thoughtful*, a phrase which I say at the end of every podcast episode and has become the signature line on my emails. When you or someone on the team is jumping to a conclusion, take a minute to ask what's missing. What haven't you thought about yet? What if that weren't true?

You may find that these initial assumptions and conclusions will work for you, and that's great. You can't go into detail every time survivorship bias comes into play (you would never get anything done!). Instead, when it is an important project or something that can impact the company's greater success (like a strategic planning initiative or new product line), take the time to be thoughtful.

Behavioral Concept: Peak-End Rule

When review time comes around, can the collective sigh and eye roll from your managers be heard around the block? While we all know reviews are important, writing one (or ten) is daunting and can feel overwhelming for managers. And while the intent is good—employees deserve to receive consistent feedback and it is good to have check-in points to confirm alignment and plan for what is to come—there is a brain quirk that keeps most reviews from showing the full picture. Depending on the employee, this could make their overall performance seem more positive (or more negative) than it is. It's called the **peak-end rule.**[120]

As our brains evaluate any experience—whether reflecting upon a meeting or having a painful medical procedure—this shortcut is used to streamline the process. Instead of performing complex calculations comparing every feature of the experience, we look to the peak (most extreme) event and the end (most recent) to shape our opinion of the experience overall.

Consider your last employee review. Did you evaluate every individual day, conversation, meeting, project, email, and interaction from the entire year to calculate an average rating? Or did you sit in front of your computer, reflecting on the most prominent moments that popped into your head to use in the review?

I'm guessing it's the latter. The problem with that is you are missing a lot of what's missing—the mundane stuff in the middle, the other positive and negative points that aren't the peak or the end—those things matter. Imagine you have two employees:

- Employee A is consistent. They get a little better each day and typically don't make mistakes. There was one missed deadline a few months ago you made a note about, and nothing else stands out.
- Employee B is all over the place. They have to be nudged often and reminded about deadlines (some before they are missed and some after), but they also have some massive wins. Like last week, they rallied at the end of the month and beat their goal in an amazing fashion. You weren't sure if they would make it, but it was exciting to follow the numbers and see how they would end the year.

I'm not going to get into a discussion about which type of employee is "better." Instead, this is about their reviews and how you reflect on their performance. When you look back at the memories of these team members, because there aren't any significant peaks for Employee A, you may have a more negative overall impression and dwell on this one missed deadline, even when everything else has been steadily improving over time (and they miss fewer deadlines than Employee B). But, because Employee B has significant positive peaks, they cancel out the missed deadlines and your brain glosses over them. This biases your reviews and impression of the team members, which leads to confirmation bias that creates either a vicious or virtuous cycle that is hard to shake.

If you aren't careful, this will start an "us versus them" mentality amongst your team members (the final section of Part 2), which can be toxic and restrict change.

Micro-Shift Moment: To help the peak-end rule have less impact on your reviews, block out a regular time to make notes on each of your employees. I recommend weekly because it isn't too often to be skipped and not so far apart to miss a bunch of stuff. Take this time to jot everything down—including the average stuff. Try to write at least one positive, one negative, and one neutral for each person, and relate it to their goals. This will make it easier come review time, so you aren't wondering, "What were we working on last February?" This practice will make the review process faster and help you reduce the peak-end rule bias creeping up and impacting morale.

I always encourage staff to keep track of their performance throughout the year as well. Come review time, you will get a list of highlights so you know what is important to them.

Bonus: While you make notes on your employees each week, do the same for yourself so you have a great list of accomplishments and opportunities from the past year to help your boss do their review of you.

Remember, Teams Are Made Up of Individuals

Survivorship bias is a symptom of the shortcuts your brain likes to take to find the quick answer to a complex question. The problem with advice like the title of this chapter, "He always meets his goals, just do what *he* does" is that, in addition to knowing that people are notoriously bad at knowing what contributes to their success, it doesn't acknowledge the differences among people.

Your team members do not all need to be nudged the same way at the same time. An approach that works for one employee will not work for another (and that is okay). Diversity is important in teams for all sorts of reasons. One of them is, much like a portfolio of investments, you don't want to be too heavily invested in one type of asset. You need to diversify your bias risk and trust the team to hold each other accountable, to have some ebb while others flow. If everyone is the same, you will get hung up on the same biases and never have a differing perspective. Much like the *Challenger* logic, just because it hasn't blown up yet doesn't mean it isn't a problem.

Worxogo is a "nudge coach" that helps employees build better work habits and take ownership of their productivity by leveraging artificial intelligence.[121] Cofounder Anant Sood shared with me a little of how it works and the amazing results they are getting for teams—more than 85,000 users across five countries. It starts by getting to know the user and building trust and transparency. It tests different nudge styles through a mix of visual and textual cues to try and see what works for each individual. This allows everyone to feel comfortable about their metrics, goals, and achievements, which increases productivity. For example, a competitive person is more interested in how their stats compare to others, whereas someone else would be more motivated by seeing how close they are to their personal best. As Anant said, "The ideal manager would understand the motivational and productivity context of every individual, but there is too much information for a human brain to fully comprehend and analyze in every moment. Our engine uses a combination of artificial intelligence and machine learning models to constantly learn and individually nudge the team."

Why This Matters

Work gets done by people, not tools. Most business leaders invest millions in CRMs and analytics tools and hope that the human at the end of the process does the task. And that's why most enterprise tools don't deliver the ROI they are expected to.

Worxogo uses real CRM data to discover what is most motivating to each user and gives them the right nudge at the right moment to help them meet the most important goal, which has been identified by management. It also gives managers feedback and lets them know when and how to optimally reach out to their team members. The manager might get a notification like, "Melina responds best to competition, so use social proof to compare them to their personal best or someone else," while simultaneously getting a message that "John responds best to teamwork, so remind him of how important he is in helping the team reach their goal."

It truly is a fascinating and amazing system getting equally impressive results. Anant told me that across the industry, for CRM systems and the like, a 30 percent daily active user count is considered stellar (and important for people to be getting the benefits of any system—if you aren't logged in, you can't get the data or the nudge). They are more than double that, with 72 percent average daily logins across industries and job roles.

Worxogo is a great example of how behavioral science, data analytics, and artificial intelligence can work with the power of people to help companies exceed their goals and have engaged employees.

Behavioral Concept: Sludge

In general, sludge is something you look to eliminate in business—this is the stuff that makes it hard to get things done.[122] Extra steps, procedures, processes, and other gunk takes up mental space and creates time pressure for your team. While looking to free up time for your team, reducing unnecessary sludge can help make everyone's job easier and more streamlined.

However, sludge is not always a bad thing. When there are significant biases that can cause you and the team to make bad decisions, sludge can help you incorporate some useful pause points. Those pause points are an opportunity to step back and look around:

- Are we being too myopic here?
- What's missing that we aren't considering?
- If we had a drill instead of a hammer, would we see a different problem or solution?
- Is my "gut" telling me to step back because of a legitimate concern, or is this a status quo/uncertainty aversion issue?

Building in sludge can help you pause before taking a misstep (remember to expect and plan for errors).

Reflection Point

Speaking of useful sludge, before moving on to the last section of Part 2 (Us vs. Them), take a moment here to pause and reflect on what you have learned in these last few chapters on status quos and shortcuts.

What is your biggest "aha" from these biases? What is one small thing you can do right now to implement some of what you have learned?

2.3
US VS. THEM

An affinity for the status quo can show up in many ways—as you know, the subconscious is continually looking for it all day every day. Sometimes, shaking things up to change the context is the best way to upend the status quo, especially when you have a team stuck in their ways and developing an "us versus them" mentality.

While we love the status quo, we also love a fresh start. It is an opportunity to leverage our optimism bias and give ourselves permission to be different. Katy Milkman, author of *How To Change*, has done amazing research with Hengchen Dai and Jason Riis on the fresh start effect, which shows why we are more likely to pursue new goals when they are tied to a fresh start.[123] This is why New Year resolutions are so appealing and why more people run marathons (or finally lose weight or quit smoking) at the age of thirty-nine, forty-nine, and fifty-nine than forty-one, fifty-one, and sixty-one.

We are also more likely to be open to change at the beginning of the week (month, quarter) than at the end. Milestones have an impact as well—starting high school felt like a fresh start for so many people, where you had an opportunity to be whomever you wanted instead of who you were the year before. Starting a new job, on a new team, a new project, being given a new purpose . . . it can all free even the most stuck person from their status quo when properly framed.

Sometimes a shift in the status quo is big and unplanned, like a global pandemic making it so billions of people around the world who said their organizations would never be remote were suddenly able to change. Hundreds of millions of status quos were taken away in an instant and we were forced to change. Even the most stubborn luddites were able to adapt—and many of them have found they *like* this virtual working thing (it's amazing how quickly our brains get comfortable in a new status quo). Often, getting people to try the new thing long enough (triggering the endowment effect, which you will learn about in this section) is all that is needed to get them on board in the long term. We like things we are familiar with after all, so much like a song on the radio we hated the first time around (but is now "our jam"), repeated exposure can make it so we like the new thing more and more.

Thankfully, shifting the status quo doesn't always need to be so extreme or negative. Sam Evans, a growth marketing and behavioral design consultant, told me about a project he did with a global, category-leading consumer packaged goods company with an extensive brand portfolio. Their typical process to develop and commercialize a new product took eighteen to twenty-four months. By developing a dedicated team with an inspiring vision and the autonomy to make fast decisions, the company could reduce that to about six months.

But what about when you can't change who is on your team? What about when you can't create a new process across the organization? "That's all fine and good for them," you might be thinking, "but I've got a team that can barely get through a meeting without shouting, shutting down, or playing the blame game." When you are in the trenches, you can still apply my change framework to get out of that current state and into one where you can finally start looking to a brighter future (you've got an extra step on the path).

In this final section, we will be talking about an "us versus them" mentality and how it can quickly become toxic on teams. This can be when team members don't trust each other or when your teams are siloed and see those in other departments as "them."

Humans are tribal by nature, and we have survived this long by relying on and trusting those who are like us more than those who are not.[124] This is important for us as a species, and it can help us rally together in companies to achieve amazing things. However, it can also create unnecessary rifts and rivalries that make us stagnant and disgruntled.

If you have a toxic team with an "us versus them" mentality, it might feel like quicksand—every step forward comes with sixty-five steps back. Don't fret; you can rally the team to come together so you can move out of the quicksand and into productive territory.

This next section (the final installment in Part 2) will look at the biases that keep people siloed, along with some behavioral concepts to help get out of that muck. We will also look at incentives, fairness, motivation, and the importance of unity. Ready? Let's get started.

CHAPTER 11

They're Out to Get Me, I Know It

Take no more than five seconds to look at the following image (I'm trusting you since this is in a printed book and you could technically take as long as you want, unlike in presentations where I will change over to the next slide). Your time starts now.

In five words or less, what is this image about?

Now that you have taken a few moments to digest it, in no more than five words, explain the focus of the painting. What was it about?

The most common responses I get to this are "water," "vacation," "calm," and the like. Perhaps you chose one of those or something similar. For most reading this book, I'm sorry to tell you that you are wrong. The painting is about the tiny little boat in the corner. It is a story about its crew, and you focused on the wrong stuff.

The Focusing Illusion and Confirmation Bias

This declaration is, of course, ridiculous. The image can be about many things, and just because I focused on and wanted it to be about the boat doesn't mean that your focus on the water or trees or how the overall composition made you feel is "wrong." Your subconscious brain merely did a scan to choose what was most important for those five seconds and filtered out everything else. As I've already said in this book, even when we are saying two different things, we can both be right.

The problem is our biased brains want to prove themselves right. The subconscious essentially evolved to believe that it is better, faster, and smarter than everyone else (including the "you" of five minutes ago). For that reason, your subconscious focuses on things that prove its assumptions. This, as you know, is confirmation bias.

While the focusing illusion and confirmation bias are not the same thing, they work closely together (as many of these biases do).[125] Think about it like this: Because your brain wants to be right, it is biased to confirm its assumptions. As a result, the subconscious will focus on certain things and ignore others, further confirming what it believes to be true (but not necessarily making it any *more* true).

Imagine you are certain your boss is out to get you and ensure you never get promoted. During a meeting while you are talking, the boss gives you a look. In the back of your mind, you begin to doubt and question, "Why is she looking at me like that? She must think I'm stupid and that I am taking too much time to talk here. Was that an eye roll? Ugh! I never get to share my opinions; I'll stop now before I make it worse and try to get through this meeting without her getting mad and sabotaging me any further."

If instead you believe that your boss supports you and values your opinions, your internal dialogue could sound something like this: "Great! She is looking at me now and giving me her full attention. I bet she is taking mental notes for how this can be valuable in our next conversation."

This could be the same conversation with the same people, but one has started a vicious cycle and the other a virtuous one.

What-If Thinking

The way our brains can question and evaluate what has happened to make a future decision is truly remarkable—this isn't something that every species can do. Sometimes, though, we can get stuck in a what-if loop: a vicious cycle of over-analysis that keeps us stuck. "Why did I say that? What must she be thinking? What if I had done something else?" This is called **counterfactual thinking**, and when you get stuck in the "what if" and "if only," it is important to calm the elephant and get out of there.

The easy way out is a simple phrase: "Next time I'll...." You and your teams can use this when you start beating yourselves up over something that didn't go well and that can't be changed. It is important to learn from mistakes, which means looking at them and seeing what happened, but then you've got to move forward. Asking what you will do next time is a powerful tool to shake the team out of the loop and back into productive territory.

The Problem with Trying to Win

Often, when I train or teach these concepts, someone will ask for my advice on a particular scenario. It could be something like, "I have this guy on my team who is focused on why things can never work, and I'm so glad to hear that this has a name! How can I show him that he is suffering from the focusing illusion and confirmation bias to help the whole team move forward together on the right path?"

On the surface, this may feel like a breakthrough—and in some ways, it is. In that way, my response may surprise you. I almost always tell this person first to consider their confirmation bias and how that is clouding the situation.

If you go into any difficult conversation believing you are "right" and wanting to figure out how you can prove to the other person (and quickly get them to accept) that they are "wrong," it is a recipe for failure. In that scenario, you will focus on all the things they do or say that can be used to your advantage, filtering out any of their valid thoughts and ideas, which they need to know are heard to move forward (calming the elephant).

Their shields are up. They focus on how you are attacking them and their confirmation bias about how you don't like them, listen to them, or care about them is constantly reinforced. This can quickly result in the **backfire effect**, which is what happens when people "double-down" on whatever they believe even when presented with facts and logical evidence for why it is wrong.[176] Just as they came into this meeting sure that you don't like them and won't listen, you went into the meeting thinking they are difficult and don't care about the rest of the team. Your confirmation biases create a lose-lose scenario where neither party is willing to budge.

When you set out to "win" in a meeting, you are essentially shooting yourself in the foot and setting the whole thing up to fail. This is true whether you are the boss or employee or meeting with someone from a different department. When it is "you" against "them," someone must lose—but as you have seen in the painting example that opened this chapter, that is rarely the case.

Of course, you can't do everything every employee suggests when solving a problem. Decisions need to be made and some people will have to defer to the group choice (but not in a false consensus effect/groupthink way). It doesn't mean they need to feel bad about it or like their opinions don't matter. When you consider your biases and those around you and use the steps outlined in Part 3, you will be amazed at how quickly people will loosen their grips on their ideas and are open to the thoughts of others (yourself included). It makes for a better working environment that is beneficial for the company because more perspectives are included in the final solutions.

Micro-Shift Moment: In your next meeting with a difficult person, instead of asking how you can show them you are right, prove to them that they are wrong, or get them to your side, ask how you can understand why their perspective can also be right. Do not leave the meeting without understanding and validating where they are coming from. You might not get time to talk about your perspective, which is okay because it isn't the goal right now. This is one small step on the path to change.

Behavioral Concepts: The IKEA Effect and Effort Heuristic

Today, you will be making some origami—either a crane or a frog.[127] No worries that you have no experience; the instructions will be provided for you and there is no set time limit so you can build until you are happy with your creation. After everyone is done building, we will have an auction. Each person can bid up to a dollar for the piece and then a random number will be drawn. If your bid is equal to or higher than that number, you can keep it. If you bid less, you cannot have it.

In this study, one group built their origami and had a chance to write down their bid for the item. A second group of non-builders went through the same bidding process for the items built by the builders and some origami made by expert folders to compare.

The non-builders valued the expert origami at twenty-seven cents on average and the ones built by the non-experts at a mere five cents. Basically, a worthless piece of paper.

What did the builders think of their creations?

They valued them nearly five times higher than non-builders. The average value was twenty-three cents, almost as much as the non-builders were willing to pay for the expertly folded origami. A separate group was tested to ensure the results weren't based on a willingness to buy something they wanted for themselves versus true value. When asked what they thought others would pay for their creations, this second group predicted that people would pay twenty-one cents, much higher than the meager five cents people would actually pay. Liking and valuing something more that you had a hand in making is known as the IKEA effect.

We are also biased to believe that more time spent equals a higher value; this is called the effort heuristic. For example, studies show that people expect to get higher grades for papers they spent more time writing.[128]

While there is often a correlation between these two items, and effort can result in a higher grade, that isn't always the case. Maybe one person "got" a concept and wrote a great paper quickly, while someone else had a hard time understanding the concept and struggled to connect the ideas, so it took them longer to understand the foundation.

Many students have argued with a professor, saying, "But I worked so *hard*! How could I possibly get a C?"

Can you see how this can be a problem in business? Someone struggling and taking a long time to complete a project might think they are providing a lot of value and deserve to be paid more for that effort. The boss might consider this to be a simple task. They would look at this situation and think, "Why is this taking so long? This person doesn't know what they are doing." That disconnect can cause a lot of problems—especially when the boss doesn't realize that the employee might think that more time = more value.

This isn't always the case, though. As you have learned throughout this book, people are more likely to rely on the rules of the subconscious when they are in unknown territory. So, if there is a new project or endeavor that no one has undertaken before, everyone might be more willing to think that increased time means increased value because of the effort heuristic.

For example, when people believed that a poem took eighteen hours to complete, they thought it was worth more money than a poem they were told took only four hours.[129] It was the same poem in both conditions, and the duration of time to create were not the only facts they were told. They were to take notes about the author's name, his age at the time of writing the poem, the title, and the time it took to write (which was the only thing that changed between the conditions). In the four-hour condition, people said the value was fifty dollars, while in the eighteen-hour version, they valued it nearly double—at ninety-five dollars!

Same exact poem.

It is important to note that people didn't necessarily like the poem more when they thought it took more time to create. People rated the quality about the same in both versions. The study also looked at paintings and suits of armor, which had similar effects.

Leaning on the effort heuristic helped the artist Jackson Pollock, whose work was hated by many when he emerged onto the art scene. Many people looked at it and said, "A child could do that," or they believe they could have splattered some paint themselves and created something similar.

When the long, painstaking process—sometimes dedicating months of hard work to a single piece—was made public, people liked, appreciated, and valued it more.

While the effort heuristic is different from the IKEA effect, they walk hand in hand. Sometimes in business, you want to let people be part of the process (more on that below), but other times, you need to show the effort to help people value the process.

The **IKEA effect** says that we value things higher when we put effort into them. So, the **effort heuristic** is present within our IKEA effects, but when someone else is putting in the work, it can trigger the effort heuristic without being the IKEA effect. The **endowment effect** (coming soon) shows that we value things we own more than things we don't.

A Plethora of Post-its

Similar to the plight of Jackson Pollock, marketing is a field where people tend to believe they could succeed if they tried. "Everyone's a marketer" is a common phrase in the field. Someone who doesn't work in that space might think that a flyer, video, or social media post can be "whipped up" in a few minutes (with stellar conversion rates, of course) and that anyone can do that job.

If you work in or close to marketing, you know this is not the case.

I once ran a marketing team that had an internal client expectation problem. I wanted the department to plan and do things strategically, which meant being at least ninety days ahead at any given time. That meant all our April campaigns would be completed and sent out by January 1 at the latest.

Do you think department heads or project leads were coming to me in December asking for a flyer they wanted to use in May? Of course not. They would come by and ask for a flyer they needed a week ago and expect my team could whip it up by the end of the day.

I could try to logic and explain to them until I was blue in the face that things take time, and we don't turn projects around that quickly. This approach would end up with someone being annoyed, perhaps complaining about how difficult the department was to work with (sometimes trying to make flyers in an attempt to solve the problem, and as you know from the biases showcased in this chapter, they felt they were a lot better than what the trained eye of a third-party observer—i.e., my team and me—would see). Trying to explain why they could not give that to customers (and that we would still not be making them a flyer for their last-minute ask) was not a great experience either—and more than once ended up with a member of the executive team in my office asking why we couldn't make this *one* flyer.

Of course, it is never just one flyer, and this is a more systemic problem. If the department is constantly doing one-off projects, we can't be strategic. We will also fall behind on the things we need to do and end up doing a lot of unnecessary work. (Don't get me started on the number of times I had someone ask for something and the team created all the materials and when we gave them what they asked for they let us know they changed their mind and didn't need that thing anymore, which was followed by a long explanation of the new thing they "need" yesterday).

This may feel hopeless, like the only option is to keep holding your ground even if you make enemies. Thankfully, there is a better way.

I discovered this by accident, but it was amazing. To keep my team productive and organize all our projects, I implemented a SCRUM method for the department. All projects were broken down into their smallest components. For example, instead of having the project be "new customer email," it would be broken down into things like:

- Determine goal of email campaign
- Discuss segmentation/audience for email
- Ask analytics for list
- Share list timeline with marketing team
- Write first draft of email
- Review draft
- Approve draft internally
- Send draft to operations for approval
- Receive approval from operations department

You get the idea. Quickly, a simple email was broken into twenty-five or more tasks, with various people responsible for each. I had a massive corkboard put up in my office (it was about half the size of one full wall) and each team member got a certain color Post-it. We each wrote our tasks (or would write tasks for another team member on their assigned color) and pinned them to the board. As tasks were in various stages of completion, they would move from "to do" to "doing" to "review" to "done."

Hundreds of Post-it notes were on the board at any time, and I constantly had team members in my office grabbing new Post-its to work on as they moved others triumphantly to the "done" section, which was full of colorful paper as a tribute to our work.

A funny thing happened when we started using this board. People from other departments would come into my office to ask for something and say, "Whoa! You guys have a lot going on; how do you get it all done?" Sometimes they would say, "Well, I was going to ask you for a quick flyer, but I can see you have a lot on your plate. When do you think your team will have time for a new project?"

In tandem with this, I would proactively ask the various departments months in advance what they would be doing in the quarters we were working on so they didn't have to remember to ask for a May promotion in January. (A little expect error/give feedback nudge.)

Explaining how much we were doing didn't make a dent in the requests or frustration. Seeing the effort in a grand, colorful corkboard of awesomeness? This made it so the workload and effort we put in were constantly visible (priming) and part of the conversation, and we never had to talk about it again.

Bring Them In

The biggest lesson from this chapter is knowing that people like to put effort into things. Effort gives them ownership.

We tend to assume people would prefer to do nothing, get everything fully assembled and complete, and they would likely tell us that on a survey because people don't know what they want most of the time.

But, as it turns out when you remove all the effort, sometimes people will rebel.

Have you ever wondered why you need to add an egg and oil to instant cake mix? Today we might say, "Ugh, why can't they find a way to include everything in the box?" The truth is they did, and sales lagged.

When instant cake mix was first introduced back in the 1950s, there was nothing to add but water—and housewives didn't want it.[130] This made it too easy. Their skills were undervalued, and it felt like a lie.

Removing the powdered egg from the mix so people had to add it themselves did the trick and soon box cake mix became the norm; these days most people don't even know how to make cakes from scratch.

It still feels like you are "making cake or cookies" when you use a box, but not quite as much as when you do it from scratch. And as an avid baker, I'm always inclined to say I made it from scratch when that is the case; the effort feels like it needs to be rewarded (or at least acknowledged).

Humans aren't the only animals who value putting in effort. When presented with two food options: one is an open, easily accessed bowl and another requires some level of work to get their food, rats and birds will choose the "work" over the freely accessible bowl.[131]

We are motivated by feeling like we did something, like we earned it, whatever "it" is. We still like convenience to a point, but when it is all done for us, we don't value the thing as much.

A word of caution: Do not ask for input if you know you will not use it. Do not give people busywork that will never turn into anything. Studies show that when people don't finish their project, whether it was too hard or because they were told to stop (and the item was super easy to finish, say, only two tiny steps left), the IKEA effect doesn't come into play. Worse than that, it can have a negative impact, resulting in regret. So, you want to ensure people will finish whatever they are working on and that it isn't too difficult or obscure.

Similarly, taking something apart can remove the effects.

Assembling a LEGO™ set of ten to twelve pieces is easy; it only takes a few minutes. When given a set to construct and a partner was making something else of similar size, people valued their items twice as much as those made by the other person unless they were told to take them apart first.

Building and then unbuilding the set made it so they valued theirs the same as the other person's build.[132] There was no customization available, it would have taken a few moments to put back together later, but the value of the IKEA effect was completely wiped away once they took the thing apart.

What Would It Take?

Yale professor Zoe Chance showcases this "magic question," as she calls it, which is a great way to trigger the IKEA effect and a little reciprocity. She shares some amazing examples in her book, *Influence is Your Superpower*, which we discussed on episode 189 of *The Brainy Business.*[133]

As an MBA student, Zoe interned at a biotech company that had way more orders than it could fill and needed employees to work tons of overtime—including on Thanksgiving and Christmas—to make it happen.

One option would have been to tell everyone it was mandatory. If they wanted to keep their jobs, they would be there—and they better have a smile on their face!

Thankfully, the person in charge of the project didn't do that. She explained the situation in which demand far outpaced their projections (giving the gift of transparency) and asked, "What would it take for us to work together to fulfill these orders?"

The team suggested a wish list, including:

- Pizza deliveries
- Late-night taxis
- Babysitting
- Christmas present wrapping

Management could deliver all those things for the employees, who worked around the clock to fulfill all the orders (and they were able to exceed expectations not by wrapping presents, but by having people do the shopping for the employees).[134] As Zoe says, "Production hit new records, sales tripled, and everyone got a fat bonus. It didn't feel like the result of a negotiation; it felt like a joint endeavor. It was both."[135]

This story (and others in her book) has many lessons. One, of course, is the magic question: "What would it take?" Write that down and plaster it all over your life. It can help you and others accomplish amazing things together.

This is because of the IKEA effect and helping people be part of the process. The other lesson is that the things people need, want, or ask for—their solutions—are often way easier, smaller, or more achievable than you would come up with.

Management could have come up with a lot of stuff—maybe even some of the things on the staff's wish list—but would the employees have felt the same way about those things if they hadn't been part of the process? Probably not. It might feel like the suggestions were a way to tempt or trick them into working more, especially if there was an "us versus them" feeling toward the management. It might feel like the company was overstepping and assuming. People might not have appreciated it as much because they didn't get their ask heard and fulfilled.

Give the gift of involvement. When you see a change coming and a roadblock to that change, ask the magic question (or any of the others in this book) and see where it takes you.

Reflection Point

Where can you bring your team into the planning (a gift they will feel compelled to reciprocate)? Ask for their opinions and let them be involved earlier in the process. You may be surprised to find that something on your plate that feels tedious would be an enlightening honor for someone else on the team to work on. Properly framed delegation can trigger the IKEA effect in a way that makes people feel valued, included, and more likely to support a project. That is a win, win, win, win.

CHAPTER 12

That's Not Fair!

Capuchin monkeys like cucumbers. They are a desirable food. Not as good as peanuts and not as valued as grapes and oranges but still a motivating reward.[136]

Capuchins are perfectly happy to do work and get paid in cucumbers—as long as everyone else gets paid in cucumbers. In the paper *Monkeys Reject Unequal Pay*, researchers found that upon seeing others getting paid in grapes while they were getting cucumber, they became furious.[137] In the video of the research, you watch as a monkey named Lance happily does her task and is content with her tasty cucumber reward. She then sees Winter do the same task and get a grape. Lance is excited now! The promise of a grape is looming, and her task is completed with some extra anticipation. When she gets cucumber again, she takes one bite—and then throws her reward back at the researcher.

Then Winter does her task again and gets another grape; Lance is obviously angry. It takes her longer to complete the task this time. When handed the cucumber, she doesn't even bother to take a bite. It too becomes a projectile to demonstrate her displeasure with the situation.

The video is funny to watch. We laugh at those silly capuchins, though on some level, we know we are the same.

What Motivates Us?

If you want your employees to participate in changes, they need to be motivated. One of my favorite books about motivation is *Drive: The Surprising Truth About What Motivates Us*, by Daniel Pink.[138] He explains that motivation can come from external incentives (a common default choice for companies) or internal motivation (which feels like something people either have or they don't and is not leveraged enough in business).

Pink classifies these as Type X (extrinsically motivated) and Type I (intrinsically motivated) people, initiatives, or programs. He says Type X is like coal: a finite resource that creates pollution, and Type I is like the sun: a clean, inexpensive, and endlessly renewable resource. If we want to be stronger, healthier organizations (incorporating that Human Capital Factor and increasing employee engagement), we need to transition from Type X to Type I.

Type X looks at short-term gains, like doing a task and getting a cucumber immediately. While it may feel tempting to focus on these, it's a tortoise-and-the-hare world, so Type I people will almost always outperform Type X people in the long run. This is one of the many reasons I stress the tree-a-day, micro-moment, snowflake approach to management, life, and work. It is also why I dedicate so much time to looking for joy in the daily routine. It is to reinforce intrinsic motivation. Because, good news, even if you operate as more Type X (or are in a Type X organization), Type I is part of our nature and anyone can learn to embrace this again. It may take some focus, but it can be done. What do you need to get there?

Intrinsic motivation requires autonomy, mastery, and purpose. This allows the individual to be self-directed and devoted to becoming better at something they care about, something that matters.

Don't Ignore Effort

Imagine you are part of a project.[139] I'm going to give you a sheet of paper with a bunch of letters on it, kind of like a word search. Your assignment is to scan the document to find when two of the same letters appear next to each other, like "s s"—once you circle ten on the sheet, bring it back. You get fifty-five cents for the first sheet you complete, fifty cents for the next, and on like that for as long as you want to keep completing sheets. Easy money, right?

This study had three different conditions for what happened when the sheets were turned in:

- **Acknowledged** participants wrote their names on the paper, and the person they handed it to reviewed their work before asking if they wanted another sheet.
- **Ignored** participants did not write their names on their paper and handed it to someone who didn't look at it before putting it on a giant pile and asking if they wanted another sheet.
- **Shredded** participants also did not write their names and when they handed in their completed sheet, it wasn't given a second glance before going straight to the shredder and then asking if they wanted to do another.

If it was all about the external motivation (payment for sheets), the ignored and shredded conditions are favorable. You don't even have to do the work to get paid! They aren't looking anyway, and your name isn't on it, so you can sit back and collect your bounty.

I'm guessing you know this isn't what happened. (And it likely won't surprise you because reading that "shred" condition probably felt soul-crushing, right? I mean, what a jerk!) Those who were acknowledged completed more sheets than those in the ignored and shredded conditions. We like to be seen, acknowledged, and believe our work has meaning—even when we are getting paid for performance.

Extrinsic Incentives Change the Dynamic

Did you get paid for good grades as a kid? Or for scoring goals on the soccer team? Or for doing chores? These are all examples of things that were once intrinsically motivating—where you have some internal drive to do well—but got turned into a transactional, extrinsic exercise. Type I people will accept the cash but still do it for themselves. Type X people become all about that short-term reward.

Once you pay a kid to unload the dishwasher, it becomes darn-near impossible to get them to do it for free. The "what's in it for me?" if/then mindset starts to take over and corrupt other areas. When we get paid to do something, it can often lose its fun and luster. Something enjoyable becomes a chore when we are motivated by an external incentive.

The Cobra Effect

A big problem with external motivations and monetary incentives is that sometimes the solution has a loophole that is obvious in hindsight but not seen when the incentive is set up. One of the best examples of this happened when the British ruled India, and the city of Delhi was infested with cobras.[140] They went to the community for help and announced they would pay for any cobra skins turned in. They received lots of skins and paid out a lot of incentives, but the cobra problem wasn't getting any better.

It turns out that a few people were exploiting the system and started up cobra farms so they could raise cobras to turn in for the bounty. When the British realized what was going on, they stopped the program to pay for the skins. The farmers freed all their cobras and the problem ended up worse than ever.

As the article says (in one of my current favorite lines), "The road to hell is paved with good intentions—and cobra skins."

A classic example of incentives gone wrong comes from a daycare that had an issue with a few parents being late to pick up their kids, so the school decided to instill a small fee (about five dollars) for any time kids were picked up late.[141] What do you think happened?

Everyone started coming late to pick up their kids! The fee turned a courteous, reciprocal sort of relationship into something monetary. It became easy to justify staying to write a couple more emails or have one more meeting when it was so affordable to be late. Introducing money into the equation changed everything.

This is not to say that all monetary incentives are bad. Sales goals and other extrinsic motivation have their place. However, it is not the only option. And often, these are thrown in with an "it can't hurt" reasoning that is downright wrong. **It absolutely can hurt.** Throwing external incentives around can become expensive and demotivating, creating a competitive environment, which feels unfair.

What Is "Fair"? It's All Relative

At this point, you may be wondering how to define fairness. Yes, it would be great if there was a recipe for "fair," but that's unfortunately tricky, as it turns out to be a bit of a moving target. One thing's for sure: when things are perceived as unfair, you'll know it. As Matthew Liebermann said, "Fairness seems a bit like air—its absence is a lot more noticeable than its presence."

To show you what I mean, let's get back to our capuchins. The same researcher discusses how, in another experiment, a group of her monkeys got peanuts for a task. One of the monkeys not included in the experiment was watching and became jealous—he wanted a peanut too.

Knowing there is no such thing as a free lunch, he started bringing over other things to the researcher to try and trade for peanuts. He started with the least desirable item, monkey chow, and worked up the chain. Eventually, he offered a quarter of an orange.

The researcher was surprised because objectively oranges are higher on the monkey food chain than peanuts. A quarter of an orange is more desirable than a single peanut, so why would he make this offer? It was not about hunger because the orange would have fulfilled that need better than a single peanut. There was something else motivating the decision.

Much like our capuchins, whenever there is a question of fairness, motivation will tank. We become distracted and disengaged—regardless of whether we are Type X or Type I. But this, as Pink explains, is why fair, transparent, and equal pay is so important. Once that is known to be taken care of, it allows the focus to come off money (external motivation) and come back to the purpose of the work itself (intrinsic).

Behavioral Concept: Relativity

Humans can't value one-off items—we need a comparison point to know if something is a good or a bad deal. My friend Brian Ahearn has a great example in his book *Influence PEOPLE* using a couch.[142]

Imagine you are in a store and find a couch you like. You ask the sales rep, "Excuse me, how much is this couch?" and they respond, "Nine hundred dollars. Oh, oops! My mistake, *seven* hundred dollars."

In that example, seven hundred dollars feels like a great deal, but what if, instead, when you asked, "How much is that couch?" their response was, "Five hundred dollars. Oh, oops! My mistake, *seven* hundred dollars." Feels a lot worse now, right?

The price of the couch never changed. It was never either of the other two prices, but the way you *feel* about it is different. And the only thing that changed was the context; the item before set an **anchor** that made the couch feel like something you were excited about buying or a waste of money.

Context Is King

When sharing information, you need to know where people are and where you want them to go—that context makes all the difference. Think back to the section on anchoring when I asked you about penguins in Antarctica. My goal was to have you be way off in your guess, which is why I set a low anchor of ten thousand penguins. If I had wanted you to be high, I could have asked about one billion penguins. If I wanted you to be close, I could have asked if there were more or less than ten million or fifteen million. (In case you forgot, there are twelve million penguins in Antarctica.)

To experience and learn the concept (my goal), you needed to have a guess that was far off from the real number (and an interesting, fun element like a story to make it memorable). I always do this twice with a high and a low example to show how your brain continues to do this even when you know it is coming.

Without a goal (purpose), I can't teach you anything. It is just random stuff—that is when I might resort to facts and boring definitions without any applicability. You will not experience and relate to the topic, making you less likely to learn and feel inspired to do anything with it, and we all waste time. Not ideal.

How often does this happen in the workplace?

You learn something and immediately share it without thinking about the context or what you want people to do with that information (or people share it with you in this way). When you don't consider the context, two problems relate to our purposes here. First, without properly framing the information, it is hard to relate it to a purpose, which is key for motivation.

Second, if you don't consider how this may relate and compare to what others are getting, what is visible, and what will feel fair to this individual (and others you don't think should care, but who absolutely notice and feel slighted behind the scenes), you can tank efforts toward building intrinsic motivation.

The Trifecta

Scenarios like the peanut and orange are all too common in business (and our personal lives). Someone complains about something, constantly wishing for something better, and then when that better thing is handed to them, they lament over what they will be giving up. Why?

There is a trifecta of concepts here: status quo bias, loss aversion, and the endowment effect. We have talked about status quo bias, so let's jump into loss aversion.

Behavioral Concept: Loss Aversion

Loss aversion is easy enough to grasp—it likely doesn't surprise you to learn that people hate to lose things. Many studies have shown that the pain felt by a loss is felt about twice as much as the joy felt for a gain.[143]

To show you how it feels, I want you to imagine two different scenarios. Try to put yourself in the moment of each. They are simple, I promise.

Scenario One: One morning, you grab a jacket you haven't worn in a while. While putting it on, you find twenty dollars in the pocket. Amazing!

How do you feel? Probably pretty good; this doesn't happen every day. You might tell a couple of people about it, or maybe not. Will you still be bragging about it tomorrow? Or next week? Will you remember, when you grab this jacket next year, that it once had twenty dollars in the pocket? Probably not.

Scenario Two: Imagine you're going to an event that only takes cash. You do some quick mental math and decide a hundred dollars is more than enough for the full day—you will probably have some money left. You swing by the ATM on your way, and when you stop to pay for parking, you realize there are only four bills there! You look in the abyss between the seats and check your wallet again—are two stuck together, maybe? No. You have *lost* twenty dollars. How does that feel?

Pretty terrible, I'm guessing. Will you tell people about *this* experience? Will you remember it every time you use that parking lot? Or see advertisements for that event? Or use that ATM? Might you even blame the bank or credit union for "stealing" twenty dollars from you when it wasn't their fault? Will this become a story you tell your grandkids about someday?

Maybe it will not be that extreme, but I'm confident you felt it more than the joy of the "found" twenty dollars. And why? Shouldn't it feel the same since it is the same amount of money? That is what conventional economics would say, but if traditional economic models were always accurate, behavioral economics would not exist!

One important thing is that giving people more things doesn't negate loss aversion. Anyone with kids who refuse to give up toys because they were "going to play with that!" can attest to this. Even as we acquire new, potentially better things, we still don't love to lose what we have.

When we see everyone else getting something, it triggers our loss aversion and fear of missing out (FOMO), so our perspectives may get a little skewed in the heat of the moment. An orange is better until everyone but you gets peanuts. Cucumbers are a great payment until you realize your neighbor is being paid in grapes.

Behavioral Concept: The Endowment Effect

When you give a monkey some peanut butter and then offer it juice, only 21 percent are willing to trade. Seventy-nine percent want their peanut butter and will resist taking the juice.

And this isn't because monkeys find peanut butter more delicious. What happens when you give them the juice first and then offer to trade for peanut butter? Fifty-eight percent of them refuse and want to keep their juice.[144]

Whatever they are given first triggers the endowment effect and they do not want to give it up. It doesn't matter what it is; that first item gets the imprint of love upon it.

It's the same for humans. One test was done with people getting mugs or chocolate bars.[145] Another with tickets to a Duke University basketball game.[146] The endowment effect still holds, and it works even when the items are given at random. I'm guessing most students on any given day would say they'd prefer to be given a chocolate bar over a mug.

When Kahneman did the study, of those who were given the mug first, 89 percent chose to keep it when presented with the chocolate bar. Only 11 percent wanted to trade! Being given the item first and told it was *yours* made it so that item was worth more to you and you didn't want to get rid of it.

Of course, if you were to give someone ten things and then ask if they want to trade any of them, they might all have some level of the endowment effect. The reason it gets triggered is loss aversion. If you keep giving people things, there is no potential loss of their items, so the endowment effect doesn't have much of an outward impact. It is only when that trade is presented and they need to give something up that we see it in action.

Autonomy Requires Trust

Trust and transparency are critical to keeping your team motivated. (And, yes, even after examples like the cobra problem, I am still advocating for giving trust first. Your team deserves to be trusted to help encourage autonomy, purpose, and an engaged working life that gives back to the organization.)

Why does transparency matter? We care what others are getting and perceived inequity can lead to some surprising decisions. Remember, the cucumber was fine until someone else got a grape—it was so infuriating that it felt better to take nothing than to accept this insulting offer; Lance threw the cucumber she earned back at the researcher. **Game theory**, a fascinating area of study, has found that people will often hurt themselves to punish another if they think they are being treated unfairly.

To demonstrate, let's play the ultimatum game.

I've been given a hundred dollars. You've been given nothing. My task is to present you with an offer for how much we will each get. If you accept my offer, we both get to keep the proposed amounts. If you reject my offer, we both get nothing.

My proposal is that we split it 50/50. Do you accept? Most people do.

Now I propose that I will keep eighty, and you get twenty. Do you accept? What if the offer was that I get ninety, and you get ten? Or ninety-nine dollars to one?

At some point, most people will reject the offer because it feels unfair.[147] You would rather get nothing than reward my selfish behavior. Logically, this doesn't make sense. If I offer you anything more than zero, you should accept because you will still get more than nothing if you reject me. This happens when there is no long-term connection to the other player—

imagine how this can compound with our long memories working on teams. A perceived slight from years back could combine with confirmation bias and the focusing illusion so one employee is sabotaging themselves and your team to keep someone in another department from "winning" anything. ("They think they're so smart—I'll show them!")

Reflection Point

Once you have trust and transparency (so fairness isn't a question), you can begin to focus on building a Type I team (knowing it is okay to sprinkle in external incentives along the way). Daniel Pink's model says that intrinsic motivation requires autonomy, mastery, and purpose. Using the **IKEA effect** gives your team the opportunity to create a shared purpose they are passionate about. Once you know that goal, you can set up **nudges** to keep them on track as they create mastery in the right areas. Make your check-ins about acknowledgment so people feel seen, not micromanaged (an autonomy killer). Is your team currently Type X or Type I? What is the first thing you will do to boost intrinsic motivation?

CHAPTER 13

Late Again? She's So Disrespectful

You're driving down the freeway, minding your business, when suddenly, someone cuts you off, causing you to slam on your brakes. "Jerk!" (or something more aggressive), you shout to the empty space in your car. The rest of your drive is now clouded with thoughts of that horrible person and what you would say to them if you ever got the chance. They are permanently labeled as "bad" in your mind, and it would take a lot for you to change that perspective.

On a different day, you are driving down the freeway again and realize you're about to miss your exit. You're running late so you make a quick maneuver to catch the exit before it's too late. Sure, you had to cut off that other car, but they should understand, right? You're a good person (and an excellent driver)! These were extenuating circumstances—you couldn't be late again!

Why was the other person a "jerk" when you gave yourself the benefit of the doubt?

Fundamental Attribution Error

This is because of fundamental attribution error, and here's a little of why it happens. When you look at your experience, you give yourself the benefit of the backstory and can blame external factors for your actions. You know that you are a good person. You understand there were unforeseen circumstances and assume others know and feel that way about you. You will also give this benefit of the doubt to those you consider part of your in-crowd (benefits of being a herding species). On the other hand, when you look at the experience of those who aren't "like you," you don't give them that same benefit and instead believe their action is due to some overarching character flaw (reflecting on the biases and examples you have learned about already, this shouldn't be too surprising).

Lateral Error

Imagine someone in another department who you've never gotten along with. They have always rubbed you the wrong way and you can tell they're always out to make you look bad to your boss. Unfortunately, you've now been assigned to work on the same project team for the next six months (ugh). It's the first meeting, and they're four minutes late.

"How rude!" you think. "Typical so-and-so doesn't care about anyone else—our time is valuable too, you know." Other adjectives you might use to describe them are selfish, inconsiderate, lazy—you get the idea.

Imagine your work best friend was also running four minutes late to that same meeting. How do you feel about them? What would you say to the others on the team to help smooth things over? Or if *you* were running late, your inner monologue might be something like, "They all know I've been in back-to-back meetings this week. I just took on this project and am spread thin right now; they know I usually make an effort to be punctual and it's not like I do this every day; they'll understand."

If they consider you part of their in-crowd, they might. But what about everyone else? Just as you don't afford others the same grace you give yourself, they aren't providing this to you either.

Whether it's:

- Running late for a meeting
- Missing a deadline
- Forgetting a report
- Complaining about a new initiative
- Bringing up that old project or system the team was forced to give up . . . again

Or any vast range of other scenarios in the office, know that this bias is running rampant in people's heads. Something happens and we might explain it away or give the benefit of the doubt to those closest to us, but for everyone else, it serves as another drop in the "I knew it" bucket. Confirmation bias, anyone? Yes, I'll take mine with a side of focusing illusion, please.

Hierarchical Error

Behavioral scientist Matt Wallaert, author of *Start at the End*, shared with me that hierarchical fundamental attribution error is one of the biggest issues he sees in organizations.[148] Much like how being at the top of a hill will allow you to see out further than someone at the bottom, as people rise in an organization, they can see and understand more than those below them (and because of the curse of knowledge, we might forget what we knew before we got to this altitude). Those looking down are aware of the pressures on the people below—whether they're coming from the side, top, or bottom. It may feel obvious and that those below should understand and see all the pressures, but we forget they have a different perspective. In addition, it is hard for someone looking up to understand the downward pressure on the layers above them.

Here's an example: an employee comes up with what they are sure is a great idea and suggests it to their boss. When it doesn't get approved, the employee is upset and assumes this was a selfish act on behalf of the manager. "They didn't approve it because they like Suzie and Steve more than me. There's no other possible reason to turn down such a great idea!"

Of course, there are plenty of other reasons for the manager to pass on the idea: money, time, and political clout within the organization—but these are hard to see from the employee's vantage point so fundamental attribution error becomes a problem.

Interestingly, if that employee manages their own team, they might not understand when their employees have a similar reaction to *their* decisions and can't predict it. Logically, they should be able to recognize the other side of fundamental attribution error as they turn their head to look down, but it doesn't work that way. They believe the reasons for their decision are obvious, common sense, so they should see and understand the motivations, "They know I'm a good boss that cares about them. They'll give me the benefit of the doubt."

What Can You Do?

The first step is to look inward. You aren't a three-dimensional creature in a two-dimensional world. Just as you see others and don't give them the benefit of the doubt, other people think the same things about *you* and your team. How might you be giving off the wrong impression? When you are going to do something that might seem inconsiderate, like any of the items from the last two sections, imagine your work nemesis was going to do that to you.

What ghastly things would your brain whisper about them? (Note, I'm not condoning this, and I recommend you work on shifting that dialogue, but we all know this happens and it is a valuable thought exercise.) Now, remind yourself that everyone in that room (physical or virtual) could say the same things about *you*. Don't develop a complex about it or anything, but think about the steps you can take to prevent these little things from ruining your reputation:

- Schedule five to ten extra minutes between meetings to ensure you have time to grab a snack and be there on time.
- If you realize a week or two out that you might struggle to hit a deadline, have a conversation about it right then to see if anyone can provide support to help the whole team while there is still time to do something about it. (Remember the **anchoring** tips from the chapter on planning fallacy. Setting a more realistic deadline will hopefully stop the problem before it starts.)
- Use that same five to ten minutes between meetings to get centered and focus on what is coming up and that you have everything you need. Even better than that, if you are calling meetings, send an agenda at least twenty-four hours in advance (with materials for review) instead of waiting until two minutes before it starts, which can prime people to think you're scattered.

Helping Others

Now, you are likely wondering about the best way to let others—perhaps someone on your team or those in another department—in on this bias so they can adjust their behaviors. The top thing to *not* do is to tell them they are biased, *so they better make a change and start giving others the benefit of the doubt*. That's a good way to create more work nemeses.

What does work is to explain that you are reading a book about the brain and how it impacts everyone's reaction to change at work. Say that you read this great segment about something called fundamental attribution error (give the cutting people off on the freeway example above) and it helped you realize that **you may have been letting yourself off the hook for little things that could be negatively impacting the team.** You can then say, "I've realized that showing up late to meetings is a habit I want to work on. I value each of you and want to be sure you know that, so this little brain quirk never comes up. Can you help hold me accountable as I get started by ensuring I always end meetings five minutes early?"

This accomplishes a few things:

1. It lets them know a bias exists, which can cause friction in the workplace.
2. You have explained how you are looking inward to work on something that many people struggle with (so they are more likely to empathize with you in the future).
3. You've invited them in (IKEA effect) to help be part of the solution, and there is a good chance they will want to reciprocate by working on something similar themselves (this gift of transparency also helps build trust).

And just like that, you've created a spark. That single conversation can become a catalyst for change in your organization. It creates a ripple effect that can go much further than you imagine, and this is the case for all the biases and concepts you've learned about.

It may be tempting to say that you're just one person and "everyone else shows up late too" (herding). How much could that one conversation do? The answer is: a lot. Remember our tree a day turning into a lush forest; a lot of small, continual efforts can quickly cause significant change.

Expanding Circles of Empathy

Most organizations create silos or have natural groupings within the business structure. Having strong bonds within teams is great, but when it puts one team against another—like marketing against finance or sales against the call center—you are creating a breeding ground for fundamental attribution error and many other biases.

If instead you consider yourself Team Company and look at how you are all working together to accomplish a shared goal, it can bring more people into that in-crowd. Also, as I advised you to think about the bad things others might think about your actions, start making a conscious effort to give other people the benefit of the doubt—especially those from other groups or whom you have locked horns with previously. They are well-intentioned people just like you.

Behavioral Concept: Unity

In 1984, the original book *Influence: Science and Practice* was published by Robert Cialdini.[149] The book introduced the six principles of persuasion, including some you've seen already in this book: reciprocity, scarcity, authority, consistency, liking, and social proof. The book was a massive hit, selling over three million copies in more than forty languages. Dr. Cialdini has published many more books, including a new and expanded version of *Influence* that came out in 2021 and added a seventh principle of persuasion. You guessed it: unity.

It was a huge honor for me to have Dr. Cialdini on *The Brainy Business* to talk about the book when it came out, and we, of course, discussed this new principle. He calls unity a universal principle hiding underneath the data all along. You might think of it as an umbrella or a foundation, but the important thing to know is that when you can bring people in and remind them (or yourself) that you are on the same team, it can be incredibly powerful.

The story he shared on the show that stuck with me had to do with a grant proposal he was working on. Late in the process (it was due the next day), he realized a critical bit of data was missing. He knew someone in the department had that data, but he wasn't the most agreeable person on the team. Nevertheless, this was an important grant and he had to ask.

He sent an email that said something to the effect of, "I have this due tomorrow and I could use your help with this. Can you go to your archives, get the data out and send it over to me so I can use it? I'm going to call you to explain further." Upon calling to explain, this colleague responded by saying, "Bob, I'm sorry. I can't be responsible for your poor time management skills. The answer is no." (Ouch.)

What he did next is important. Bob told me that before reading the research on unity, he would have said something like, "Come on, I really need this. I've got this thing due tomorrow." Even though he had already said no to that (asking the same question louder or quicker doesn't make it more appealing, as you might have learned over time).

Instead, he said, "Come on; we've been members of the same psychology department now for twelve years. I really need this." He had the data that afternoon.

Showing people how you are on the same team, or maybe reminding them of it when you make an ask, can make all the difference. Remember, this was after that, shall we say, harsh response of "I can't be responsible for your poor time management skills." Many of us would hear that, put our tail between our legs, and sheepishly back away. To follow up with this statement—and get the person who has a reputation for being difficult to do a complete 180 and give you what you are asking for? It's amazing to behold. And it shows the power of unity.

Remember back to reciprocity when I shared Stephen M.R. Covey's insights about trust. In his book, he shared how he gained trust after a difficult merger filled with animosity by having a large, impromptu Q&A session with the whole company in which he was completely transparent and answered every question. During this process, he helped the two "sides" of the newly merged company to realize they were a united front. He started them on the path to unity and trust. After that meeting, he told me one of his managers said, "You know, I think we built more trust in this one meeting than we have in the entire year."

Whether you like the snowflake/iceberg analogy, or the idea of planting a tree a day, or anything else from within these pages or outside—remember that change starts with you. You now have an awareness of these biases and can start to see them in your daily working life (and likely at home too). Get curious. Look around and ask questions. "I wonder why that happened?" or "How could that have gone differently?" or "What can I do next time to get a better reaction?"

One More Bias: Not Invented Here

The not invented here bias (or syndrome) makes us believe that our ideas or creations are better than those created or thought up by others.[150] Even when great ideas are presented right to us, we reject them in favor of something that came from in-house. This bias could rear its ugly head to defend ideas from the full company, within a specific department, or inside your mind from one project to the next.

Countless great ideas have been ignored, written off, ridiculed, or rejected because of this bias, but it doesn't have to be that way.

You might notice that **confirmation bias** can be coming into play here because as you are being presented with an idea from some other source, your brain might be scanning for why it won't work (**negativity bias**) or isn't a good idea. When looking at your idea, though? The **focusing illusion** helps you scan the data for anything that supports how great it is and why it *will* work (**optimism bias**).

Phrases like:

- We can do that better/faster/stronger/cheaper ourselves.
- They don't know what they're talking about; that'll never work.
- I've tried this before; it's a waste of time.
- Our customers have never asked for that/won't want that.

are signs of the not-invented-here bias and are an opportunity to dig a little deeper.

Treating a Toxic Team

Picture this: You are a division president at a global pharmaceutical firm, overseeing sales and marketing. When in meetings with your two direct reports, James and Sarah, they are on board and ready to cooperate. They say all the right things when the three of you are together, but their teams are constantly battling and don't work well together. You bring in a consultant to help fix the problem because it is too toxic to continue.

Tim Houlihan was one of those consultants,[151] and he told me about how, during one-on-one interviews with James and Sarah (names changed), both said something like, "It's not us. Everything would be fine if (s)he would listen to what my team is advising them to do." While in meetings with each other and the boss, they would politely acknowledge their differences and act like they were playing nice but were more divisive when with their teams or the consulting firm.

They were stuck in this status quo of blaming the other person and feeling like they were on opposite sides. Step one was to get them to realize this problem and agree to *really* support their teams (starting by removing their biased statements) to shift and focus on trusting each other as one big team.

So, Tim and his colleague (and cohost of the fantastic *Behavioral Grooves* podcast) Kurt Nelson facilitated an all-day meeting with both teams (about fifty people) to hash things out and build some trust. As he explained to me, one of the main things they did was to have people from each team explain who they were, what their job was, what they did, why, how . . . getting into the details of it.

As someone on the marketing team explained their job and what they were doing to support the sales team, it was eye-opening for those on the other side of the aisle. They didn't realize how the other side was trying to support them. When they asked questions like, "Well, why would you do X when Y is the case in my territory?" The answer was, "I didn't know that about your territory."

They heard what the other side said and then shared some national insights that helped influence the decision they made, including some stuff that the sales rep didn't know.

This level of transparency built a trust that helped them realize they were all on the same team, working toward the same goals. They developed a **unity** that allowed them to work better together in the future and achieve their goals.

Building on this, in their book *The Power of Us*, Dominic Packer and Jay Van Bavel go into great depth about how people support each other in groups and how our demeanor or approach can change when we are supporting someone from "our team" or opposing someone from the "other" team.[152]

People have many different pieces of their identities, and the groups they identify with can vary throughout the day. In the morning, I have my "mom" identity on while getting the kids ready and out the door. I have my consultant identity and my teaching identity or keynote speaker or Kate Spade lover or chai tea latte drinker or friend or sister or runner or any other number of things at various times throughout the day.

While many pieces of our identity are essentially static, we often shift back and forth between our respective identities. This fluidity is important as you look for opportunities to leverage unity when it may be lacking in an organization.

If your company is overly siloed right now, with departments that disagree and undermine each other, it may feel like a tall order to get them to be a unified team. However, if you start small and focus on building up the snowball, it can be done. Don't try to get anyone and everyone on board from the get-go. Instead, start with your most influential team members. These could be leaders of departments or people within teams who others listen to—not always the person with the most experience.

Once you get them on board with the unity principle (we are no longer the "marketing" team and the "sales" team, but we are "team company"), work on using reinforcing language to keep triggering thoughts about that larger group. Remove competitions between departments. Look for company-wide language. Give people assignments to find someone from another department who likes the same music as they do or who enjoys the same sports. Help them find the humanness in others and reinforce that they are all people working together toward a common goal. That they are in this together.

And keep in mind that bringing together a larger group is not always better. Tim shared about another project to increase sustainable farming in South Dakota.[153] For that one, they brought in small groups from micro-communities (small towns) to address problems relevant to what was happening in their town—not the entire county. Tim used the IKEA effect by asking them to build their ideal state for the future of their farm. It helped the farmers understand the problems, which caused them to pledge to solve the problems of their farms. Ironically, all of them made the same pledge. When asked how they might have felt if it was farmers from the next county over (only a few miles away), they said, "They won't understand; they don't know anything about what we are dealing with over here."

Understanding how the "us versus them" mentality is at play and what is needed to get to your specific goal is critical in solving the problem. In the pharmaceutical company, getting the teams to work together was the goal, so everyone needed to be involved. For the farmers, individual participation was the goal, and bringing everyone together would have been detrimental.

This is why understanding your specific situation is so important—no tactics are perfectly generalizable.

As Jon Levy shares in his book *You're Invited*, when you can have everyone come together and have a shared trust-building experience (like pledging a sorority or fraternity), it creates continuous vulnerability loops, elevating feelings of belonging.[154] This can help people to rally together and form lifelong bonds within a few minutes or hours that would otherwise take years. This is why things like trust-falls and other teambuilding rituals can work so well (though you don't have to be so extreme or create scenarios that feel forced and one-off—there is a full chapter dedicated to fun in Part 3 to help get your brain thinking about options here).

Activating **unity** can get people to do amazing things. They can help and support each other for the common good. Your team can rise up and achieve massive goals and come together through change. Their snowflakes can become something bigger than themselves. Being a unified team is an important step in that process.

Keep that in mind as we move into Part 3. It was intentional to have this as the last chapter of this section. I want you to be thinking about the whole group and what the company is trying to accomplish as you move forward.

Now that you have learned about many biases that can be blocking your way and concepts to leverage to help your team overcome those natural tendencies (or reframe them so they work to your advantage), it is time to talk about application. Part 3 introduces my "It's Not About the Cookie" framework and how every manager can use this to help their teams be naturally better at change.

I hope you're as excited as I am—let's do this!

PART 3

CHANGE FRAMEWORK

CHAPTER 14

Where Are We Going?

> *"Alice: Would you tell me, please, which way I ought to go from here?*
>
> *The Cheshire Cat: That depends a good deal on where you want to get to.*
>
> *Alice: I don't much care where.*
>
> *The Cheshire Cat: Then it doesn't much matter which way you go.*
>
> *Alice: …So long as I get somewhere.*
>
> *The Cheshire Cat: Oh, you're sure to do that, if only you walk long enough."*
>
> —LEWIS CARROLL, *ALICE IN WONDERLAND*

A big piece of my job as a content creator includes nurturing my platform and engaging with people on social media. I, of course, love this part of the job. It is fun to chat with people, share content, and scroll around the various platforms to see what's new. When it is time to work on my social media, it helps me move toward my goals. When it is a **bikeshedding** tool that keeps me from writing this book (or a podcast episode, finalizing a keynote presentation, or grading papers), it is a distraction.

In his book *Indistractable*, Nir Eyal helps the reader be more productive by removing distractions.[155] One of the greatest insights from this book is that you cannot call something a "distraction" until you know what it is distracting you *from*.

If I didn't take the time to define my goals and what I needed to do each day to reach them, it would be easy to procrastinate productively on Twitter or LinkedIn and never make progress. Like Alice, I would be walking a lot but never getting anywhere.

My other favorite insight from *Indistractable* is that the opposite of distraction is *traction*. When the distraction is removed, you can be more effective and gain traction toward your goal.

Identify the Path

In the case of leading your employees through change—the first thing you need to know is what you want people to *do*.

- Where do you want them to end up?
- Where are they now?
- What is the next step on the path?
- What is keeping them from doing the thing you want them to do?

And think big picture here. Don't compromise the long-term win on short-term churn. If you let **time discounting** and **optimism bias** run the show, it will be tempting to think that you can be better at this "tomorrow" when you have more time. Until you do something today, nothing will change tomorrow. If you want a forest, you need to plant some trees.

If you only look at today, the goal might be about getting everyone on board quickly so you can get a few minutes back in your day to finish that report before your three o'clock meeting. This could lead you to lean on the **false consensus effect** or **groupthink** to get through your meetings without questions. Perhaps useful today, but is that helping you get to the ideal team and culture you want to create?

Take a step back and think about what that ideal team would be like. If you woke up tomorrow and had the dream team, how would you describe them? What do they do? How does everyone work together? What are the days like?

Let's say you have a **functional-fixedness** driven, **status quo**–loving team. They do things a certain way and they like it. Any time you have presented a change in the past, they fight you every step of the way: excuses, tantrums, and negative side-conversations abound. That's where they *are*—where do you want them to end up? What is the goal? A non-exhaustive list of options includes:

- To be more **creative**
- To **proactively** look for **efficiencies** and ways to **innovate** processes
- To be more **open** to change when it is presented to them
- To **trust** each other more
- To be more **flexible**

Now, I know you are inclined to say, "I want all of those things!" But if you try to do too many things at once, you are setting yourself and the team up for bikeshedding and spiraling in a space where you never get anywhere because you don't know where you want to go. Much like the advice of the Cheshire Cat to Alice, if you don't know where you're going, it doesn't matter which way you go.

As the manager, you first need to determine the most important thing for the team. If you only get ***one thing*** your department will be known for, what would it be? Thoughtful? Flexible? Innovative? (Note: The bolded words in the list above are more possibilities.)

A thesaurus is your friend as you choose your word. This will allow you to understand the associations others might have in their brains as you pick the perfect one thing you can strive for. Depending on the goal and the team, you can leverage some **IKEA effect** goodness to have them help come up with the word (choosing their purpose to help create some **intrinsic motivation**, or a team of Type I people, to use language from Daniel Pink). In the case of the rigid, change-hating team, that is probably a bad strategy. You want to do a little work and **nudging** first to get the snowball forming before bringing them into the plan.

Write **at least ten** words here that could be your department's one thing:

1.	6.
2.	7.
3.	8.
4.	9.
5.	10.

Circle three possibilities and look them up in the thesaurus. If there is a new word you like better, add it to the list. Ruminate on it for a bit, and choose your one word:

____

What does that word mean to you? Why did you choose it?

____

____

____

Small Steps and Nudgeable Moments

Throughout this book, I have stressed the importance of micro-moments. Now that you know where you want the team to end up, it is important to think about where everyone is starting. While everyone might be on their way to Oz, not everyone needs to take the yellow brick road to get there. Some people are closer than others. Some can travel quickly by magic bubbles, others will stick it out and walk every step, and others need to find a flying monkey to carry them over a dark, scary forest.

Your job as the manager is to zoom out and get some perspective on the big picture. Where is each person now and where might they take a wrong turn if you aren't there to **nudge** them back on the right path? Glinda may be a good witch, but she was a terrible manager. She knew the path was full of monsters, traps, and tricksters but still sent Dorothy off with one piece of guidance (stay on the yellow brick road) and no way of contacting her when she got stuck along the way. Are you doing something similar with your team?

You don't need to create a path for them and micromanage every step, but it is good to know the check-in points and general direction for those small steps. It is also important to note that if Glinda had given a long list of all the nightmares that awaited Dorothy on the journey, she probably wouldn't have gone. Staying where she was would have felt like the better option (after all, her house was already there). A few well-timed check-ins along the way would have been welcomed; if she had popped in to tell her not to pull apples off the trees because they were alive and might not like it, that would have been helpful, well-timed information at a nudgeable moment.

What Do I Mean by Nudgeable?

While it is important to be thoughtful about all the small steps and micro-moments, you don't need to try and do something with every one of them. (Talk about an overwhelmed brain!) Instead, some moments are more likely to be receptible to a nudge; those are the ones to focus on. Here are a few of my favorite examples to get your brain buzzing with ideas:

Reducing Opportunistic Insurance Fraud

If I asked you to come up with an example of insurance fraud, it would likely be something massive. A long-planned, devious scheme to actively steal millions. This happens, sure, but a more common form of insurance fraud can create problems for everyone in the system. Opportunistic fraud is when you know your sixteen-year-old son will be the primary driver on this car you're adding to the plan, but instead of listing his name, you say it is you for a lower payment. This may seem negligible, but these little actions added up and were estimated to cost one billion pounds per year in the UK (which causes everyone's premiums to go up, creating a vicious cycle).

Unlike the premeditated fraud examples that come to mind, opportunistic fraud is not typically something people spend hours, days, or weeks planning. It is an on-the-spot decision by otherwise good people, meaning it is nudgeable.[156]

If you worked for the insurance industry, you might assume nothing can be done. How do you solve this problem? You could call every person to ensure they fill the form out correctly, increase auditors, and have harsher punishments for those caught trying to cheat the system, but many of those interventions are expensive and can cause a ripple of unintentional normalizing (negative **herding**), making people think the problem is more rampant than it is, so they choose to do what you are trying to stop (remember the **cobra effect**). It probably would feel like a thing you have to accept. A known problem that was expensive but not worth the effort.

Thankfully they hired Dectech, a behavioral research consultancy in the UK. Dectech tested five concepts (norming/**social proof**, self-consistency, **priming**, **framing**, and **reciprocity**) over eighteen scenarios to see what worked best. These included an "honesty pledge" (self-consistency), providing statistics showing how honest others were (**herding**), and (my personal favorite) setting up the captcha so people have to select the words that have to do with "honesty" from a list (**priming**). Nearly all the eighteen interventions had a positive impact and reduced dishonest responses in a simulated claim process. The least effective had a 5 percent lift (still not bad considering it was a one-billion-pound problem and essentially a free tweak), and the most impactful reduced lying by 74 percent!

Putting in the work up front to consider the problem helped Dectech find this nudgeable moment and create some tests using the concepts most likely to have an impact (the art in the science). Before moving to the next example, I want to note the importance of testing. Everything worked and saw some lift, but there was a huge difference from one to the next.

The only way to know which concepts work in your context (and to what degree) is to test. And it is important to consider each of your team members individually when you think about change. Bringing it back to Oz, blasting out generic information about the talking trees when it is convenient or top of mind for *you* isn't helpful for those who won't encounter them on the path, those who already passed them (and are annoyed you didn't give them a heads-up at the right time if you knew it was there), and those battling another monster and can't think about that.

> **Timely feedback at the right moment in the right way makes the nudge work.**

The Power of a Post-it

Imagine you are an accountant at an insurance company. It's December, and you find an error: All 150 insurance agents have been double-paid on their commissions—a $700,000 mistake.

This is back in the days when you couldn't fix it electronically. The only way to get the money is to ask each person to write you a check—some as high as $10,000. You're leading a small team in the effort to get the money back. How would you approach this sensitive situation?

Fortunately, you remember a training about the brain and how studies had found that a handwritten Post-it on a cover letter doubled the chances someone would complete and return a survey. You pull out a pad of Post-its and get to work, hoping for the best (but with a skeptical logical brain contemplating plans B, C, and D).

After a couple of weeks, you're shocked to find 130 of the 150 agents have sent back checks, and a few weeks after that, all but three have paid in full. How could a Post-it be so powerful?

There are a couple of factors at play here, which I discussed with my friend and Cialdini-certified trainer Brian Ahearn, who was on the team at the insurance company all those years ago and included this fascinating example in his book *Influence PEOPLE.*[157]

The first benefit is from drawing the attention of the conscious brain with the colorful Post-it (which has shown to be much more impactful than the same handwritten message on a cover letter without the contrast of the sticky note that calls attention to the **effort** put in). For something out of the norm like this, it is important to make sure the subconscious brain realizes something is different and worth a second glance (the small decision they need to make to get to the next, critical step).

The second piece is the power of going the extra mile to write the note by hand. This triggers **reciprocity** and can **nudge** the recipient to take the desired action.

In the years that have followed since these studies came out, many companies have tried to emulate the result in less time with a laser-printed note made to *look like* it was handwritten. Of course, anyone with reasonable vision can tell in a fraction of a second that it was not—and the result can be worse than no note. You've basically called attention to the fact that you don't care enough to put in the effort, so why should they?

You can't put everything on a Post-it and expect it will always have such a huge impact—you need to pick your Post-it moments wisely. Imagine you get one per person per quarter. One time to make a big gesture (hopefully not always asking for things). What would you use them for? What nudgeable moments matter the most along the way to building **trust**, showing **flexibility**, or fostering **innovative** tendencies?

Getting back to the theme of the chapter, if you don't know where you want people to go, you can't know which moments are most nudgeable, what nudge to incorporate, and if it worked.

Corporate Social Responsibility in Saudi Arabia

Why would Rawabi Holding,[158] a large oil and gas company, start a career fair, Rawabi Talent Exhibit (RTE), for youth across the country, showing the benefits of having jobs like being a chef or professional mountain climber? It may seem random, but as Wiam Hasanain,[159] a social impact and behavior change advisor, explained to me, this initiative was the result of careful planning toward a corporate social responsibility (CSR) program.

At the time, she explained, research revealed a stigma toward certain careers and a social norm that encouraged the brightest students to pursue careers in medicine and engineering. Rawabi Holding believed in CSR and needed many other roles, including maintenance staff and graphic designers. To help empower the future generation to see these valuable roles, they started at the source—students. They created a multipronged program[160] to encourage youth to identify their passion. It consisted of 1) RTE, 2) internships, and 3) career guidance tools.

This wasn't one random event—it was a strategic and methodical process that involved company executives, management teams, and key employees (**IKEA effect**) for over eighteen months of work before the first RTE. The company worked with schools to set up visits to RTE and make it easy for the students to get there (removing the **sludge**). They invited the press and influencers to talk about the fair and its values (**social proof**) and shared engaging videos about each profession on a dedicated portal.

While entering RTE, students received a personality assessment highlighting their unique talents and matching roles. The most traditionally desirable jobs (doctor, engineer) were placed at the back, and you had to walk through other careers with fun booths to get there. Students gained a new perspective from inspirational young professionals volunteering at each booth. They shared what they wished they knew about their jobs when they were younger and wished someone had told them to help them find their passion in life. Upon leaving, visitors received a career guidance kit on planning for their future careers (bridging the intention-to-action gap).

Wiam was involved for several years[161] in the CSR program and said that the company was motivated to have the second one—as a public private partnership[162] in various cities—because of the obvious results: double-digit growth in students' consideration of fields that were not a consideration before. While this is only one example, it is fair to say it sparked a change.

The country's national strategic plan, Vision 2030,[163] outlined the approach for a diversified economy—including appreciating several careers and roles.

Today, many more careers are valued in Saudi Arabia and students continue to pursue their dreams.

Identifying Your Small Steps

Hopefully, you have already gotten lots of tips along the way and this is reinforcing what you have learned rather than feeling like brand-new information. From years of teaching and consulting on this stuff, I know this is where you're probably thinking, "Where do I start?" Once you know your big goal, it's time to get small.

As you consider your change initiative, especially a larger one, it is common to think of your tasks in more grandiose terms. Your to-do list might include something like "tell the team" among twenty-five or fifty other items. While it is tempting to lump the entire task into this top category, there are lots of little factors to consider within a step like "tell the team." When leveraging micro-moments, you need to consider:

- Is it best to tell the group together or one at a time?
- What if you did it the other way?
- When will they be most receptive to the idea?
- Why are you telling them now?
- What are you asking them to do?
- What is the best result of this first notification?
- What do you want to avoid?
- Is this something to send via email or discuss in a meeting?
- What sort of burnt popcorn will come from the invite?
- What are you naming the meeting (if there is one) and how is that priming the experience?

- What subject line will encourage opens and prime the experience you want?
- What questions will they have? Which should be addressed here?
- When will you follow up?
- Do they know what is coming next (as well as when to expect it)?

Once you have thought through all those pieces, you can break "tell the team" into small steps to find your nudgeable moments. Let's assume you are telling the whole team in one meeting; your small steps include:

- Select optimum time of day and day of the week for the meeting (i.e., when will the elephants be most calm and receptive to change?)
- Will it be mandatory to attend? (If most of your meetings don't have a "(!)Required" note on them and this one does, what message will that send?)
- Determine how long is needed for the meeting (Remember to set a high anchor)
- Determine a name for the meeting (Don't burn the popcorn)
- Decide if anything should accompany the meeting invite (description, attachments, prep materials, agenda)
- Create items to go with meeting invite
- Determine how to answer questions if you get them from curious team members before the meeting
- Draft body for email/invite
- Review and edit email/invite
    - » Wait at least thirty minutes and then read with "the worst" interpretation to find items to be edited; get a trusted colleague to review if needed
- Is there any opportunity to include priming words?
- Is the message framed to meet your goals?

- Draft agenda for meeting (just for you)
- Draft public agenda for meeting
- Send invite/schedule meeting

If you're thinking, "Every time?!" don't worry. Yes, at first, this is more of a manual process while training your conscious brain to take over some of these tasks and write new rules for the subconscious. I promise it will quickly become a **habit** and you can zip through these more quickly (while still keeping **thoughtful sludge** like delaying before sending important emails to ensure they are conveying the most important stuff).

If you still doubt the importance of this critical step, here's a **reframe**. The longer question is essentially, "You mean I have to care about the other person *every time* I communicate with them?" And if that one doesn't resonate, here's another: How would you feel if your boss didn't care enough to put thought into the emails they sent you? Not great? That's why you make it a priority. And one more, remember that putting a little more thoughtfulness up front will save countless hours of correcting miscommunications on the back end. **It is always more effective and efficient to plan and communicate better the first time.**

Reflection Point

Before we move on to the "It's Not About the Cookie" framework, take a moment to consider a project at work where you need others to get on board.

- How many choices and micro-decisions are there?
- Is it well-structured and easy for someone to choose?
- What do people need to know at each moment?
- What can they learn later?

- **What pieces are there for your short-term benefit but making it harder to reach long-term goals?**
- **Where can some thoughtful sludge help you to communicate better?**

CHAPTER 15

It's Not About the Cookie

Imagine you're walking down the street with your best friend. You haven't seen each other in a while and are having a particularly engaging conversation, catching up on all that's happened over the last few months. Suddenly, a delicious scent wafts into your nose—sugar, butter, chocolate, and a hint of salt. Those are delicious cookies baking!

Your nose is now on the hunt to find the source of the delightful smell, and while you're still half-listening, you've both become distracted. You're essentially cartoon characters now with your nostrils leading you down the street.

When you finally find the store and see a line, you think, "These cookies must be amazing!" and can't help but wander inside. You're handed a sample to try and are told there is a sale today only—*buy three, get one free*. Before you know it, you and your friend leave the bakery, each eating a cookie with a bag in hand.

Alternate Version: You are walking with the same friend, same engaging conversation, when, out of nowhere, someone waves a flyer in your face and says, "Today only! Buy four cookies and only pay for three! I've got samples!" while shoving a tray at you.

Ugh.

How rude is this guy? You and your friend, annoyed, decline the samples and begin a one-upping contest of worst sales experiences. By the time you're in front of the bakery and smell the cookies, you're so irritated, you grab your phones to write a Yelp review about how awful their tactics are, vowing that you will never buy from them (pitying those fools in line whose standards are lower than yours).

Same bakery. Same cookies. Completely different experience.

Buying and Selling Change

The most important thing to note is that price was never a factor. The cookies could have been three dollars each in the first scenario and fifty cents in the second, but it didn't matter. Your elephant decided if you needed or hated those cookies before the price even came up (and the rider was there to logic you into supporting the idea even more). Sure, if they were astronomically priced, you may have said no (though there is a $214 grilled cheese sandwich on a menu in New York that may disagree with you),[164] but in general, pricing is never about the price. Everything that happens before the price matters more than the price itself.

And did you notice that all the same things happened (just in reverse)? There are several concepts at play here, making up my "It's Not About the Cookie" framework:

- Priming (the scent of the cookies)
- Herding / Social proof (the line, reviews)
- Loss aversion / Perceived ownership (from the tasting, scent, and scarcity)
- Reciprocity (free sample)

- Framing ("Buy three, get one free" vs. "Buy four cookies and only pay for three")
- Scarcity (Today only!)

Using the right concepts in the right order is necessary for change to flow naturally. Even the right stuff out of order can make for a rebellious brain. As you will see below, it always starts with the scent of the cookies.

In case you are wondering why I am talking about pricing strategy in a book about change management, it's because I use this same framework for both. Why? Because just like whether someone chooses to buy isn't about the price, whether someone *buys in* on a change isn't about the change—it's about how well you *sell it to them.*

It's Not About the Cookie

Even when no money is exchanging hands, in a change conversation, you still **need someone to buy the idea you are selling them.** This is why behavioral economics is relevant for change management. Just like pricing isn't about the price, the likelihood of a change initiative working isn't about the change. It's all about how it is presented.

Have you ever had the experience of putting together a plan, strategy, or proposal that you knew was in the best interest of the person you were presenting it to, only to have them immediately get hung up on some small detail and turn it down?

This could be anything, but I like to start with a reorganization. Whether it is a shift of departments where a large group of people will now report to another executive or have title changes, or perhaps the most dreaded of all, they need to move their desks. (*bum bum buuum*)

While money could be involved in some of this, let's assume, for the sake of this conversation, there is no money factoring in here. No one is losing salary or being expected to move down into the basement like Milton in *Office Space.*

The movie, and of course, Milton, are a great example of how change can easily go so badly when the brain is left out of the equation. First, if you haven't seen *Office Space*, you need to. It's hilarious and totally holds up. If you have seen *Office Space*, he is the one who gets moved to a storage space and all he cares about is his red stapler. The situation escalates as there is downsizing throughout the organization. He gets worse and worse circumstances—including no longer receiving paychecks. But at the end of the day, all he cares about is keeping his stapler. He even says, "If they take my stapler, I'll set the building on fire"—and when someone finally takes his stapler, what happens?

Let's just say he is not happy.

And, the thing is, it could have been prevented. He repeatedly said what mattered to him, and no one listened. What about the other employees in the movie? In some cases, they cared about money, but they potentially would have been just as happy with a copy machine that worked instead of saying "PC Load Letter" and being treated like they mattered.

Yes, that is a movie that exaggerates reality for the sake of humor, but is it that far off?

You already know the concepts from Part 2, but let's break down the cookie framework to show how these can start combining as you think about how to lead your team through change.

Priming—The Scent of the Cookies

The "good" bakery story started with the smell of the cookies. This is so interesting to your subconscious—so appealing and distracting that it breaks through the clutter and causes it to flag your conscious brain (or pull focus under the surface).

Change conversations are even more likely to have the brain flagged and on high alert than pricing situations. Think about it—the rumor mill might have already started and preceded your conversation (thanks to some burnt popcorn). Good news travels fast, sure, but change-inducing, potentially threatening news? Wildfire.

As you know from Part 2, priming is about more than scent. Powerful imagery, great verbiage, video, and emojis can all prime people to feel a certain way or take action.

When it comes to change, the wrong prime could make people rebel against what you're proposing and fight you at every turn (the right prime and everything could be smooth sailing). When priming is done right, people don't consciously realize it is happening. It is like a deep current, slowly helping you drift in one direction instead of another.

Begging and shoving logic in their face does not work—remember the cookie flyer. You got irritated and shunned the whole establishment in that scenario. This is also why you can't jump right in with the ask, logic, or facts of the change. If you have a team with low trust and you want them to work well together, saying, "We need some trust around here!" or "Why don't you just trust each other already?" or "Stop being so judgmental!" won't get you far (at least not far in the right direction; you might go far away from your ultimate goal).

A Deep Dive Using Trust

To show how priming can be applied to the "one thing" you identified in the last chapter, let's take a deep dive into the concept of trust since it is the foundation of any well-functioning team.

As you consider the scent of the cookies, everything matters. Seemingly insignificant things can be important micro-moments adding to the iceberg instead of the snowball. Remember back to the short emails from my boss. They were about her convenience and likely something she didn't think about too much, but they had a huge, lasting impact on me.

Doing some mind mapping can help find the associations that might exist and whether they are working for you or against you. Combining priming with the **peak-end rule** lets you start with two categories:

- What positive primes are already working for you or that you can add?
- What are the negative primes you need to eliminate?

As you look at each item, put it in the positive or negative camp. As you can see, "emails" isn't going to cut it here. There are lots and lots of emails going around. What are emails like when you are stressed or busy? Those short emails from my boss usually showed up when she was in a specific meeting each week. Something would pop into her head during the meeting that she didn't want to forget about. She was already taking notes on the iPad, so it was easy to send a quick email to move the task down the line and cross it off her mental to-do list.

How do your "before I forget…" emails come across to the recipient? How are they different than your more thoughtful emails? Scheduling emails? Asking for a favor? Assigning a project? To your most trusted team member versus the one you are skeptical about? When you send an email from your phone, does it have that "Excuse my typos, I didn't care about you enough to proofread this email" signature line? How is that fostering or killing trust?

Hopefully, this reinforces why having one word and one goal at a time is important. There is a lot to consider and if you are trying to split your primes into a bunch of subcategories, it will be a jumbled mess soon. **Increase the chances of success by narrowing to one thing at a time you can focus on until it is achieved, then you can move on to the next.**

Priming is why the word choice for your goal is important. Images, words, actions, and activities for "creative" are different than for "innovative," "open," "trust," "balance," or "flexible."

A quick image search on the word "trust" has:

- people helping others up a mountainside
- bees working together
- a tiny bird in someone's hand
- tandem skydiving
- a circle of hands
- a child jumping to be caught by their parent

Remember, you don't want to include images of the stuff you want to *avoid*. Remember the "Don't think about white bears" phenomenon. Putting an image of someone stressed to remind you not to be stressed will have the opposite effect.

Don't stop at the images, though; remember, you have four other senses. What does trust *sound* like? Smell? Taste? Feel? It may seem silly, but it is important to go through each area of this exercise. Even if you don't use everything, you want to understand your word in as much depth and breadth as you can.

The firm Olson Zaltman focuses on metaphor elicitation research.[165] As they have demonstrated, we think in images and metaphors. Understanding the metaphors people have can help them understand where they are coming from and where they want to go. When two of their associates, Hannibal and Malcolm Brooks, joined me on the podcast, we discussed all the water metaphors people have around money: frozen assets, liquid funds, and drowning in debt. Those words mean something to our emotional subconscious brains. Tapping into that is key when you are thinking about change. You need to know what associations someone already has, which are working for you, and which are a hindrance.

- To you, trust might feel like a warm hug, sweater, or cup of cocoa. If it were a fabric, it would be fleece.
- To someone else, trust could be more like intricate lace—if one part gets snagged, it all comes apart.
- Another might say it is mesh because you can see through it.
- To another, trust may be like a wetsuit—you feel safe jumping into the icy water because you know it is there to protect you.

As you can see, assuming that the way you think about your word (whether it is trust or anything else) will land perfectly with the group is a biased belief. Using "wetsuit" language to a "lace" person could work against you. Instead of guessing, this is a great opportunity for the team to create some common language and ownership by bringing them into the process (IKEA effect).

Once you have sorted through your micro-moments and have your priming associations, you can start to match them.

Videoconferencing Background

Do you let everyone see your space or do you have a virtual background or blur set up? What does a blurred background or virtual one say about trust? Does it convey that you trust the team enough to see where you are? Or does it show that you are guarded? Keeping something secret from them? You remind their subconscious of that lack of trust three times per second as their eyes scan the environment around them. Even if they can't articulate it, it can still add constant snowflakes to the iceberg.

Creating a space you feel good enough to let the team see in all its glory is an important prime for trust. What image might you hang on the wall to help continually prime trust in every conversation?

Email and Conversation

What trust words can you weave into your emails? Sometimes, it might include saying the word itself: "I have complete trust in you." Other times, it is less overt. Remember Gene Kranz telling the team before the Apollo 11 mission, "Whatever happens, I will never second-guess any of your calls. Now let's go—let's go land on the moon." That statement is deeper than saying, "I trust you." There is an explicit promise there, a verbal contract of trust.

In *Fierce Conversations*, Susan Scott says you can delegate a task, but not the responsibility.[166] This is an important path for trust. I always tell my teams, "I will never throw you under the bus. Whatever choice you make, know how it will make our department proud." While this builds trust, it also helps them get out from the myopic view of their work and think, "Would I feel good if Melina had to defend this to the CEO? Do I have a good enough reason to make this choice, or should I think about it a little more?"

I didn't have to ask them to do this continually because I also lived up to my end of the promise. They saw me walk that walk, even when it was hard. If a deadline was missed, I didn't say, "Ugh, Susie didn't get me the file. I'll talk to her." I would own it on behalf of the team (reciprocity) and say something like, "I'm sorry for missing the deadline. Next time, I'll be more thoughtful. What can I do now to be most supportive of you?" In case you're wondering, my team didn't miss many deadlines (and I never had to harp about them).

Your Turn

As you think of your word, what images, sounds, smells, and literal associations align with it?

____

____

____

____

____

____

Where can you incorporate those into your:

Emails: ______________________________

Office: ______________________________

Zoom background: ______________________________

Daily language: ______________________________

Signature line: ______________________________

Other: ______________________________

Scarcity

As you know, when you and your team are spread thin and pulled in different directions, it creates **time pressure**. This stressful state is a way to ensure your change initiatives don't get far and are full of drama. Relieving this pressure is accomplished with planning, thoughtfulness, and intention.

For any team in every industry, in every situation, I recommend you start by narrowing your goal so you are working on the right problem (the focus of the last chapter). It is foundational for change (revisit Part 2.1 for specific insights and tips about calming the elephant) and has a big bang for the buck.

Even as you have read all of this, you probably still like the idea of having ten things on your to-do list. It makes us feel better to think we will get a lot done—there is a reason "hustle culture" was a thing for such a long time. To frame it differently, let me say this:

Busy is not important. Stressed is not productive. Overcommitted does not equal successful.

Don't Wait

I know what it is like to have multiple deadlines and priorities pulling you and the team in a thousand directions. I've been in environments with back-to-back meetings and too many projects with far too few hours in the day. I get that in this state, the idea of putting in the work so what is already on your plate takes more time today for a win tomorrow can be a tough sell. When time is scarce and your team is spread thin, you are more likely to lean on time discounting; it is hard to justify spending more time today to save some indeterminate amount of time later that doesn't feel tangible. Your optimism bias will lead you to believe that once *this* project is over, you will have time to be better.

It's a fallacy.

Until you take action, it will not get better. There are always more projects, more deadlines, more stress. This is why all change starts with you. As a manager, one of the biggest things you can do for your team is protecting their time and ensuring they are focused on the right things and don't get stretched too thin working on extra projects. How might things be different if you were to make it so their scarcest resource—their time and cognitive capacity—is used (but not depleted) each day?

For one thing, when you present them with a change they need to get on board with, they are more likely to be willing to work with you because they know you have their best interests at heart. They will also be more likely to have a better output on their work, so win-win-win. You don't have to do everything all at once (no need to bikeshed on coming up with the perfect plan and tactic). Start sprinkling in little things from throughout this book.

Planning better so you and your team have enough time to get things done creates a huge, positive ripple effect. Limiting goals and priorities allows you to get more of the right stuff done better in less time. Remember from Chapter 6 that 17 hours of communication per week is spent clarifying something previously said, and 62 percent of emails are considered unimportant.

If you are more thoughtful about the emails you send—you know why they are being sent and the recipient gets the right information at the right time with everything they need to move forward on the right path, you could conservatively cut your communications in half. Even if you were to reduce it by 25 percent, what impact would that have?

- A quarter of scheduled meetings for you and your teams are no longer needed.
- A quarter of the emails are gone.

- A quarter of the "Do you have five minutes?" drop-ins that take an hour don't happen.
- A quarter of the Slack or chat questions never come in.

How much more time would you and your team gain back if 25 percent of all of it never happened? If your team was 25 percent more efficient, you could get more done in less time. And, because people are less stressed, they make better decisions, are more creative, and are nicer to each other. When you focus on the right stuff and narrow your priorities, everything is easier.

If you do nothing else after completing this book, do this one thing: be more thoughtful up front to reduce time pressure for yourself and your team.

Your Turn

Effective immediately, I want you to stop sending any communication without being thoughtful about it first. No one-off emails or off-the-cuff chats for a quick question. Whenever you want to communicate with anyone else, **expect an error** and incorporate **sludge** to slow yourself down. Your new self-talk could be: "You care about others enough to always be thoughtful. You don't send one-off messages."

For emails, this could mean you have to review all drafts at least an hour after you wrote them before hitting send. If you want to call/text/IM/email/schedule a quick Zoom with anyone: Stop. Ask yourself, "Why do I feel the need to do this? What is the goal? Is there anything else I might need to ask them?"

Remember to read the communication with the worst possible intent before sending it. If this was sent to someone who has a **confirmation bias** against you (your work nemesis), how might they read it? Or imagine that same person sent you this email; how would you interpret it?

Once you have thought about it through that lens, you can look for opportunities to clean things up.

What are common points where people have questions? It could be clarifying what time zone the proposed meeting is in or who will send the calendar request when a time has been finalized (include those details in your initial email to avoid future back-and-forth). At each phase, ask yourself how to make this easy and reduce the need for more conversation.

For example, if someone sends you times for a meeting, don't respond with, "Sure, any of those work," because that needs additional communication to complete the task. Saying, "Let's do three o'clock," is better, but you could have closed out more steps.

Instead, send a calendar invite for the proposed time and instructions (i.e., a meeting link or your phone number). Follow up with an email that says something like, "You should now have a calendar invite in your inbox for three o'clock Eastern on Thursday. It includes my Zoom link. If you prefer to meet another way or need a different time, please let me know and I will be happy to update accordingly. See you then."

It may feel forward, but I promise you almost everyone appreciates this reduction in tasks on their to-do list. It cut out several emails that could have delayed the meeting days or weeks and primes them about how easy it is to work with you—another win-win.

Being more thoughtful about your communication reduces miscommunications and follow-ups. A little thoughtfulness now can save hours on the back end. And, because you will send less communication overall, it makes people more likely to pay attention to your important emails when they come through. Win-win.

Commit to the following for thirty days (I'm starting with email, and ideally you will do this across all areas):

- **Before sending any email,** consider, "If this was the only email I could send them today, is there anything else I would want to know?"
- **For every received email,** consider the intent and not just the surface question, "What are they really asking? Why was this sent? What peripheral questions might exist?"
- **Every email must be proofed before sending.** You wait at least ___ (minutes/hours/days) before hitting send.

When you commit to #BEthoughtful let me know on social media with that hashtag. You'll find me as @thebrainybiz everywhere.

Reciprocity

When we look at change, the gifts you give your team are often not monetary. Instead, reciprocity is the gift of trust, transparency, clarity, direction, involvement, time, thoughtfulness, passion, and/or purpose.

When you present options or have other communication with your team, consider how they will feel inclined to reciprocate.

One way to trigger reciprocity is with the **IKEA effect**. Where can you invite someone to participate in shaping their job role, the department's focus, or other items that can boost intrinsic motivation?

Remember, don't ask if you know their ideas will not be implemented—that will make things worse than if you didn't ask at all. Find the right place and give them the freedom to come up with areas *they* are excited about. (This is about them, not you.) If your organization would support it, consider something like "20 percent time" to give people the freedom to let their minds wander (especially if your focus words were "creative," "innovation," or "trust").

Your Turn

Where is a place that you could leverage the IKEA effect for your team?

___

How will you show people their suggestions were used?

___

Where can you incorporate transparency?

___

What is the purpose of the team?

___

Do the individual members rally behind it? Why or why not?

___

Where can you let go and trust them?

___

Herding and Social Proof

Wherever you want to nudge people, it is important to know where your herds are. Showing that other people like them are behaving how you want to encourage is important. In the cookie example, this was the line in the bakery (and your outraged Yelp review).

Beware of unintentional normalizing and don't use short-term herding benefits that compromise your long-term change goals.

Remember that because of **false uniqueness bias**, people will be likely to overestimate the people who do the same negative behavior and underestimate the number of people who do as much good stuff as they do.

If you have a team member who is always late to meetings, social proof is a great way to show them the importance of being part of the team (**unity**) and that others are on time.

Your Turn

As you consider the next step in the process for your team member, where is the herd that will support the behavior you want them to take?

Who is this for?

____

What is the action you want them to take?

____

What do they believe is going on?

___

What is motivating them to not do the action?

___

Where is the herd you can lean on?

___

Remember, team members are all unique, so you need to consider the context for each. What motivates one will not motivate another and not everyone is at the same place on their journey. (In other words, they are coming from different locations, and you need to be nudging each along on their way to Change City so they don't get lost.)

Loss Aversion

Imagine you have an employee who constantly makes little side jabs about their projects—one isn't challenging enough; on another, the rest of the team isn't doing enough so they can't make progress; another is downright confusing. Your employee has had these same projects for the full year they have been on your team, and you are starting to worry about overall morale and the great promise you saw when they joined the team.

One day, a miraculous opportunity presents itself. Another department has asked for one employee to take on loan for six months to a year to support their initiatives. Your unhappy employee's skill set matches the requirements and you're ecstatic to share the news. This will allow them to shake things up, move out of those stagnant projects, and try something new.

You call a meeting with them and say, "Great news! Sally is taking over all your projects. I know you have been agonizing over them this past year, so you can stop all your work immediately and start fresh. Bob's department asked us to send someone from our team to be on loan for up to a year, and I've decided you're the one! You start Monday."

"But I've been working on these projects for a year already!" they protest. "How could you take them away from me? I was just starting to make progress. I have so many ideas." After an exhausting thirty minutes of complaints and reasons why they shouldn't be the one to be forced onto this other team for the project, you decide to put a pin in this and revisit it in a meeting tomorrow.

What the heck just happened?

You were so sure they would be delighted with this change of workload, so it was jarring to have this response. You already told Bob the employee would start next week and now you worry they might quit instead of taking on the new opportunity. Frazzled, you start compiling a stack of arguments to present in the next meeting to convince them this is something they should be happy about.

The problem here is that you are triggering loss aversion, status quo bias, and the endowment effect on what they have *now*. You jumped too quickly to the new state and reminded them of everything you are asking them to give up. And because the brain fears the unknown, it is more likely to dig in its metaphorical heels. To put it another way, you told them to put on their graduation goggles and all the things to look at while wearing them.

The lesson is to shift the focus of the trifecta. **Do not remind them of what they are giving up; instead, help them feel ownership over the new opportunity.** You want to lead with the endowment effect and the rest of the trifecta will follow.

For this opportunity, you introduced the idea by 1) saying all their projects were being given to someone else (scaring the elephant), 2) reminding them about all the effort and time they had put into their existing projects—the year of work they have already put in, and 3) assuming they would be happy, jumping in with a decision already made (bias alert!)—they had no say in the matter and with such a quick shift the brain can get scared about this looming change.

A better approach would be to help them take ownership of the new opportunity. Remember the mugs and chocolate bars, though; the current trifecta is working against you, so you need to combat it by making the new opportunity real for them. One way to do this would be to ask a question like, "Imagine if you had a fresh start with a project you could build from the ground up, where you had a dedicated team of people working only on getting that one thing done. What would be exciting about that for you?"

Notice, I strategically framed this question by asking, "What would be exciting about that for you?" and not, "Would you like that?" or something similar. There is an opportunity that someone could say, "No, not really." With that second question, now you have made your job that much harder. When you ask them to come up with something that would be exciting about that for them, they are essentially talking themselves into the new space, which makes them more likely to take ownership of it. Of course, you want to align the set-up scenario (the thing they imagine) with the real benefits they will get in the next phase.

They will then give you the language you can use to help explain why the new opportunity is a great fit for them. If they say, "Not having to deal with X anymore would be exciting," then you can be sure to stress that in the new scenario, they will not have to deal with X. Or if they say having a dedicated team focused on the one thing is exciting, you can stress that benefit.

There is no need to dwell on or remind them of what they are giving up—that will only work against you and the goal of this one step in the process. Remember our small steps approach and don't try to do too much now. All you need from this introductory meeting is to get them excited about the change. Once you get them excited about it, don't squelch it all by spending forty-five minutes going through all the old projects (which can bring up loss aversion before their new excitement solidifies), next steps, and a long list of to-dos (creating overwhelm that could make them revert to status quo bias).

Instead, it's okay to have this be a quick meeting where you pump them up. Let this be one of those meetings that end early; schedule thirty minutes and ideally you can give them back fifteen or twenty, where they are left to dream about their new opportunity and how exciting it is. They will continue to talk themselves into loving this new idea, which will make the transition easier when you have those "next steps" conversations later (it doesn't have to be far into the future; the follow-up could be later that same day). If they have more questions and additional conversation is necessary, you have the time, but ideally your thoughtful approach will make it so this isn't needed.

Note: When the thing they are stepping away from is an "elephant in the room" that will cloud everything else being discussed until it is addressed, you should talk about it early. You still don't want to apologize or lament over how they must give it up but ignoring it will make things worse, not better.

A simple example of this is employee reviews. If you give performance-based pay increases along with reviews, the employee will be bogging down their brain with tallying and concern about how this might impact the number that will be revealed at the end of the conversation. Because the brain gets easily overwhelmed when trying to remember facts and figures, they will not internalize anything you are saying during the important part (feedback, goals, areas for improvement), creating a lost opportunity.

Giving them the information they care most about up front is a gift. This can either be done at the beginning of the meeting or perhaps even sent twenty-four hours in advance, which has the double benefit of giving them time to reflect and come up with thoughtful questions. You may be thinking, "Most people get some sort of raise, so this is a good change. They should know that it will be positive and be pleasantly surprised with whatever happens at the end."

That would be too logical! They might be **anchored** on what they got last year or how much they could get if they hit the top tier like Sally did in accounting (and I work way harder than her—it wouldn't be fair if she got a bigger raise than me). These "what ifs" and "if onlys" are constantly floating around. The expectations create anticipation, which can cause someone to lose focus as they are trying to do a mental tally and constantly worry about what might come next. Alleviate the pressure on situations like this before they derail everything.

Your Turn

Consider a change moment coming up soon. For practice purposes, I recommend something small. That means one aspect of someone's job is changing. This could be needing to switch to a new software system, step in a process, or working together through the insights in this book so they can be more thoughtful before sending communications out.

Who is the person being asked to change?

____

What is the change?

____

What question can you ask to get them excited about the new scenario?

____

What are they most concerned about?

___

Do you need to address that first in some way?

___

Are you *absolutely sure* you need to? Would I agree?

___

Framing

As you know, how you say something matters much more than what you say. This entire section (and most of the book) is an exercise in framing. In my opinion, framing is the most important concept you can learn regarding behavioral economics. It is the easiest to apply and you can see quick results, often with little to no cost.

The good-cookie scenario had a rhyming phrasing ("buy three, get one free") compared to the bad scenario's clunky "buy four cookies and only pay for three" statement. Our brains believe that rhymes are more truthful[167] and that those who communicate simply are more knowledgeable. Putting in the time up front to be thoughtful about the goal (bringing it back to the tips that started this section) will help you have more organized thoughts and clearer communication. This will help establish trust and make it so people are more likely to want to follow you with whatever you are recommending.

For example, if I were to say, "The precipitation in one month makes it so there are likely to be flora appearing at some point within the following month," you would likely say, "Uh . . . what?" Saying instead, "April showers bring May flowers" is simple, clear, and easy to remember. Even if it isn't true, it *feels* true and sounds like I know what I am talking about.

> *"If you can't explain it to a six-year-old, you don't understand it yourself."*
> –ALBERT EINSTEIN

> *"I apologize for such a long letter–I didn't have time to write a short one."*
> –MARK TWAIN

Reflect on both of those statements for a moment.

As you consider the information to share and how to best share it with the recipient, what would make it most effective? How could you say it in fewer words? Is there an analogy or story that can help make your point?

One study by Johns Hopkins put this to good use.[168] They posted signs in convenience stores that read, "You have to run fifty minutes to burn off the calories in one bottle of soda." (Yikes!) Less sugary drinks were purchased when the signs were out.

Understanding and highlighting the right context—framing the message to showcase the right thing at the right nudgeable moment—makes a difference.

It may feel like stories are unnecessary fluff that distracts from the point, but remember, we need to emotionally engage to decide.[169] The story helps us internalize what is going on and want to act. Stories are how you can relate the circumstance to them, what you want them to do, and why it matters.

Say you have a new software system you need someone to use, and they are resisting (they might be skipping meetings about it, making excuses, conveniently forgetting to use the new system). Instead of saying, "Hey, this is the policy, just do it," you can find a way to get them out of their status quo with a good story and a different frame.

You could share about a customer named Suzie that was stranded with her infant daughter Nora in the car and no way to get gas when her debit card stopped working last month and end with something like, "If we have an easy and affordable solution to fix that in the future, so no one has to feel the stress and discomfort like Suzie and her daughter Nora that day, do you think we have an obligation as her bank to do so?"

While someone could say "no" to this, it is harder than the simple "I want you to change your process" statement. When the person likely says, "Yes," you can then present the simple fix in the process, and that it can be done in a few minutes or whatever the case is.

Note: The framing of the question at the end of the story is important. You need to consider the person you are speaking to, what matters to them, what you want them to do, and everything else outlined at the beginning of this chapter. A badly framed question can end in them saying no in a way that gets you even more stuck. **Thoughtfulness matters.**

Your Turn

Let's start small. Take a moment to look at some common phrasings—either that you are saying or those from others. Remember my "Does that make sense?" example as inspiration here. Where is there a "10 percent fat" phrasing that could be easily reframed as "90 percent fat-free" to be more appealing?

Common Phrase 1:

Why isn't this phrasing optimal?

How might you say that differently?

What is another way to say it?

Common Phrase 2:

Why isn't this phrasing optimal?

How might you say that differently?

____

____

What is another way to say it?

____

____

Reflection Point

We've now completed the basic "It's Not About the Cookie" framework, which can be applied to all sorts of scenarios, from micro-moments of change to all-encompassing initiatives. The concepts outlined here should be considered in every conversation about change. And, since every conversation is essentially a change conversation (either in the aftermath of something that has already happened, a present change, or prepping for something to come), it is important to be thoughtful and keep these concepts in mind all the time.

I've created a free one-sheet printable you can put up to help prime you so you are always thinking about the cookie framework elements.

Scan this QR code or visit www.thebrainybusiness.com/cookie to get your free "It's Not About the Cookie" printable and other resources.

CHAPTER 16

Where's the Fun?

"If it was supposed to be fun, they wouldn't call it work."

–TOO MANY PEOPLE

In 2021, a book came out called *Four Thousand Weeks: Time Management for Mortals*.[170] This is a clever **reframe** from author Oliver Burkeman to help everyone get out of their own way in the constant striving for productivity for productivity's sake. Why is it called *Four Thousand Weeks*? It's your entire life; about seventy-seven years. Something he says is "absurdly, terrifyingly, insultingly short." (I agree.)

Considering you spend a third of that time at work, do you want to spend 1,333 of your 4,000 weeks feeling stressed and overwhelmed by busywork? Or would you prefer to do something that matters? To have fun in your days and help your team to be motivated toward the same? To have a purpose and make a difference?

Focusing on the stuff that matters is energizing. And people like to have fun!

Millions of people get their news from comedians. We share gifs and memes that make us laugh. We relate to others through the power of stories and are more likely to want to put in the effort for people we like and who care about us. So, as you identify your big goals, small steps, nudgeable moments and begin applying the "It's Not About the Cookie" framework, don't forget to build in some fun.

It is important to remember that your idea of "fun" is not the same as everyone else's idea of fun (**false consensus effect**). There are some things that people universally agree are *not* fun, like virtual happy hours. *The Atlantic*, *Slate*, and *Fast Company* all have articles about why workers hate these forced fun activities.[171]

Trying to replicate what was fun (for some people) in person and "make it virtual" doesn't work. First, it is important to know why people like to get together and what camaraderie is doing for your organization. (Again, what is the *goal*?) Then you can look for ways to incorporate that throughout the day and other interaction points—virtually or in person.

We have all zoned out during a long check-in meeting where everyone takes five (or fifteen) minutes to give their update from the week. Far too many of them get long-winded (because there isn't a clear purpose to the meeting), and people distract themselves by doodling or having their minds wander during the updates. This experience is made even worse in a virtual environment, where people feel like they can be checking their email on the computer while half-listening to their coworkers' updates.

One choice would be to eliminate these meetings, but they can be important. Knowing what the team is working on and having some accountability/checking in to regularly align priorities is good. That makes them a perfect opportunity to build in some fun and an ability for the team to bond.

Matthew Confer, VP of strategy and business development at Abilitie, shared with me a practice they incorporated in 2021 that has helped boost engagement and interest among their team in this type of meeting.[172] Each person answers three questions on the call:

1. A fun question of the week like, "Who would you want to play you in a movie?" or "What is your favorite board game of all time?"
2. A reflective question, "What is the most important thing you thought about this week?"
3. A forward-looking question, "What is your most important thing for next week?"

There are a few great things here. First, having the fun question of the week helps you to relate to the people on your team as people and, according to Matthew, boosts engagement throughout the meeting. It isn't that everyone shares their answer to question one and then you get to the "boring work stuff." Instead, each person shares their three things one at a time.

You naturally find yourself interested in what the next person will say and are more likely to listen to the other updates. It is a constant wave of engagement that keeps the meeting moving forward in a fun way.

The phrasing of the second question is also important. It isn't the same boring, "What did you work on this week?" but rather, "What is the *most important thing you thought about* this week?" This says something about the organization and what matters to them. It isn't about busy work, but important work—*thoughtful* work. This encourages people to stop and think about what they are doing. Does it add value? Is it worth sharing about each week? It also encourages them to ask good questions. A well-framed question incorporated at the right time can increase engagement and intrinsic motivation, prime a better experience and environment, shape culture, and encourage questions and discussion without costing anything. It is one of my favorite things—a small change that makes a big difference.

The third question is also important because it helps shape the priorities and narrow them down to one thing (you know how much I love that!). It is short enough (for next week) that it can be actionable, and by asking in advance, there is an opportunity to shift if it is out of alignment. Notice too, it doesn't ask, "What deadlines do you have coming up next week?" or "What is your team working on next week?" but, "What is the *most important thing* for next week?"

Naming and claiming your most important thing (and being limited to only one) increases the likelihood of completion. This helps the organization keep moving forward thoughtfully toward future goals as individuals and as a team. A great use of fun to boost engagement and thoughtfulness.

Emoji-Intelligence

A 2020 article in *Entrepreneur* (just before the pandemic began) shared that 60 percent of two-word emails, like "Nice work" or "Good job," are interpreted sarcastically.[173] How to fix that? Emoji.

These aren't frivolous cartoons; they are becoming more commonplace, help communicate emotional intent (research shows the same part of the brain that processes human faces is also where we process emoji[174]), can enhance relationships, and close generational gaps. Plus, they're fun!

Emojis, gifs, and memes aren't your style? Remember, it isn't only about you—it's about the team. Integrating emojis with a common language can help foster team building across an organization, increasing unity and circles of empathy while boosting morale and reducing miscommunications (for free). Sounds like a win to me.

Making Meetings Engaging, Effective, and Cool

When Troy Campbell, who has previously worked at/for Disney, Netflix, and Nike, was on the podcast, he talked about the science of "cool" (yes, there is a science to it!), and we specifically had a conversation about making meetings cooler and more effective.[175]

In our conversation, he shared how his company, On Your Feet, incorporates the idea of a "portal" from Disney parks to the start of a meeting. This is that area you go through before you get onto the ride, a "slow transitional space that transitions you into the right mindset while creating a metaphor of going somewhere different." Using the portal concept at the beginning helps people be primed for the outcome of the meeting so they are more effective.

Much like my "one word" approach for your team that kicked off Part 3, Troy talked about some of the goals for a meeting and their corresponding warmups to increase the likelihood of the team performing in that way.

For example, if you need **collaboration** from the team, start with the one-word story. Use the prompt of "In a world where…" (important to read this using your best movie trailer voice) and then each person adds one word at a time to create the story. The story itself doesn't matter; the exercise does the necessary job to prime the meeting for collaboration.

If the meeting is more **strategic** in nature, you want to use an if/then prompt. He gave the example of "What is the best doughnut place to go when visiting Portland?" and his suggestions for possible answers were, "*If* you value bacon on your doughnut, *then* you should go to Voodoo." And "*If* you are a hipster elitist, *then* you should go to Blue Star." It's all in fun and jest, which helps the team bond together while being psychologically primed for the theme of that meeting. He says these warmups usually take one to five minutes but completely transform the effectiveness of the meeting. A few minutes well spent.

He also mentioned how the power of narrative and story could be used to make meeting objectives more likely to be relatable to people. If you want your meeting objective to resonate, you want to tell the story of the meeting. Instead of an agenda, walk through this format:

- We used to be here
- We did X, Y, and Z
- Now we are here
- Today we are going to do this
- After today we will do this

This little shift (also free!) can make meetings more engaging, productive, and strategic. They are more likely to resonate with the team and are a simple way to incorporate fun that is targeted without being contrived.

The moral of this story? You spend a third of your 4,000 weeks at work, at least 87,500 of your micro-decisions each week—shouldn't it be enjoyable? People appreciate fun. It is a gift, so have more fun!

Let's take a moment to recap all we have covered as we move through the portal to the final chapter. Since we have covered a ton, and much like the peak-end rule having an impact on reviews, it can also make you gloss over most of the things you have accomplished through reading this book. In our time together (which hopefully won't end here—this book is intended to be a resource you reach for again and again), you have learned:

- Part 1
    - » How the brain works
    - » That relationships are memories

  - What makes a great manager and how everyone can become one (even without natural talent for this area)
  - That thinking about change should not be reserved for giant, company-wide initiatives but is fostered as part of the culture one micro-moment and decision at a time
  - Why you need to plant a tree a day—do something now instead of waiting for the perfect forest opportunity to come tomorrow
- Part 2
  - We will never be completely unbiased, but we can understand and work with these tendencies to be more effective
  - A carefully curated assortment of biases and concepts from behavioral economics to help lead your employees through change
  - Several "Micro-Shift Moments" you can apply immediately to overcome time discounting and kick off your change journey
- Part 3
  - Why you need to be thoughtful about one goal and where people are coming from
  - The importance of small steps
  - What nudgeable moments are and how to find them
  - Why it's not about the cookie and how to apply that framework
  - The importance of fun and some simple ways to incorporate it to boost effectiveness and engagement in your organization

Reflection Point

Take a moment to celebrate your accomplishment. Pause and reflect, even for a moment, on what you learned in this book. What is your favorite concept? What is the first thing you will do (or what have you already done)? What do you want to be sure you don't forget? Make some notes here:

CHAPTER 17

Application and Final Thoughts

So, what's left? There are a couple of final important aspects to keep in mind as you begin applying what you have learned in this book. We close with two real-world examples where I have used the "It's Not About the Cookie" framework from this book to help traditionally difficult situations go over smoothly. One small (physical move) and one big (that corporate rebrand I mentioned way back in Chapter 1) to inspire you on your journey.

Why Timing Matters

As you know, change comes micro-moment by micro-moment. While you have the tools to set yourself up for success, I know that pressures (both internal and external) will make it tempting to try and take on too many changes at once. Whether it is optimism bias, herding instincts, or any other of the plethora of examples from Part 2, you will feel compelled to do *one more thing* on occasion. Sometimes it will be a direct ask (or order) from your boss; in others, it could be your brain nagging you to implement two or three change projects at a time. Remember what you learned about the value of dissent earlier in this book. Yes, it can be hard, but standing up for limiting priorities is about standing up for the good of the organization.

Framing the intent properly can help to get others on board instead of making them feel like you aren't being a team player.

What might happen if you explained the value of reshuffling priorities to increase the chances of all the important things being more likely to succeed while reducing inefficiencies in the organization?

Lean on the lessons you have learned from this book—the IKEA effect, priming, and framing, to name a few. When your boss says, "What could it hurt?" or "I know your team is busy, but I just looked at the quarterly projections and we need to do X, Y, and Z before the end of the month if we have a chance of meeting our numbers!"

Think back to my example of the "plethora of Post-its" and the giant corkboard in my office. Sometimes there is a priming benefit elsewhere that can help. You could also respond with something like, "I hope you know how much my team and I care about hitting the quarterly goal. May I share some thoughts on how doing less can help us achieve more now and for the rest of the year?"

It may help to provide some details about the brain (if you haven't shared this book with them already, I recommend it!). Think back to the information I shared about habits way back in Part 1 of this book; our life and experience are made up of our habits. We need our habits so that subconscious processing can handle the bulk of the mental load. Without existing rules, our slower, more manual conscious processing must take over. Even seemingly small changes can have a big ripple effect throughout someone's life and how they show up at work.

You don't get to say, "Well, I know my habits will be upended right now, so I am going to be more efficient in my conscious brain and use up a hundred bits per second now instead of the typical forty." It doesn't work that way. You have the bandwidth you have, and when small things shift (and you lose your habits), it leads to a tired, overwhelmed brain. Which, as you know, leads to worse decisions.

During the early days of the pandemic, people around the world felt exhausted. People said things like, "I'm doing less than I used to, but for some reason I can't seem to get through the day without feeling like I need a nap/coffee/cookie/Netflix break." One of my favorite ways to describe this was when a client called it the "COVID blahs"—that feeling of exhaustion that you couldn't shake.

Sure, the stress of a scary situation is part of it. Your brain was buzzing with fear and anxiety about the unknown. But there is more to it than that. Losing your habits creates a strain on your brain that makes you more tired.[176]

- The route you drive to work
- Where you put your keys
- Where you placed your coffee cup
- How you find a file
- Where your phone is
- Where you reach to grab a pencil, pen, or notepad
- Who you meet with (and when and where)

All these little habits were part of your subconscious processing, and when they are upended, it causes stress on the brain and makes you more tired. It doesn't take a global pandemic to experience this; any change or disruption in habits will make it so people use more of their conscious bandwidth on these simple things until the subconscious learns new habits.

This could be adapting to a new system or process, adjusting to a new reporting structure, incorporating a new project, remembering to loop in a new person on team emails, and moving locations (to name a few).

Moving is incredibly disruptive to all those little habits. Think of all the stuff you and the team have in your space at any time: pens, papers, files, keyboard, mouse, screen, chair, desk layout, route to walk to get there/to the bathroom/lunchroom/coffee break/meeting rooms, where you set your coffee or water cup, where you set your bag, phone or tablet, and countless other little things that add up and steal mental bandwidth.

Think about your kitchen and how it is set up. Imagine you are preparing a meal for a dinner party tonight with lots of moving parts: multiple courses for at least eight people. You are creating some old staples and a couple of new things, so you need your recipes handy (those ones aren't set up as habits yet). It will take coordination, but you have a plan and are confident.

Imagine you come home to prepare the meal and realize that while you were gone, some well-intentioned person reorganized your entire kitchen to optimize the flow. All the essentials: plates, silverware, glasses, knives, cutting boards, pots, pans, spices, pantry items, food in the refrigerator and freezer—none of the items are where you instinctively expect them to be.

How much more difficult is the preparation? You are focused on the new recipe and open the cabinet that used to have the salt and pepper and grouchily remind yourself that it is in a drawer on the other side of the kitchen now. You will likely mutter under your breath about how annoying it is as your stress mounts. You make mistakes while cooking, even on the recipes you know by heart: forget to set timers, take the rolls out too late because you couldn't find an oven mitt, and it all spirals in a way that ruins your mood and the entire dinner party for you. You're exhausted before the guests even arrive!

When you ask your team members to change too many things at once, they have this same bandwidth issue. This is why thoughtfulness on the *timing* of a change and the effort to calm the elephant are so important. In addition, you should expect an error in far-reaching places when someone is going through a change. Give them space and support. And, yes, this is a time when it makes sense to tell someone you know this can happen, so they should be patient with themselves. Encourage them not to take on too much and to expect their error.

Ayelet Fishbach has done great research into how people motivate themselves and prepare for when things will be hard.[177] Sometimes, knowing that something is going to be difficult will help you get through and weather the storm. She gives the example of being on a diet and going to a holiday party. If you don't have a plan, you are likely to indulge in the delicious food and drink when it is placed in front of you. If you instead think through what is coming and say, "Aunt Millie loves to hand out drinks, and I know if I start with the wine I will be on a slippery slope to desserts and fried foods. Right when I get there, I will get a club soda with lime so she doesn't feel the need to place a glass in my hand."

Having a plan is important so you aren't caught off guard. While on *The Brainy Business* podcast, Ayelet shared a great example of how people brace differently when you tell them what they are about to lift is heavy—you prepare for the weight, bend your knees, and instinctively increase your chances of successfully lifting the object without injuring your back.[178]

Brace for big changes and clear the way so you don't use up energy on unnecessary stuff that will reduce the chances of success. Everything can be done—successfully—when you are thoughtful about timing.

Don't Change Too Much

Because of this mental bandwidth, no matter how small the change you present to someone is, you want to be aware of what is going on at the same time so you don't change too much at once. It is better to stagger change requests and increase the likelihood of success for all of them than to pile them on and have everything fall apart.

Remember, you can't ask them if they are too busy or preoccupied. Because of planning fallacy, optimism bias, and a desire to prove themselves to you at work, people will be inclined to say they can handle it. Instead, before presenting a change as the manager, ask yourself, "Is now the right time for this?" If there is a massive cultural shift, it likely isn't the right time to ask someone to move their desk or reorganize their electronic files.

The "small" change will endanger the big one—delay it whenever possible. Remember, you need different management strategies during times of "war" and times of "peace." Times of peace are an opportunity to make little tweaks to get better through nice-to-have changes (and know this is where the creativity and best business moves often come from—Gmail, Post-its, and many other great ideas were only possible through the value of letting minds wander and wonder). During times of war, it is more about triage and having enough bandwidth for the big task at hand (being in this state too long, even by constantly spreading your team too thin, is a recipe for stagnation and being a victim of others changing while your company is stuck in the status quo). It all comes back to our theme of thoughtfulness—plan more up front so you can incorporate a nice ebb and flow into the organization.

Applying the Framework

The "It's Not About the Cookie" framework applies to every type of change. It is structured enough to give a few things to keep in mind without getting overwhelmed while being big enough to support you through even the largest company-wide initiatives. And, because you have an idea of the biases that might be blocking your path, you know the best ways to navigate through change (for yourself and those on your teams). To close out this book are two examples, one small and one big, where I have personally used the framework to help inspire your new life of thoughtful change.

Small Change: We're Moving

I worked in one company during a time of significant growth. Whenever one big move of departments was done, it felt like another started. My team moved three times in six years, and we weren't included in every move. By the third time, it would have been easy to introduce it by saying something like, "Hey everyone, I know you just started getting comfortable over here, so don't shoot the messenger, but I've been told it's time to move again." (Insert collective groan here.)

That message is framed as a loss aversion triggering prime that will derail the entire move (and subsequently all the work my team needed to work on simultaneously). Because I had invested in my team and knew what was important to them (not assumed based on my preferences but from past conversations where they had a chance to share), I was able to frame the message differently.

Instead of giving them information too early in the process (when nothing could be done), I did some due diligence to prepare for the conversation. I met with the head of facilities to see the available options for us in the move:

- Which locations could we choose from?
- What choices could my team have in the process? (This included desk height, wall height, sit/stand options, and color of the wall near them—I wanted to know every option that might be of value to them.)
- Who else might be moving at the same time?
- When was the move taking place? (Are there any projects or deadlines I should be thinking about now and move up or back to make this transition easier?)

After gathering the information, I knew we had a short turnaround time to pick our optimal location because multiple departments were moving at the same time. The goal (our "one thing") was a successful move where we got all our projects done on time, and the team was happier in the new location than they were in the current one. In this first meeting, I needed them to agree on which block of desks we wanted to claim as our new promised land.

My presentation of the options went something like this: "I got a chance to review all the available spaces, and based on what I've heard from you over the years as your top priorities, I kept an eye out for those with the best window options and proximity to the HR team—they are moving to the space right next to this. This spot has an unobstructed window view, and because it is on the other side of the building, it shouldn't have glare hitting your computer in the morning. I'm pretty confident I captured everything on your wish list when I designed this, but I want you to have the ability to weigh in before finalizing anything with facilities. Can you see yourself enjoying working in this space?"

Hopefully, you can feel the difference in this approach. It includes reciprocity, priming, framing, a shifted trifecta, trust, autonomy, nudging, IKEA effect, and scarcity, all in one thoughtful presentation. The pitch wasn't the same for each team member because not everyone had the same interests or deal-breakers.

Ending on a thoughtful, well-framed question is critical to keep the conversation moving with their attention focused on the positive (a nudge). Asking, "Can you see yourself enjoying working in the space?" is different than "What did I miss?" or "What should I tell them?" or "Are you on board?" or "What do you think?" (Note: I'm not saying these questions are bad; they serve a different purpose than mine in this instance.)

Not only is it not asking them to compare the existing desk (which can trigger the trifecta against the change), but it also helps to guide the way they think about the opportunity. It is intended to nudge them to start thinking about what would make that space enjoyable.

It is important to know your team and shape the thoughtful question to match their style. The worst thing that could happen with a question like that is if someone said no.

I knew I had a team that was used to change and adaptable. They were easygoing and used to big sweeping opportunities that they embraced at every turn. If I had a different team, I would have phrased the question differently.

Zoe Chance's magic question of "What would it take…" is a great option for most situations.[179] When in doubt, I say this is an easy frame that can be applied to most situations. In the case of the desks, you could ask:

- What would it take to make you love the new space?
- What would it take to have you excited about the space?
- What would it take to get you on board with the move?
- What would it take to make the transition seamless?

This, of course, is not the only prompt to use. And, again, consider the end goal (and most important next step) as you create your thoughtful question.

The presentation I shared was intentional about some other things as well. The language was all set up to:

- Remind them of what they asked for (either directly or indirectly)
- Show that I put in the extra effort on their behalf
- Show them that they matter
- Shift the endowment effect so they are already bought in
- Make it easy for them to agree to the proposal (and be happy about it!)

It's Not About Convincing

One question that comes up a lot in my classes and during consulting projects is how you can convince someone that this is the best thing for them. Whatever the change, if you go in with the intent of "winning" by showing them why they are wrong and you are right, it is a recipe for failure.

Remember back to what you learned about **confirmation bias** and the **focusing illusion**. If the other person can sense you are trying to convince them they are wrong, they will double down and fight you every step of the way. If you ask for their opinion and give them an opportunity to weigh in, be ready to listen and open to discovering *you* are wrong.

If that employee would have said, "I love being friends with so-and-so in HR, but I'm worried if we sit that close, I might not get as much work done; he is chatty and that concerns me," I needed to be ready to shift the plan. No matter their concern, I was prepared to have a conversation about it and listen. They need to know they are psychologically safe and can present concerns because I am there to listen and do what I can to support them.

With any change, big or small, give the person space to ask questions and share their insights and concerns—and listen to them. Hearing and internalizing the concerns (shaking up your biases) is important in them feeling comfortable and heard (calming the elephant) so they are more willing to change. Be open to changing the plan (whenever possible) if they present a valid alternative. If you can't do anything, change the approach so you don't ask and set them up to be disappointed.

Big Change: Corporate Rebrand

In case this hasn't been made clear yet, I am going to be explicit here: **When you propose a big change, you need to do your homework. When the stakes are high, your prep work needs to be significant.**

While running a marketing department, I wanted to convert our entire approach and essentially gamble the entire marketing budget (which was not insignificant) on a new focus. This meant I needed to get the executive team on board with leaving the status quo (which had decent growth and numbers) to come over to my new approach: shifting away from product marketing to a more cohesive brand message. To make it potentially even scarier for those who needed to buy in, the recommendation included having local bands and artists create all the assets for the brand, which we would not know in advance or have control over. It was a big ask. It was a huge change. And I would not have gotten unanimous approval if I had not done my homework in advance.

The initial groundwork was laid months in advance with thoughtful anchoring and priming. When explaining the process to the teams involved, including the CEO, I said, "If we do this, we need to be ready to implement anything to have this rebrand be successful. That means everything, including the name and tagline, will be on the table. We need to be open to any possible change, and I promise it will be undertaken thoughtfully."

This was absolutely true. I was hopeful (and pretty sure) that the name would stay, but I didn't want to bias the results and how we would integrate the recommendations from our research. This also set an anchor on the gravity of the possible change that made the thing I ended up asking for feel more reasonable than if I would have tried for a small ask to get my foot in the door and gradually built up to this bigger change (a strategy that would have failed in this application).

My team was given the same message, and I also leveraged the IKEA effect to bring them into the process with ownership early. They were empowered to find opportunities to build this brand into something they were passionate about. Before we had approval on the project (before the big, quick changes could begin), I had them do foundational work that would be critical when it was time to pull the trigger, like: collecting lists of everywhere the name and brand currently existed, from pens to building signs and the website and starting to sort these into phases for the rollout. If the project wouldn't have been a go, this was still useful, so it wasn't busy work that would be undone. We could use it in another way if needed. They had a purpose and were intrinsically motivated by the task—they were excited about working hard to achieve our collective dream.

In the lead-up to the official pitch meeting, I sat down individually with each executive team member to get their insights and input. I learned what they cared about, their concerns, and what would make them say "no" before the meeting—and what would make it easy for them to say yes. For the more fearful (or those who would be most significantly impacted), I had multiple meetings.

These meetings were framed about learning from them—it wasn't about winning or forcing them to my side. I didn't go in and say something like, "I need you on board with this. Let me tell you all the reasons you need to go along with my suggestion." This language would have likely caused them to dig in their heels and fight against me.

Instead, I genuinely asked more thoughtful and curious questions that leveraged **unity**, like: "What would need to be included in the project for you to feel good about supporting it?" and "What would be a big red flag that would make you not want to support it?" and "What am I not seeing that needs to be considered?"

Thoughtful questions are a valuable frame. They have a magical power to turn adversaries into advocates. If you are open and ready to listen and ask good questions, people will tell you what they need most of the time.

Everyone in the final pitch meeting knew without discussion who the most likely adversaries were. Herding instincts and a false consensus effect could have derailed everything if one of those key people had expressed concern in that meeting. When they were not skeptically accepting but *excited* by the idea in the meeting, it made it easy for everyone else to be excited and supportive as well.

In every meeting, I thoughtfully leveraged the power of story, priming, framing, and scarcity at specific moments to be supportive and not cause overwhelm. This process took about eight months of prep from my initial "our brand awareness is low; I think we need a change" moment to the pitch.

Keep in mind, no one asked me to do this. I had been researching and evaluating for months because I wanted the company to succeed—and I knew a new brand and culture shift were the way to get us there. We had been arguably successful up to this point (though remember that flawed logic from the *Challenger* story—I could see a better world and wanted to change before we had to). And I want you to know, this initiative meant stepping out of my comfort zone—it was scary to put all my career eggs in this basket. But I channeled that into making it amazing and my passion came through because I knew this was the right thing to do. Yes, it was scary for all of us—as I said, I was gambling my reputation on this change. What if I put in all that effort to sell my idea to the team and it didn't work? Let's just say the stakes were high.

But putting in the groundwork meant I had advocates, and let me tell you, having advocates is key in culture work. This was more than a "rebrand." We aligned the entire culture and incorporated changes in every department, from the onboarding process for new hires to individual meeting structures and the images on the walls in the headquarters building. Culture shifts need everyone on board. Company missions and values need everyone on board. And not reluctantly—you need advocates. You need to think long term.

The "It's Not About the Cookie" framework was applied constantly and concurrently in various areas throughout this big change initiative.

- It was a way to be thoughtful about the entire process—considering the end goal, how to prime, frame, and use reciprocity and fun to help get there.
- It was also applied to every meeting, email, and offhanded conversation along the way—in countless micro-moments.

Remember the opening part of this book; it was named "Big Plans and Micro-Moments" for a reason. The framework in this book and everything you have learned applies to both (and everything in between) and they all need to work together to reach the common goal. Every big change is made up of many micro-moments that each get their own "It's Not About the Cookie" framework application.

After the pitch was approved, we had about six weeks to complete the entire rebrand and launch it to the organization. This included finding our bands and artists, redesigning the logo, creating our new commercials, doing a new kind of media buy, and planning a launch event for the entire company and board of directors to reveal the new change.

Oh, did I forget to mention I had a team of three? It was me and my two amazing team members making this all happen in a ridiculously short time. Because I knew this was coming and could not be successful without their buy-in, I brought them in as early as possible to be part of the planning. They helped shape the brand and the dream became ours collectively, instead of my vision that I dropped on their plates at the last minute.

If I had not used the "It's Not About the Cookie" framework, this would have been a terrible experience that made them hate coming to work (and resenting the resulting brand when everything was said and done)—instead, it had the glow of a vulnerability loop, something we worked on together that bonds us to this day. I look back on that time with fond memories, and I know they do as well. We did something amazing in record time, and it was a rush. The entire company was excited about the reveal; we kept everything a secret to build anticipation for the final launch party, which included live bands featured in our commercials.

In the days and weeks leading up to that event, people tried to get a sneak peek at what marketing was working on to be part of the fun. We dropped the occasional riddle or tiny gift to all employees and presented physical invitations to everyone in the company for the launch.

When the event finally came, the anticipation and excitement were palpable—the room was buzzing with potential (and it wasn't just the reverb from the electric guitars). As we showed the first commercials and explained the new direction, the faces in the room were something to behold.

Captivated is a word that comes to mind. We had some short speeches, but it was about them. Everyone clapped, cheered, and celebrated together from across the organization.

When the commercials began running the next day, all employees and the board were excited to talk about how great the new direction was. They were energized by being part of the process (even though many of them had no impact on the outcome, they were still brought in and felt ownership over our new shared identity).

If there had been siloed teams before, they melted away. It was no longer an "us" in marketing versus "them" in finance (or wherever else). It was "us"—a united organization—empowered to take on the world together.

That's the power of thoughtful application of behavioral economics in a business. Big dreams are achieved in the right micro-moments. It's not about the cookie, but you can be sure it will be the most delicious cookie when you stop to take a bite.

So, I ask you: What will your first change be?

Whatever it is, remember to *BE thoughtful*.

—Melina

Resources

Many amazing terms and concepts were shared throughout this book. Some only got a sentence or two within these pages but know they are all fascinating topics with large amounts of research. Do you want to keep learning? Many of these topics also have episodes on *The Brainy Business* podcast (and freebie worksheets) so you can take a deeper dive.

Get Your Freebies

Your virtual glossary and more supporting materials await at thebrainybusiness.com/employees-need

Consulting?

Visit melinapalmer.com/consulting to learn more

Speaking or Corporate Training?

If you are looking for an engaging speaker for your next event or training, Melina is a perfect fit.
Check dates and details at melinapalmer.com/speaking

Got a question?

You can always send an email to melina@thebrainybusiness.com—I'm happy to help and love to connect!

Endnotes

1 Buzhardt, L. (n.d.). Can old dogs learn new tricks? *VCA Animal Hospitals blog*. Retrieved from: vcahospitals.com/know-your-pet/can-old-dogs-learn-new-tricks

2 Isaacson, W. (2012, September). How Steve Jobs' love of simplicity fueled a design revolution. *Smithsonian Magazine*. Retrieved from: smithsonianmag.com/arts-culture/how-steve-jobs-love-of-simplicity-fueled-a-design-revolution-23868877/

3 Kaku, M. (2014, August 20). The golden age of neuroscience has arrived. *Wall Street Journal*. Retrieved from: wsj.com/articles/michio-kaku-the-golden-age-of-neuroscience-has-arrived-1408577023

4 Graff, F. (2018, February 7). How many daily decisions do we make? *Science*. Retrieved from: science.unctv.org/content/reportersblog/choices

5 Palmer, M. (Host). (2020, November 20). Good habits, bad habits: An interview with Wendy Wood (No. 127) [Audio podcast episode]. In *The Brainy Business*.

6 Morse, G. (2002, June). Hidden minds. *Harvard Business Review*. Retrieved from: https://hbr.org/2002/06/hidden-minds; Walesh, S. G. (n.d.). Using the power of habits to work smarter. *Helping You Engineer Your Future blog*. Retrieved from: helpingyouengineeryourfuture.com/habits-work-smarter.htm

7 Wood, W. (2019). *Good habits, bad habits: The science of making positive changes*. Farrar, Straus and Giroux.

8 Bergland, C. (2012, November 29). The neurochemicals of happiness. *Psychology Today*. Retrieved from: psychologytoday.com/us/blog/the-athletes-way/201211/the-neurochemicals-happiness; Palmer, M. (Host). (2020, October 23). Get your D.O.S.E. of brain chemicals (No. 123) [Audio podcast episode]. In *The Brainy Business*.

9 Palmer, M. (Host). (2020, November 20). Good habits, bad habits: An interview with Wendy Wood (No. 127) [Audio podcast episode]. In *The Brainy Business*.

10 Field, H. (2019, July 18). 5 science-backed ways to boost your creativity. *Entrepreneur*. Retrieved from: entrepreneur.com/article/311870

11 Kahneman, D. (2011). *Thinking, fast and slow*. Farrar, Straus and Giroux.

12 Shiv, B., & Fedorikhin, A. (1999). Heart and mind in conflict: The interplay of affect and cognition in consumer decision making. *Journal of Consumer Research, 26*(3), 278–292.

13 Horowitz, B. (2014). *The hard thing about hard things*. Harper Business.

14 Edland, A., & Svenson, O. (1993). Judgment and decision making under time pressure. In: Svenson, O., & Maule, A. J. (eds), *Time Pressure and Stress in Human Judgment and Decision Making*. Springer, Boston, MA.

15 Amabile, T. M., Hadley, C. N., & Kramer, S. J. (2002, August). Creativity under the gun. *Harvard Business Review*. Retrieved from: https://hbr.org/2002/08/creativity-under-the-gun

16 Harvard Business Review Analytics Services. (2013, September). The impact of employee engagement on performance. *Harvard Business Review*. Retrieved from: https://hbr.org/resources/pdfs/comm/achievers/hbr_achievers_report_sep13.pdf

17 Zhang, H. (2022, January 25). Looking for a good investment? Find a company that understands its employees. *Institutional Investor*. Retrieved from: institutionalinvestor.com/article/b1wh5htywlzjbz/Looking-For-a-Good-Investment-Find-a-Company-That-Understands-Its-Employees; Palmer, M. (Host). (2020, May 22). Shapa, the numberless scale, interview with Dan Ariely (No. 101) [Audio podcast episode]. In *The Brainy Business*.

18 Beck, R., & Harter, J. (2014, March 13). Why good managers are so rare. *Harvard Business Review*. Retrieved from: https://hbr.org/2014/03/why-good-managers-are-so-rare

19 List, J. A. (2022). *The voltage effect: How to make good ideas great and great ideas scale*. Currency; Palmer, M. (Host). (2022, February 4). The voltage effect, with John List (No. 190) [Audio podcast episode]. In *The Brainy Business*.

20 Kahneman, D. (2011). *Thinking, fast and slow*. Farrar, Straus and Giroux.

21 Pradeep, A. K. (2010). *The buying brain: Secrets for selling to the subconscious mind*. John Wiley & Sons.

22 Haidt, J. (2006). *The happiness hypothesis: Finding modern truth in ancient wisdom*. Basic Books.

23 Shiv, B., & Fedorikhin, A. (1999). Heart and mind in conflict: The interplay of affect and cognition in consumer decision making. *Journal of Consumer Research*, *26*(3), 278–292.

24 Mani, A., Mullainathan, S., Shafir, E., & Zhao, J. (2013). Poverty impedes cognitive function. *Science*, *341*(6149), 967-980.

25 Neal, D. T., Wood, W., & Drolet, A. (2013). How do people adhere to goals when willpower is low? The profits (and pitfalls) of strong habits. *Journal of Personality and Social Psychology*, *104*(6), 959-975.

26 Ash, T. (2021). *Unleash your primal brain: Demystifying how we think and why we act*. Morgan James Publishing; Palmer, M. (Host). (2020, October 30). Unleash your primal brain, interview with Tim Ash (No. 124) [Audio podcast episode]. In *The Brainy Business*.

27 Price, M. E. (2013, June 25). Human herding: How people are like guppies. *Psychology Today*. Retrieved from: psychologytoday.com/us/blog/darwin-eternity/201306/human-herding-how-people-are-guppies

28 Palmer, M. (Host). (2021, August 13). The era of applied behavioral economics with Matej Sucha (No. 165) [Audio podcast episode]. In *The Brainy Business*; Zemko, T. (2021). Case study: How a job search portal increased conversions by 154% without changing a single word in job ads. *InsideBE.* Retrieved from: https://insidebe.com/articles/social-proof-increased-conversions-by-154/

29 Asch, S. (1955). Opinions and social pressure. *Scientific American, 193*(5), 31–35.

30 There is an ever-growing number of studies within the fields of behavioral economics and behavioral science from around the world, which I expect to grow faster in the coming years. I highly recommend *behavioraleconomics.com* as a starting resource for anyone looking for more academic research from the field as well as the back catalog of episodes from *The Brainy Business* podcast.

31 Bohns, V. (2021). *You have more influence than you think: How we underestimate our power of persuasion and why it matters.* W. W. Norton & Company; Palmer, M. (Host). (2022, March 25). You have more influence than you think, interview with Vanessa Bohns. (No. 197) [Audio podcast episode]. In *The Brainy Business.*

32 Tatam, S. (2022). *Evolutionary ideas: Unlocking ancient innovation to solve tomorrow's challenges.* Harriman House; Palmer, M. (Host). (2022, May 13). Evolutionary ideas with Sam Tatam. (No. 204) [Audio podcast episode]. In *The Brainy Business*; Wu, K., & Dunning, D. A. (2019). Hypocognitive mind: How lack of conceptual knowledge confines what people see and remember. *PsyArXiv.*

33 Chance, Z. (2022). *Influence is your superpower.* Penguin Random House; Cialdini, R. B. (2021). *Influence, new and expanded: The psychology of persuasion.* Harper Business; Bohns, V. (2021). *You have more influence than you think: How we underestimate our power of persuasion and why it matters.* W. W. Norton & Company.

34 Graves, K. (n.d.). How memories (or lack of) influence our relationships. *Communicating Psychological Science.* Retrieved from: communicatingpsychologicalscience.com/blog/how-memories-or-lack-of-influence-our-relationships; Heath, C. (2017, August 8). Your memories make you who you are. *Psychology Today.* Retrieved from: psychologytoday.com/us/blog/psychoanalysis-unplugged/201708/your-memories-make-you-who-you-are

35 Palmer, M. (Host). (2019, May 17). An overview of memory biases (No. 48) [Audio podcast episode]. In *The Brainy Business.*

36 Gardner, R. W., & Lohrenz, L. J. (1960). Leveling-sharpening and serial reproduction of a story. *Bulletin of the Menninger Clinic, 24*(6), 295.

37 Arkowitz, H., & Lilienfeld, S. O. (2010, January 1). Why science tells us not to rely on eyewitness accounts. *Scientific American.* Retrieved from: scientificamerican.com/article/do-the-eyes-have-it. *Note: the language of the story getting lost in the mall is one I wrote for the example within the book and is not the exact language used by the researchers in the study.*

38 Begg, I. M., Anas, A., & Farinacci, S. (1992). Dissociation of processes in belief: Source recollection, statement familiarity, and the illusion of truth. *Journal of Experimental Psychology: General, 121*(4), 446–458.

39 Nickerson, R. S. (1998). Confirmation bias: A ubiquitous phenomenon in many guises. *Review of General Psychology, 2*(2), 175–220.

40 Loewenstein, G. (1994). The psychology of curiosity: A review and reinterpretation. *Psychological Bulletin, 116*(1), 75-98.

41 Palmer, M. (Host). (2021, April 30). You're invited, interview with Jon Levy (No. 150) [Audio podcast episode]. In *The Brainy Business.* (Quote and permission to use it provided via private interview with Jon Levy.)

42 Bourtchouladze, R. (2002). *Memories are made of this: How memory works in humans and animals.* Columbia University Press.

43 Burman, P. (2015, April 27). Assamese who created a 1,360-acre dense forest in a river island is the Forest Man of India. *The Weekend Leader, 17*(6). Retrieved from: theweekendleader.com/Heroism/2155/forest-maker.html

44 Cialdini, R. B. (2021). *Influence, new and expanded: The psychology of persuasion.* Harper Business.

45 Palmer, M. (Host). (2021, November 12). The power of us, interview with Dominic Packer (No. 178) [Audio podcast episode]. In *The Brainy Business*; Van Bavel, J. J., & Packer, D. J. (2021). *The power of us: Harnessing our shared identities to improve performance, increase cooperation, and promote social harmony.* Little, Brown Spark.

46 Steindl, C., Jonas, E., Sittenthaler, S., Traut-Mattausch, E., & Greenberg, J. (2015). Understanding psychological reactance: New developments and findings. *Z Psychol, 223*(4), 205-214.

47 Winerman, L. (2011). Suppressing the white bears. *American Psychological Association, 42*(9), 44.

48 Lakoff, G. (2009). *The political mind: A cognitive scientist's guide to your brain and its politics.* Penguin Books.

49 Palmer, M. (Host). (2020, April 17). How to make it easy to do business with you, with Nikki Rausch (No. 96) [Audio podcast episode]. In *The Brainy Business*; Rausch, N. (2016). *Buying signals: How to spot the green light and increase sales.* Pacelli Publishing.

50 Gilbert, D. T., & Ebert, J. E. J. (2002). Decisions and revisions: The affective forecasting of changeable outcomes. *Journal of Personality and Social Psychology, 82*(4), 503-514.

51 Wendel, S. (2020). *Designing for behavior change (second edition).* O'Reilly Media; Palmer, M. (Host). (2020, September 4). Designing for behavior change with Steve Wendel (No. 116) [Audio podcast episode]. In *The Brainy Business.*

52 Scott, S. (2004). *Fierce conversations: Achieving success at work & in life, one conversation at a time.* Berkley.

53 Bruckmaier, M., Tachtsidis, I., Phan, P., & Lavie, N. (2020). Attention and capacity limits in perception: A cellular metabolism account. *The Journal of Neuroscience, 40*(35), 6801-6811.

54 Pronin, E., Gilovich, T., & Ross, L. (2004). Objectivity in the eye of the beholder: Divergent perceptions of bias in self versus others. *Psychological Review, 111*(3), 781-799.

55 Ross, M., & Sicoly, F. (1979). Egocentric biases in availability and attribution. *Journal of Personality and Social Psychology, 37*(3), 322–336.

56 Kruger, J., & Gilovich, T. (1999). "Naïve cynicism" in everyday theories of responsibility assessment: On biased assumptions of bias. *Journal of Personality and Social Psychology, 76*(5), 743-753.

57 Kruger, J., & Gilovich, T. (1999). "Naïve cynicism" in everyday theories of responsibility assessment: On biased assumptions of bias. *Journal of Personality and Social Psychology, 76*(5), 743-753.

58 Staff. (n.d.). False uniqueness bias. *Psychology.* Retrieved from: http://psychology.iresearchnet.com/social-psychology/social-cognition/false-uniqueness-bias/

59 Dolcos, S., & Albarracin, D. (2014). The inner speech of behavioral regulation: Intentions and task performance strengthen when you talk to yourself as a You. *European Journal of Social Psychology, 44*(6), 636-642.

60 Patrick, V. M., & Hagtvedt, H. (2012). "I don't" versus "I can't": When empowered refusal motivates goal-directed behavior. *Journal of Consumer Research, 39*(2), 371-381.

61 Pradeep, A. K. (2010). *The buying brain: Secrets for selling to the subconscious mind.* John Wiley & Sons.

62 Terao, Y., Fukuda, H., & Hikosaka, O. (2017). What do eye movements tell us about patients with neurological disorders?—An introduction to saccade recording in the clinical setting. *Proceedings of the Japan Academy. Series B, Physical and Biological Sciences,* 93(10), 772–801.

63 Burmester, A. (2015, November 5). How do our brains reconstruct the visual world? *The Conversation.* Retrieved from: theconversation.com/how-do-our-brains-reconstruct-the-visual-world-49276.

64 Macknik, S., Martinez-Conde, S., & Blakeslee, S. (2010). *Sleights of mind: What the neuroscience of magic reveals about our everyday deceptions.* Henry Holt.

65 Palmer, M. (Host). (2022, February 11). Using semiotics in retail, with Rachel Lawes (No. 191) [Audio podcast episode]. In *The Brainy Business*; Lawes, R. (2022). *Using semiotics in retail: Leverage consumer insight to engage shoppers and boost sales.* Kogan Page.

66 Dillon, R., Sperling, J., & Tietz, J. (2018, October 29). A small nudge to create stunning team results. *McKinsey Organization Blog.* Retrieved from: mckinsey.com/business-functions/people-and-organizational-performance/our-insights/the-organization-blog/a-small-nudge-to-create-stunning-team-results

67 Duke Today Staff. (2008, March 18). Logo can make you 'think different'. *Duke Today.* Retrieved from: https://today.duke.edu/2008/03/apple_ibm.html

68 Jenkins, R. (2020, February 27). 50 percent of emails and texts are misunderstood, but there's an easy way to change that. *Entrepreneur.* Retrieved from: entrepreneur.com/article/346802

69 Jouany, V. (2020, June 4). 10 shocking internal communications stats you can't ignore. *Smarp Blog.* Retrieved from: https://blog.smarp.com/10-shocking-internal-communications-stats-you-cant-ignore; Staff. (2016, August 4). How much of our workdays do we spend communicating? *Quantified Blog.* Retrieved from: quantified.ai/blog/how-much-of-our-workdays-do-we-spend-communicating/

70 Kahneman, D. (2011). *Thinking, fast and slow*. Farrar, Straus and Giroux. (pp 325-326); Asch, S. (1946). Forming impressions of personality. *Journal of Abnormal and Social Psychology, 41*, 258-290.

71 Shih, M., Pittinsky, T. L., & Ambady, N. (1999). Stereotype susceptibility: Identity salience and shifts in quantitative performance. *Psychological Science, 10*(1), 80-83; Steele, J. R., & Ambady, N. (2006). "Math is hard!" The effect of gender priming on women's attitudes. *Journal of Experimental Social Psychology, 42*(4), 428–436.

72 Colye, D. (2018). *The culture code: The secrets of highly successful groups*. Random House.

73 Sharot, T. (2012, February). *The optimism bias* [Video]. TED Conferences. ted.com/talks/tali_sharot_the_optimism_bias; Palmer, M. (Host). (2019, February 8). Optimism bias: The good and the bad of those rose-colored glasses (No. 34) [Audio podcast episode]. In *The Brainy Business*.

74 Kahneman, D., & Tversky, A. (1979). Intuitive prediction: Biases and corrective procedures. *Management Science, 12*, 313-327.

75 Kahneman, D. (2011). *Thinking, fast and slow*. Farrar, Straus and Giroux. (pp. 325-326); Palmer, M. (Host). (2020, August 21). Stressed and overcommitted? Tips to tackle planning fallacy (No. 114) [Audio podcast episode]. In *The Brainy Business*.

76 Buehler, R., Griffin, D., & Ross, M. (1994). Exploring the "planning fallacy": Why people underestimate their task completion times. *Journal of Personality and Social Psychology, 679*(3), 366-381.

77 Dragicevic, P., & Jansen, Y. (2014). Visualization-mediated alleviation of the planning fallacy. *DECISIVe: Workshop on Dealing with Cognitive Biases in Visualizations*. Retrieved from: https://hal.inria.fr/hal-01500560/document

78 Sunstein, C. (2013). *Simpler: The future of government*. Simon & Schuster.

79 Palmer, M. (Host). (2020, May 8). Bikeshedding: Why the simplest tasks can keep you stuck (No. 99) [Audio podcast episode]. In *The Brainy Business*; Wigmore, I. (April 2015). Parkinson's law of triviality (bikeshedding). *WhatIs.com*. Retrieved from: https://whatis.techtarget.com/definition/Parkinsons-law-of-triviality-bikeshedding

80 Thaler, R. H., & Sunstein, C. R. (2008). *Nudge: Improving decisions about health, wealth, and happiness*. Penguin Books.

81 Thaler, R. H., Sunstein, C. R., & Balz, J. P. (2012). Choice architecture. *The behavioral foundations of public policy*, Ch. 25, Eldar Shafir, ed. (2012).

82 Palmer, M. (Host). (2019, February 15). Introduction to NUDGES and choice architecture (No. 35) [Audio podcast episode]. In *The Brainy Business*. (Note: This is the first episode in a seven-part series on NUDGES, which runs from episode 35–41.)

83 Staff. (2009, October 22). 52 percent opted to donate to state parks in September. *Washington Policy Center*. Retrieved from: washingtonpolicy.org/publications/detail/52-opted-to-donate-to-state-parks-in-september

84 Eskreis-Winkler, L., Milkman, K. L., Gromet, D. M., & Duckworth, A. (2019, July 23). A large-scale field experiment shows giving advice improves academic outcomes for the advisor. *Proceedings of the National Academy of Sciences (PNAS), 116*(30), 14808-14810.

85 Tversky, A., & Kahneman, D. (1974). Judgment under uncertainty: Heuristics and biases. *Science (New Series), 185,* 1124–1131.

86 Stibe, A. (1999, December 15). Designing transformation for sustainable behavior change and organizational management. EM Normandie Business School Metis Lab, France; Palmer, M. (Host). (2022, June 17). Interview with Agnis Stibe (No. 209) [Audio podcast episode]. In *The Brainy Business.*

87 [Mr. Beat]. (2019, July 20) *The space shuttle Challenger disaster explained* [Video]. YouTube. youtube.com/watch?v=TJIXIhypGL0; Staff. (2005, December 5). NASA – STS-51L mission profile. *NASA.* Retrieved from: nasa.gov/mission_pages/shuttle/shuttlemissions/archives/sts-51L.html; The Editors of Encyclopaedia Brittanica. (2022, January 21). Challenger disaster. *Brittanica.* Retrieved from: britannica.com/event/Challenger-disaster

88 Ross, L., Greene, D., & House, P. (1977). The "false consensus effect": An egocentric bias in social perception and attribution processes. *Journal of Experimental Social Psychology, 13*(3), 279-301.

89 Leonhardt, M. (2022, January 4). The great resignation rages on as a record 4.5 million Americans quit. *Fortune.* Retrieved from: https://fortune.com/2022/01/04/great-resignation-record-quit-rate-4-5-million/

90 Staff. (2022, March 9). Interactive chart: How historic has the great resignation been? *SHRM.* Retrieved from: shrm.org/resourcesandtools/hr-topics/talent-acquisition/pages/interactive-quits-level-by-year.aspx

91 Tsipursky, G. (2021). *Returning to the office and leading hybrid and remote teams: A manual on benchmarking to best practices for competitive advantage.* Disaster Avoidance Experts; Palmer, M. (Host). (2021, October 22). How to lead hybrid and remote teams, interview with Gleb Tsipursky (No. 175) [Audio podcast episode]. In *The Brainy Business.*

92 Sutherland, R. (2019). *Alchemy: The dark art and curious science of creating magic in brands, business, and life.* HarperCollins.

93 Sullivan, B. (2019, December 10). Know your nuggets: False consensus and groupthink. *PeopleScience.* Retrived from: https://peoplescience.maritz.com/Articles/2019/Know-Your-Nuggets-False-Consensus-and-Groupthink

94 Feynman, R. P. (n.d.). Volume 2: Appendix F – personal observations on reliability of shuttle. *Rogers Commission, via NASA.* Retrieved from: https://science.ksc.nasa.gov/shuttle/missions/51-l/docs/rogers-commission/Appendix-F.txt

95 *Psychology Today* Staff. (n.d.). Bystander effect. *Psychology Today.* psychologytoday.com/us/basics/bystander-effect

96 Walsh, N. (2021, February 4). How to encourage employees to speak up when they see wrongdoing. *Harvard Business Review.* Retrieved from: https://hbr.org/2021/02/how-to-encourage-employees-to-speak-up-when-they-see-wrongdoing; Palmer, M. (Host). (2021, May 21). Only 1% of people blow the whistle at work—let's change that, interview with Nuala Walsh (No. 153) [Audio podcast episode]. In *The Brainy Business.*

97 German, T. P., & Defeyter, M. A. (2000). Immunity to functional fixedness in young children. *Psychonomic Bulletin & Review, 7*(4), 707-712; Palmer, M. (Host). (2022, March 4). Functional fixedness (No. 194) [Audio podcast episode]. In *The Brainy Business.*

98 Want help figuring out if you are working on the right problem? I do this as a consultant for all kinds of businesses and would love to work with you!
Email melina@thebrainybusiness.com for details and to see if we are a fit for each other.

99 Hansen, A., Harrington, E., & Storz, B. (2017). *Outsmart your instincts: How the behavioral innovation approach drives your company forward.* Forness Press; Palmer, M. (Host). (2021, October 29). Outsmart your instincts, interview with Adam Hansen (No. 176) [Audio podcast episode]. In *The Brainy Business.*

100 Delizonna, L. (2017, August 24). High-performing teams need psychological safety. Here's how to create it. *Harvard Business Review.* Retrieved from: https://hbr.org/2017/08/high-performing-teams-need-psychological-safety-heres-how-to-create-it

101 Kruger, J., & Dunning, D. (1999). Unskilled and unaware of it: How difficulties in recognizing one's own incompetence lead to inflated self-assessments. *Journal of Personality and Social Psychology, 77*(6), 1121-1134; Palmer, M. (Host). (2022, April 1). Dunning-Kruger effect (No. 198) [Audio podcast episode]. In *The Brainy Business.*

102 Levitt, T. (1960). Marketing myopia. *Harvard Business Review, 38*, 45-56. Retrieved from: https://hbr.org/2004/07/marketing-myopia

103 Staff. (2020, January 24). Storytelling and cultural traditions. *National Geographic.* Retrieved from: https://education.nationalgeographic.org/resource/storytelling-and-cultural-traditions

104 Zak, P. (2014, October 28). Why your brain loves good storytelling. *Harvard Business Review.* Retrieved from: https://hbr.org/2014/10/why-your-brain-loves-good-storytelling

105 Auerbach, M. (2020). *The life-saving skill of story.* Changemakers Books; Palmer, M. (Host). (2021, March 26). The power of story, interview with Michelle Auerbach (No. 145) [Audio podcast episode]. In *The Brainy Business.*

106 For more information on the Human Behavior Laboratory at Texas A&M University including the Certificate in Applied Behavioral Economics, visit https://hbl.tamu.edu/certificate-program/ or email me: melinap@tamu.edu

107 Loranger, H. (2016, October 23). The negativity bias in user experience. *Nielsen Norman Group.* Retrieved from: nngroup.com/articles/negativity-bias-ux/ psycom.net/negativity-bias; Palmer, M. (Host). (2022, September 23). Negativity bias (No. 223) [Audio podcast episode]. In *The Brainy Business.*

108 Ellsberg, D. (1961). Risk, ambiguity, and the savage axioms. *The Quarterly Journal of Economics, 75*(4), 643-669.

109 Thaler, R., & Benartzi, S. (2004). Save more tomorrow™: Using behavioral economics to increase employee saving. *Journal of Political Economy, 112*(S1), S164-S187.

110 Thaler, R., & Benartzi, S. (2004). Save more tomorrow™: Using behavioral economics to increase employee saving. *Journal of Political Economy, 112*(S1), S164-S187.

111 Schwartz, B. (2004). *The paradox of choice: Why more is less.* HarperCollins; Palmer, M. (Host). (2021, September 24). Paradox of choice (No. 171) [Audio podcast episode]. In *The Brainy Business.*

112 The 6 Principles of Persuasion by Dr. Robert Cialdini [Official Site]. (2019, June 25). influenceatwork.com/principles-of-persuasion; Palmer, M. (Host). (2021, June 18). Influence and the (now!) 7 principles of persuasion, with Robert Cialdini (No. 157) [Audio podcast episode]. In *The Brainy Business*.

113 Covey, S. M. R. (2008). *The speed of trust: The one thing that changes everything*. Free Press; Palmer, M. (Host). (2021, April 16). The speed and economics of trust, with Stephen M. R. Covey (No. 148) [Audio podcast episode]. In *The Brainy Business*.

114 Covey, S. R. (2020). *The 7 habits of highly effective people: 30th anniversary edition*. Simon & Schuster.

115 Govindarajan, V., & Srinivas, S. (2013, August 6). The innovation mindset in action: 3M Corporation. *Harvard Business Review*. Retrieved from: https://hbr.org/2013/08/the-innovation-mindset-in-acti-3

116 Pink, D. H. (2009). *Drive: The surprising truth about what motivates us*. Riverhead Books; Palmer, M. (Host). (2022, July 22). The power of regret, with Dan Pink (No. 214) [Audio podcast episode]. In *The Brainy Business*.

117 [TedX Talks]. (February 3, 2015). *Missing what's missing: How survivorship bias skews our perception | David McRaney | TEDxJackson* [Video]. YouTube. youtube.com/watch?v=NtUCxKsK4xg; Palmer, M. (Host). (2020, July 24). Survivorship bias: Are you missing what's missing? (No. 110) [Audio podcast episode]. In *The Brainy Business*; Palmer, M. (Host). (2022, June 24). How minds change, with David McRaney (No. 210) [Audio podcast episode]. In *The Brainy Business*.

118 For more great behavioral cartoons check out 100behaviors.com brought to you by Bon Granlund and Kurt Nelson of The Lantern Group. Kurt is also a cohost of *Behavioral Grooves* and was my guest on episode 187 of *The Brainy Business* podcast.

119 Le Cunff, A. (n.d.) Confirmation bias: Believing what you see, seeing what you believe. *Ness Labs*. Retrieved from: https://nesslabs.com/confirmation-bias; Palmer, M. (Host). (2020, May 29). Confirmation Bias (No. 102) [Audio podcast episode]. In *The Brainy Business*.

120 Kahneman, D., Fredrickson, B. L., Schreiber, C. A., & Redelmeier, D. A. (1993). When more pain is preferred to less: Adding a better end. *Psychological Science, 4*(6), 401-405; Palmer, M. (Host). (2020, April 24). Peak-end rule (No. 97) [Audio podcast episode]. In *The Brainy Business*.

121 Palmer, M. (Host). (2022, June 10). Worxogo, the AI-powered nudge coach, with Anant Sood (No. 208) [Audio podcast episode]. In *The Brainy Business*. (Additional details and permission to use them provided via private interview with Anant Sood.)

122 Sunstein, C. R. (2021). *Sludge: What stops us from getting things done and what to do about it*. The MIT Press; Palmer, M. (Host). (2021, November 19). Sludge: What it is and how to reduce it (No. 179) [Audio podcast episode]. In *The Brainy Business*.

123 Milkman, K. (2021). *How to change: The science of getting from where you are to where you want to be.* Portfolio; Dai, H., Milkman, K. L., & Riis, J. (2014). The fresh start effect: Temporal landmarks motivate aspirational behavior. *Management Science, 60*(10), 2563-2582; Dai, H., Milkman, K. L., & Riis, J. (2015). Put your imperfections behind you: Temporal landmarks spur goal initiation when they signal new beginnings. *Psychological Science, 26*(12), 1927-1936; Beshears, J., Dai, H., Milkman, K. L., & Benartzi, S. (2021). Using fresh starts to nudge increased retirement savings. *Organizational Behavior and Human Decision Processes, 167*, 72-87; Palmer, M. (Host). (2021, May 7). How to change, interview with Katy Milkman (No. 151) [Audio podcast episode]. In *The Brainy Business.*

124 Ash, T. (2021). *Unleash your primal brain: Demystifying how we think and why we act.* Morgan James Publishing; Palmer, M. (Host). (2020, October 30). Unleash your primal brain, interview with Tim Ash (No. 124) [Audio podcast episode]. In *The Brainy Business.*

125 Palmer, M. (Host). (2020, February 28). Focusing illusion (No. 89) [Audio podcast episode]. In *The Brainy Business.*

126 Le Cunff, A. (n.d.) Confirmation bias: Believing what you see, seeing what you believe. *Ness Labs.* Retrieved from: https://nesslabs.com/confirmation-bias; Palmer, M. (Host). (2020, May 29). Confirmation Bias (No. 102) [Audio podcast episode]. In *The Brainy Business.*

127 Norton, M. I., Mochon, D., & Ariely, D. (2012). The IKEA effect: When labor leads to love. *Journal of Consumer Psychology, 22*(3), 453-460; Palmer, M. (Host). (2020, August 7). The IKEA effect and effort heuristic (No. 112) [Audio podcast episode]. In *The Brainy Business.*

128 Kruger, J., Wirtz, D., Van Boven, L., & Altermatt, T. W. (2004). The effort heuristic. *Journal of Experimental Social Psychology, 40*(2004), 91-98; Palmer, M. (Host). (2020, August 7). The IKEA effect and effort heuristic (No. 112) [Audio podcast episode]. In *The Brainy Business.*

129 Kruger, J., Wirtz, D., Van Boven, L., & Altermatt, T. W. (2004). The effort heuristic. *Journal of Experimental Social Psychology, 40*(2004), 91-98; Palmer, M. (Host). (2020, August 7). The IKEA effect and effort heuristic (No. 112) [Audio podcast episode]. In *The Brainy Business.*

130 Shapiro, L. (2008). *Something from the oven: Reinventing dinner in 1950s America.* Viking.

131 Sexton, C. (2021, August 13). Most animals prefer to work for their food, but not cats. *Earth.com.* Retrieved from: earth.com/news/most-animals-prefer-to-work-for-their-food-but-not-cats/

132 Ariely, D., Kamenica, E., & Prelec, D. (2008). Man's search for meaning: The case of Legos. *Journal of Economic Behavior & Organization, 67*(3-4), 671-677.

133 Chance, Z. (2022). *Influence is your superpower.* Penguin Random House; Palmer, M. (Host). (2022, January 28). Influence is your superpower, with Zoe Chance (No. 189) [Audio podcast episode]. In *The Brainy Business.*

134 Graham, G. L. (2002, April). If you want honesty, break some rules. *Harvard Business Review.* Retrieved from: https://hbr.org/2002/04/if-you-want-honesty-break-some-rules

135 If you're looking for a great resource and expert on negotiation with compassion and psychology, I highly recommend the *Negotiate Anything* podcast by Kwame Christian. He has been a repeat guest on *The Brainy Business*, including episodes 107, 146, and 221.

136 Brosnan, S. (2020, December). *Why monkeys (and humans) are wired for fairness* [Video]. TED Conferences. ted.com/talks/sarah_brosnan_why_monkeys_and_humans_are_wired_for_fairness/reading-list#t-112812

137 Brosnan, S. F., & de Waal, F. B. M. (2003). Monkeys reject unequal pay. *Nature, 425*, 297-299; Palmer, M. (Host). (2022, September 30). That's not fair! (No. 224) [Audio podcast episode]. In *The Brainy Business*.

138 Pink, D. H. (2009). *Drive: The surprising truth about what motivates us*. Riverhead Books; Palmer, M. (Host). (2022, July 22). The power of regret, with Dan Pink (No. 214) [Audio podcast episode]. In *The Brainy Business*.

139 Ariely, D., Kamenica, E., & Prelec, D. (2008). Man's search for meaning: The case of Legos. *Journal of Economics Behavior & Organization, 67*(3-4), 671-677.

140 Hartley, D. (2020, October 14). The cobra effect: No loophole goes unexploited. *Psychology Today*. Retrieved from: psychologytoday.com/us/blog/machiavellians-gulling-the-rubes/202010/the-cobra-effect-no-loophole-goes-unexploited; Palmer, M. (Host). (2022, September 2). The cobra effect (No. 220) [Audio podcast episode]. In *The Brainy Business*.

141 Gneezy, U., & Rustichini, A. (2000). A fine is a price. *Journal of Legal Studies, 29*(1), 1-17.

142 Ahearn, B. (2019). *Influence people: Powerful everyday opportunities to persuade that are lasting and ethical*. Influence People, LLC; Palmer, M. (Host). (2020, June 12). How to ethically influence people: Interview with author Brian Ahearn (No. 104) [Audio podcast episode]. In *The Brainy Business*.

143 Kahneman, D., & Tversky, A. (1979). Prospect theory: An analysis of decision under risk. *Econometrica, 47*(2), 263-292; Palmer, M. (Host). (2018, August 17). Loss aversion (No. 9) [Audio podcast episode]. In *The Brainy Business*.

144 Brosnan, S. F., Jones, O. D., Lambeth, S. P., Mareno, M. C., Richardson, A. S., & Schapiro, S. J. (2007). Endowment effects in chimpanzees. *Current Biology, 17*(19), 1704-1707; Palmer, M. (Host). (2021, February 12). The endowment effect (No. 139) [Audio podcast episode]. In *The Brainy Business*.

145 Knetsch, J. L. (1989). The endowment effect and evidence of nonreversible indifference curves. *The American Economic Review, 79*(5), 1277-1284; Palmer, M. (Host). (2021, February 12). The endowment effect (No. 139) [Audio podcast episode]. In *The Brainy Business*.

146 Ariely, D. (2009). *Predictably irrational: The hidden forces that shape our decisions (revised and expanded)*. Harper Perennial; Palmer, M. (Host). (2020, May 22). Shapa, the numberless scale, interview with Dan Ariely (No. 101) [Audio podcast episode]. In *The Brainy Business*.

147 Thaler, R. H. (1988). Anomalies: The ultimatum game. *Journal of Economics Perspectives, 2*(4), 195-206; Palmer, M. (Host). (2019, August 23). Game theory (No. 62) [Audio podcast episode]. In *The Brainy Business*.

148 Palmer, M. (Host). (2020, November 27). How to build products that create change, interview with Matt Wallaert (No. 128) [Audio podcast episode]. In *The Brainy Business.* (Additional details and permission to use them provided via private interviews with Matt Wallaert.)

149 Cialdini, R. B. (2021). *Influence, new and expanded: The psychology of persuasion.* Harper Business; Palmer, M. (Host). (2021, June 18). Influence, and the (now!) 7 principles of persuasion, with Robert Cialdini (No. 157) [Audio podcast episode]. In *The Brainy Business.*

150 Katz, R., & Allen, T. J. (1982). Investigating the not invented here (NIH) syndrome: A look at the performance, tenure, and communication patterns of 50 R&D project groups. *R&D Management, 12*(1), 7–20.

151 Palmer, M. (Host). (2020, July 17). Secrets of motivation and incentives, Tim Houlihan interview (No. 109) [Audio podcast episode]. In *The Brainy Business*; Palmer, M. (Host). (2021, January 14). Motivation and incentives at work, with Kurt Nelson (No. 187) [Audio podcast episode]. In *The Brainy Business.* (Details about this case study and permission to use them provided via private interviews with Tim Houlihan.)

152 Palmer, M. (Host). (2021, November 12). The power of us, interview with Dominic Packer (No. 178) [Audio podcast episode]. In *The Brainy Business*; Van Bavel, J. J., & Packer, D. J. (2021). *The power of us: Harnessing our shared identities to improve performance, increase cooperation, and promote social harmony.* Little, Brown Spark.

153 Details about this case study and permission to use them provided via private interviews with Tim Houlihan.

154 Levy, J. (2021). *You're invited: The art and science of cultivating influence.* Harper Business; Palmer, M. (Host). (2021, April 30). You're invited, interview with Jon Levy (No. 150) [Audio podcast episode]. In *The Brainy Business*; Palmer, M. (Host). (2022, November 4). Vulnerability loops (No. 229) [Audio podcast episode]. In *The Brainy Business.*

155 Eyal, N. (2019). *Indistractable: How to control your attention and choose your life.* BenBella Books; Palmer, M. (Host). (2019, December 13). How to become indistractable, interview with author Nir Eyal (No. 78) [Audio podcast episode]. In *The Brainy Business.*

156 Mitchell, T., & Benny, C. (2020). Using behavioural science to reduce opportunistic insurance fraud. *Applied Marketing Analytics, 5*(4), 294–303; Palmer, M. (Host). (2021, February 19). Interview with Dr. Benny Cheung (No. 140) [Audio podcast episode]. In *The Brainy Business.* (Additional details about this case study and permission to use them provided via private interviews with the Dectech team.)

157 Ahearn, B. (2019). *Influence PEOPLE: Powerful everyday opportunities to persuade that are lasting and ethical.* Influence People, LLC; Palmer, M. (Host). (2020, June 12). How to ethically influence people: Interview with author Brian Ahearn (No. 104) [Audio podcast episode]. In *The Brainy Business.*

158 Staff. (n.d.). About Rawabi Holding. *Rawabi Holding.* Retrieved from: https://rawabiholding.com/#Rawabi_holding_home

159 Palmer, M. (Host). (2022, July 1). Corporate social responsibility programs (that work), with Wiam Hasanain (No. 211) [Audio podcast episode]. In *The Brainy Business.*

160 Staff. (n.d.). Youth empowerment. *Rawabi Holding.* Retrieved from: https://rawabiholding.com/csr/youth-empowerment/

161 Staff. (2014, August 26). Rawabi Holding plans to launch fifth talent exhibit. *Arab News*. Retrieved from: arabnews.com/corporate-news/news/620701

162 Staff. (2012, January 28). Rawabi talent exhibit empowering youth. *Arab News*. Retrieved from: arabnews.com/node/405035

163 Staff. (n.d.) Vision 2030 website. Retrieved from: vision2030.gov.sa/

164 [BuzzFeedVideo]. (2017, August 20). *People try world's most expensive grilled cheese* [Video]. YouTube. youtube.com/watch?v=ryZYOA4nalY; Palmer, M. (Host). (2018, August 10). What is value? (No. 8) [Audio podcast episode]. In *The Brainy Business*.

165 Zaltman, G., & Zaltman, L. H. (2008). *Marketing metaphoria: What deep metaphors reveal about the minds of consumers*. Harvard Business Review Press; Palmer, M. (Host). (2021, December 3). The power of deep metaphors, with Olson Zaltman (No. 181) [Audio podcast episode]. In *The Brainy Business*.

166 Scott, S. (2004). *Fierce conversations: Achieving success at work & in life, one conversation at a time*. Berkley.

167 Kahneman, D. (2011). *Thinking, fast and slow*. Farrar, Straus and Giroux.

168 Bleich, S. N., Barry, C. L., Gary-Webb, T. L., & Herring, B. J. (2014). Reducing sugar-sweetened beverage consumption by providing caloric information: How black adolescents alter their purchases and whether the effects persist. *American Journal of Public Health, 104*, 2417–2424.

169 Auerbach, M. (2020). *The life-saving skill of story*. Changemakers Books; Palmer, M. (Host). (2021, March 26). The power of story, interview with Michelle Auerbach (No. 145) [Audio podcast episode]. In *The Brainy Business*.

170 Burkeman, O. (2021). *Four thousand weeks: Time management for mortals*. Farrar, Straus and Giroux.

171 Palmer, M. (Host). (2021, October, 22). How to lead hybrid and remote teams, interview with Gleb Tsipursky (No. 175) [Audio podcast episode]. In *The Brainy Business*.

172 Palmer, M. (Host). (2021, June 25). 3 steps to better decision making, with Matthew Confer (No. 158) [Audio podcast episode]. In *The Brainy Business*. (Additional details and permission to use them provided via private interviews with Matthew Confer.)

173 Jenkins, R. (2020, February 27). 50 percent of emails and texts are misunderstood, but there's an easy way to change that. *Entrepreneur*. Retrieved from: entrepreneur.com/article/346802; Kaye, L. K., Malone, S. A., & Wall, H. J. (2017). Emojis: Insights, affordances, and possibilities for psychological science. *Trends in Cognitive Sciences, 21*(2), 66-68.

174 Gantiva, C., Sotaquira, M., Araujo, A., & Cuervo, P. (2019). Cortical processing of human and emoji faces: An ERP analysis. *Behaviour and Information Technology, 39*(1), 1-9.

175 Palmer, M. (Host). (2021, September 10). The science of cool, with Troy Campbell (No. 169) [Audio podcast episode]. In *The Brainy Business*; Warren, C., & Campbell, M. C. (2014, May 15). What makes things cool? How autonomy influences perceived coolness. *Journal of Consumer Research, 41*(2), 543-563; Wilson, M. (2016, March 29). How to design happiness. *Fast Company*. Retrieved from: fastcompany.com/3058237/how-to-design-happiness

176 Palmer, M. (Host). (2020, November 20). Good habits, bad habits: An interview with Wendy Wood (No. 127) [Audio podcast episode]. In *The Brainy Business*.

177 Myrseth, K. O. R., & Fishbach, A. (2009). Self-control: A function of knowing when and how to exercise restraint. *Current Directions in Psychological Science, 18*(4), 247-252; Fishbach, A. (2022). *Get it done: Surprising lessons from the science of motivation.* Little, Brown Spark.

178 Palmer, M. (Host). (2022, January 7). Get it done, with Ayelet Fishbach (No. 186) [Audio podcast episode]. In *The Brainy Business.*

179 Chance, Z. (2022). *Influence is your superpower: The science of winning hearts, sparking change, and making good things happen.* Penguin Random House; Palmer, M. (Host). (2022, January 28). Influence is your superpower, with Zoe Chance (No. 189) [Audio podcast episode]. In *The Brainy Business.*

About the Author

Melina Palmer is a globally celebrated keynote speaker with a mission to help great brands and the people within them do greater things by leveraging the power of behavioral economics. She is CEO of The Brainy Business, which provides behavioral economics training and consulting to businesses of all sizes from around the world. Her podcast, *The Brainy Business: Understanding the Psychology of Why People Buy*, has downloads in over 170 countries and is used as a resource for teaching applied behavioral economics for many universities and businesses. Melina teaches applied behavioral economics through the Texas A&M Human Behavior Lab and obtained her master's in behavioral economics from The Chicago School of Professional Psychology. A proud member of the Global Association of Applied Behavioral Scientists, Melina has contributed research to the Association for Consumer Research, Filene Research Institute, and writes the Behavioral Economics & Business column for *Inc* Magazine. Her first book, *What Your Customer Wants and Can't Tell You*, was a finalist in two categories of the International Book Awards. *What Your Employees Need and Can't Tell You* (what you are reading right now!) is her second book in the series.

@thebrainybiz
Twitter, Instagram, Facebook

/thebrainybusiness
YouTube

Melina Palmer
LinkedIn

About the Forewordist

Dr. Gleb Tsipursky is a behavioral scientist and CEO of Disaster Avoidance Experts, a consultancy in futureproofing, decision-making, and cognitive bias risk management in the future of work. The author of seven books, he is best known for his global bestseller, *Never Go with Your Gut: How Pioneering Leaders Make the Best Decisions and Avoid Business Disasters* (Career Press, 2019), and *The Blindspots Between Us: How to Overcome Unconscious Cognitive Bias and Build Better Relationships* (New Harbinger, 2020). His newest book is *Returning to the Office and Leading Hybrid and Remote Teams: A Manual on Benchmarking to Best Practices for Competitive Advantage* (Intentional Insights, 2021). His writing has been translated into Chinese, Korean, German, Russian, Polish, Spanish, French, and other languages. He has been featured in over 550 articles and 450 interviews in *Harvard Business Review, Fortune, USA Today, Inc., CBS News, Time, Business Insider*, and elsewhere. His expertise comes from over twenty years of consulting, coaching, speaking, and training for mid-size and large organizations ranging from Aflac to Xerox. It also comes from his research background as a behavioral scientist. After spending eight years getting a PhD and lecturing at the University of North Carolina at Chapel Hill, he served for seven years as a professor in Ohio State University's Decision Sciences Collaborative and History Department. He published dozens of peer-reviewed articles in academic journals such as *Behavior and Social Issues* and *Journal of Social and Political Psychology*.

Mango Publishing, established in 2014, publishes an eclectic list of books by diverse authors—both new and established voices—on topics ranging from business, personal growth, women's empowerment, LGBTQ+ studies, health, and spirituality to history, popular culture, time management, decluttering, lifestyle, mental wellness, aging, and sustainable living. We were recently named 2019 *and* 2020's #1 fastest-growing independent publisher by *Publishers Weekly.* Our success is driven by our main goal, which is to publish high-quality books that will entertain readers as well as make a positive difference in their lives.

Our readers are our most important resource; we value your input, suggestions, and ideas. We'd love to hear from you—after all, we are publishing books for you!

Please stay in touch with us and follow us at:

Facebook: Mango Publishing
Twitter: @MangoPublishing
Instagram: @MangoPublishing
LinkedIn: Mango Publishing
Pinterest: Mango Publishing
Newsletter: mangopublishinggroup.com/newsletter

Join us on Mango's journey to reinvent publishing, one book at a time.

CPSIA information can be obtained
at www.ICGtesting.com
Printed in the USA
LVHW040839290922
729325LV00004B/8